Ruth Goldstraw was born in 19 Archaeology at University Colle seventeen years as an antiquities i sometimes working on site on ex abroad. After that she lived in working at the County Court. The the north of the county, and the fascinating history of the area, inspired her to write *The Witchfinder's Assistant*.

Ruth then moved to the Cotswolds and until recently worked in a care home. She started writing novels at primary school, and has continued to do so, in many genres, though is most passionate about historical fiction. She has won short story competitions and is particularly proud of coming second in a limerick contest. In 2012 and 2013, writing as Aaron Adams, she had two Westerns published by Robert Hale. She lives with her husband, David, who is both her fiercest critic and greatest champion.

THE WITCHFINDER'S ASSISTANT

RUTH GOLDSTRAW

One More Chapter
a division of HarperCollins*Publishers* Ltd
1 London Bridge Street
London SE1 9GF
www.harpercollins.co.uk
HarperCollins*Publishers*
Macken House, 39/40 Mayor Street Upper,
Dublin 1, D01 C9W8, Ireland

This paperback edition 2024
1
First published in Great Britain in ebook format
by HarperCollins*Publishers* 2024
Copyright © Ruth Goldstraw 2024
Ruth Goldstraw asserts the moral right to
be identified as the author of this work

A catalogue record of this book is available from the British Library

ISBN: 978-0-00-869784-6

Printed and bound in the UK using 100% Renewable Electricity
by CPI Group (UK) Ltd

In memory of dear friends Tim Cooke and Ray Edwards

Chapter One

My children are everything to me, yet my husband cannot bear to look upon them. Is that why I, in turn, cannot welcome my husband's touch? Or is there more? Sometimes I can almost remember what it was like before—

I was about God's business—
But I cannot even write my own story.

Journal of Zipporah Carne

WEM, SHROPSHIRE, 1643

Why was it, wondered John Carne as he limped miserably along High Street, that just because he was married to a whore everyone assumed he enjoyed more pleasure in life than most?

Farmer Laycock, scuttling by on his way to the market, muttered 'Good day' to everyone he passed, except for John. 'Good night, eh, Master Carne?' he said with a salacious chuckle and a wink.

1

John automatically touched the brim of his hat by way of response, but Laycock was already far ahead of him.

John wasn't going to the market, though. He swung into Noble Street, and stopped just before the turning into New Cripple Street. He paused and looked at the modern brick-built house in front of him. It was at least five times as large as his own home, and stood back from the road. He walked to the iron-studded oak door, and rapped it loudly with the end of his stick. Moments later the door opened and John gave his name to the small bald-headed man who stood in the doorway.

'Oh, yes, Sir Moreton is expecting you,' said the man in a melodic Welsh accent.

After a short while, waiting in the lobby, John was shown to a room upstairs at the back of the house.

Sir Moreton Spibey was a magistrate. His study was panelled, but the wood was plain and undecorated. Spibey was dressed in a puritanical dark grey jacket with a broad off-white collar draped over the top. His small, shiny black eyes peered keenly at John, through his saggy wrinkled face, with skin the colour and texture of old dough.

'Shall we sit,' said Spibey, settling himself behind a large table and indicating that John should take the chair on the other side.

There were three books on the table – The Bible, Michael Dalton's *Countrey Justice* and King James' *Daemonologie*. John was familiar with the first two.

The magistrate remained silent, looking down at the letter he had placed before him. A burning log in the fireplace fizzed, crackled and then spat loudly. That seemed to rouse him from his reverie. He looked up. 'I see you still have the look of a soldier about you.'

John presumed that referred to the fact that he kept his sandy hair short and preferred his chin shaved. Yet many of his Roundhead comrades had been as ringleted and bearded as their Cavalier foe. Still, if his appearance encouraged Spibey to think he was a Parliamentarian with a godly bent, then so much the better.

Spibey rested his own clean-shaven chin on the tips of his fingers. 'I believe you're here because you've heard I need an assistant and you think you can do the job.'

John nodded. 'That is correct, Sir Moreton.'

'It'll be no easy position, assisting a Justice of the Peace in a time of war, when our land froths with blood.'

John knew all about frothing blood, most of it spouting from his shattered leg. Yes, he'd seen plenty of that, together with mangled sinew and broken bone during his short time in the army. He blinked away the memories and returned his attention to Spibey, who was still talking.

'There is evil in this land, Master Carne. Evil as tangible as this table.' He thumped the piece of furniture as if to prove his point. 'I mean devilry, in all its most heinous forms. What do you think?'

'I've seen this war at first hand; I understand the wickedness of violence.' He wasn't sure what he actually meant by that but Spibey seemed satisfied.

'Then we are in agreement. Whether Satan, coward that he is, is hiding behind these unhappy events, or is the author of them, I neither know, nor care. What I believe, most fervently, is that I must destroy witchery wherever I find it, root and branch. Only when every last speck of this depravity is removed can we hope for peace to return to our land.' He stopped and took a sip from the plain pottery mug before him. 'What do you think, Master Carne?'

'Evil is an abomination, anyone sound of mind knows that.'

'Indeed.' Spibey was silent for a while. 'You think you can help me, but you're not sound of body.'

John shifted slightly in his chair and swallowed. His own mouth was dry but there was no drink for him. He glanced across the table, his clear blue eyes linking briefly with Spibey's. 'My left leg was mangled at Edgehill and is beyond complete repair, and yet I continue to improve, even though progress is slow. At the beginning of the year I could take barely three steps, now with my stick, though ungainly, I shift about well enough. I flatter myself that my wits are sharp and I write a neat hand.'

The corners of Spibey's mouth twitched briefly, as he examined the letter John had written by way of application. 'That I see for myself. You say you were destined for the law.'

'That was my ambition. Had the war not curtailed my studies and had I not joined Parliament's forces, my father would have set me up with a practice in Shrewsbury.'

'I hear you're estranged from your family.'

'From some of them, yes. Let me assure you, that will have no effect on my ability to be of assistance to you. Let me be perfectly honest, Sir Moreton. It is because I now find myself alone in the world that I need employment. If possible, with you.' He hoped he hadn't said too much, as he was sure Spibey would dislike anything that could be interpreted as flattery.

The magistrate's eyes narrowed. He pushed the letter towards John. 'How do I know this is your hand? You may have dictated it. There's space at the bottom, cut a nib and write something there.' His podgy finger tapped the paper.

John reached across the table to the quills and ink and carefully did as he was instructed. '*John Carne of The Dial, High Street, Wem, Salop,*' he wrote in a hand that was indeed neat.

Spibey twisted the letter round and nodded approvingly. 'It is your own hand for sure. This is good. I shall need written reports of all my investigations. You will execute this duty well. I will accept your broken body; ours is not a fight with muskets and pikes. We do battle with our minds, with our souls, with God's grace. You can do this as well as any man with sound limbs.' He paused. Those beady eyes twinkled suspiciously. 'There is one problem.' He rested his chin on his fingertips again. 'The woman.'

John said nothing.

Spibey raised his eyebrows.

'You mean my wife?' said John.

Spibey nodded gravely.

'She is my wife. We were married by the rector. You may check the book; our names are there.'

'I have,' said Spibey. 'No doubt the rector thought he could do no less than attempt to raise a woman from the gutter.'

Spibey didn't know how true his words were. The image of Zipporah when he found her swam before John's eyes. He remained silent.

'And there are those', continued Spibey, 'who consider a church wedding nothing more than a relic of our pagan, Popish past, and not binding.'

'We took vows before God and exchanged rings,' said John. 'I believe myself to be truly married.'

'Regrettable,' said Spibey under his breath, with a dismissive sigh. 'Still, I need never meet her.'

'I shall make sure you never do,' said John, firmly.

'Good, yes, good,' said Spibey, softly, not looking at John. Then he got up and walked around the table and motioned John to stand. Spibey gripped his hand. 'I believe you'll do, Master Carne. You'll start tomorrow morning.'

'Thank you, Sir Moreton. Tell me what time and I'll be here.' John was truly grateful.

Spibey sniffed. 'You don't use tobacco do you? I consider it a foul substance, as much a work of the devil as an extra nipple or a talking familiar.'

John enjoyed his pipe as much as any man. 'I do not smoke,' he lied.

'No, of course you don't. Tomorrow morning, seven o'clock sharp, Master Carne. We shall pray together every day, before we start our great work. You've cast aside the armour of steel to take up the cudgel of righteousness, which we will use to beat evil back down into the very depths of hell.'

As John left, Spibey's servant announced that Sir Moreton's son-in-law wished to see him.

'Bring him to me,' said the magistrate.

Out in the lobby waited an old man, with sparse wispy hair and a deeply lined face. He and John merely nodded to each other.

'You may let yourself out,' said the servant to John before turning to the other man. 'Sir Moreton will see you now, Master Perks,' he said.

John frowned as he stepped back into the daylight. He must have mis-heard as Master Perks was clearly much older than Spibey. Then again, he reasoned, why not? It wasn't unknown for an old man to take a young woman as his wife.

John stopped where High Street twisted slightly, and his house, The Dial, so named because of the sundial set into the wall above the front door, came into view. He couldn't help a smile tweaking the corners of his lips when he saw Zipporah tending their garden. She pushed the fork in and out of the soil and occasionally stopped to twist a stray lock of hair back under her cap.

He felt the usual rush of emotions, first amongst them, as always, love. Ever since the first time he'd seen her, when he was a young man who'd barely reached maturity, he knew there would never be another for him. Then came the constant companion to his love, anger. Rage at the situation he found himself in. Anger born of frustration, both of body and mind. He walked on a little more, then stopped again. She hadn't noticed him. There was another strand of hair to be repositioned. It was growing back nicely and though it hardly reached her shoulders, its former chestnut glossiness was returning. She was tall, only an inch or two shorter than himself and her body was slim, strong and supple. He noticed a group of children beginning to assemble by the wooden fence. He resumed his ungainly progress, and heard the children's laughter.

His wife confronted the group, raising her cap. 'See, no horns, two hands, two feet, one nose, what did you expect?'

He reached the gate and shook his stick at them. 'Be gone! Off with you,' he shouted.

They ran away, still laughing maliciously.

'Why do they do that?' he snapped.

She shrugged. 'No doubt I'll soon lose my novelty value. You'd think they'd never seen a whore before. I can't believe Wem doesn't boast one or two of its own.'

John snorted and shook his head. 'If I thought I could catch them I'd tan their hides, rather than stand here like a feeble old man.'

'Perhaps I shouldn't assume it's my harlotry they come to tease. Perhaps they've never seen a woman of quality digging her own garden before.'

'I've told you, Zipporah, I've no money to pay a man, even to till this little patch. We keep it well enough ourselves.' His inability to care properly for his wife stung him and made his words harsh.

She shrugged a second time. 'Then again, maybe they've never seen anyone who hails from so exotic a place as Nantwich, or indeed someone to whom they are not related.' She shot him her wickedest most alluring smile. 'I watched them go off to market this morning, the good people of Wem. They have but three features between them. There's many a sister in these parts lain with her brother, I'll wager.'

'And you, wife, keep that thought to yourself.'

She snorted. 'So, how did you get on with that mad bigot, Spibey?'

He grabbed her by the arm and marched her into the house. 'You keep that sharp tongue of yours silent outdoors, understand?

We're new here and I need a job. Sir Moreton has engaged me as his assistant, though I doubt you care.'

'Indeed I do. Now you have employment perhaps we can get some help and I can cultivate more of our land. We could grow enough to sell, I'm sure.'

'No one comes into this house but us. That's my rule, Zipporah. Dear God, woman, you obey me in so little, I insist you obey me in this. If only you kept to your wedding vows and did all my bidding, but I know better than to expect that.'

She laughed one of her nasty tinkling laughs. 'You know me well enough, husband. Expect nothing, for you'll get nothing.' Despite her words she poured him a mug of ale from the cask that stood on the sideboard.

He drank a large gulp, and watched her as she turned her attention to the pot resting on the trivet across the fire. She stirred it, increasing the already appetising aroma of sage, garlic and rich meaty sauce that filled the room. He smiled wistfully and sipped his drink this time. His bed might be as cold as the grave, but she kept his belly warm with her tasty victuals.

'So, how many lies did you have to tell Sir Holier-than-thou to convince him you were the man for the job?'

'Just the one,' he replied, reaching for his pipe, and pushing tobacco into the bowl. 'Sir Moreton considers a good smoke as sinful as kissing the devil's arse.'

'Now, you watch your tongue, husband.' He heard real amusement in her voice as she passed him a taper lit from the fire.

He squinted his eyes as smoke snaked from the pipe. 'Sir Moreton, as we suspected, is one who believes that anything pleasurable must not only be bad for you, but perilous to the soul.'

'Even in Nantwich we heard of him. His austerity is legendary. And yet, so I believe, his wife died exhausted, not thirty years of age after numerous confinements.' She paused. 'A man must do his duty I suppose.'

She was still standing next to him and he dared to reach his hand out to hers. 'As this man longs to do his duty.'

She slapped his arm with her ladle, splashing gravy onto his sleeve.

'Look what you've done! I need to wear this tomorrow.' He stood up and removed his jacket.

She threw him a cloth from the pail of clean water. 'It'll rub off.' She returned to her pot and stirred it determinedly. 'I've told you, John, you may take your lusts, your duties, whatever you like to call them, wherever you want. It's nothing to me.'

He returned to the table, hurt, as always by her attitude. A plate of food was thrust in front of him. 'At least eat with me,' he said softly.

She did, in silence.

After a while he spoke. 'So, as from tomorrow, you'll see a lot less of me. Which should please you.'

Her expression seemed more of confusion than anything else.

He persisted in making conversation. 'I saw an old man at Sir Moreton's today, by old I mean well on his way to his dotage. Apparently, he's Spibey's son-in-law. Isn't that curious, as I doubt Spibey's daughter is hardly any age at all. Didn't you say you knew her? By the way, this is most delicious, as always.'

'Don't try to flatter me, John.'

He shook his head; he wasn't.

Zipporah ran some bread around her bowl as she thought. 'Young Mistress Margaret Spibey was a minx, and by my reckoning would be twenty or so by now. I cannot say I knew her as a friend. She attended my father's academy for young ladies, for sure, but stayed hardly any time at all. She was one of the stupidest creatures on earth, that much was instantly apparent. Virtually unteachable, and I tried, truly I did. But she was only interested in making a good match to a rich man. So there, maybe I've answered your question, for rich men are often old men.' She picked up their empty bowls. 'I must see to my babes.' She put the vessels in the tub used for washing and went up the narrow stairs to the attic rooms above.

John refilled his mug with ale and re-lit his pipe. An outsider peeping through the window would have seen a contented man. In fact his mind whirled. What exactly would his employment with Sir Moreton entail? Would he be able to do it? Not that he had any choice, Wem was a small town and since physically demanding work was now beyond him, he was grateful that he would be able to provide for Zipporah and keep her safe. That was all that mattered. He raised his eyes to the ceiling as he heard his wife's footsteps above. His desire for her overwhelmed him.

'I'll finish tilling that patch,' he called up the stairs.

'Don't strain your leg,' she shouted down.

Chapter Two

My babes kept me awake most of the night. Or was it the thought of John working for a man I must fear? Sometimes I almost understand why my husband keeps me prisoner in this house. The rabbit stew was good, John ate well.

Recipe for Rabbit Stew
Half a rabbit —
I was about God's business —
Will I ever be able to write my story?

Journal of Zipporah Carne

The next day, John and Spibey were an hour at prayer before they started their work. John imagined that he would be dispatched to a desk with pens, ink and paper. Instead the magistrate asked him an unexpected question.

'Are you able to ride, Master Carne?'

'I was a cavalryman when I fought for Parliament, but now, I don't know. Once aboard I imagine I shall manage well enough, though I may need help getting on.'

'I have a mounting block and you've one good leg; you'll manage.' Spibey wasn't about to allow any weakness. 'A strange phenomenon has been reported, something found in the Moss. It'll save time if we go on horseback. I've a pony at your disposal.'

'That would suit me better than a charger in my present condition.'

The day was slightly warmer than it had been recently. Winter had started to bite early that year and now, a week into October, few ventured out without thick coats and cloaks. As the two men set off, however, a light mist warmed the air but dampened their clothes.

John was uncomfortable. No, more than that, even using the mounting block, his leg had strained abominably as he stepped onto the solid pony, and now he felt his scars, still red and vivid after nearly a year, stretching. He hoped they wouldn't burst.

The magistrate nodded to the guards as they approached the gates of the town. For the last few weeks, Wem had been garrisoned by Parliamentary troops. They, together with some of the inhabitants, were busy building ramparts of heaped earth around the town. It was slightly better than nothing thought John.

'God bless you, Captain Carne,' called one of the guards.

Trying to save a foot soldier's life might not have done much good to John's health, but it left him much admired by the rank and file.

As they rode away from town, Spibey explained that some of the peat cutters who worked on the Moss had discovered a body. Or part of one.

'They're strange people,' he said. 'Spending all their time out there, looking down onto nothing but damp sod after damp sod. It'll probably turn out to be a sheep, or someone's lost dog, but I must be sure.'

John knew of the Moss, a vast uncultivated area a few miles to the north of Wem, but he'd never been there before.

He and Spibey stopped their mounts at the ragged tree line that ringed the bog and stared out at its magnificent bleakness. Acres and acres of reeds, heather and bracken, broken by the occasional scrappy bush or shrub, and crisscrossed with thin streams running with water tanned brown as dark ale. A pair of kites wheeled around above them, and with a rush and rustle that made them both jump, a mighty heron heaved itself into the air and began its powerful ascent to the heavens.

Spibey sniffed. 'Evil,' he said with a knowledgeable air. 'Only evil could flourish here.'

The sights and sounds were those of nature and industry, though. In the distance John could see the peat cutters, and as the wind swirled, he occasionally caught the sound of their singing as they worked. So did Spibey, who sniffed again with disapproval. John wasn't surprised; he might have guessed that Spibey disproved of singing as much as tobacco and probably anything else that made life bearable. He kept an even expression on his own face.

'It's a strange landscape, Sir Moreton, I'll grant you that. But whether it is any more naturally evil than anywhere else I cannot say.' He was still unsure if he should voice his own opinions. He suspected the magistrate was a man who disliked any disagreement with his ideas. John wanted, or more to the point, needed, to gain Spibey's trust. It was essential that he kept his employment.

Fortunately, Spibey interpreted his words favourably. 'How right you are, Master Carne. The whole world is an abomination of sinfulness.'

John kept his peace. There was no room in Spibey's world for beauty, for love, or emotions like the sheer bubbling up of joy he'd felt when he'd first set eyes on Zipporah.

'The position of the thing, the remains,' said Spibey, 'the

creature, whatever it may be, has been marked with a flag. Do you see it fluttering over there, Master Carne?'

John nodded and painfully nudged his pony back into motion.

Dismounting was torture and he put the thought of remounting without a block to the back of his mind, sufficient unto the moment being the evil thereof. Biting his lip to stop crying out in pain, he followed Spibey who was jumping from tuft to tuft of peat and moss towards the marker, until they reached a ditch. Resting heavily on his stick John looked down, his breath ragged.

Spibey turned to him. 'You're in pain.'

'I haven't ridden for some time; I'll get used to it.'

'I hear you ran back to save a fallen comrade, a cannon exploded and the metal pierced your leg.'

John didn't answer.

'Come then, Master Carne, let's meet this devilish thing. I fear we must descend into the gully. Can you manage?'

'My staff will support me,' said John, indicating his stick. Now the initial pain had passed he was curious to see exactly what they'd been called out to investigate.

'I'll go down first, rest your hand on my shoulder and I'll support you.' Spibey was graciousness itself, though they made an untidy couple, slipping and staggering into the gully. They approached the flag and both men stopped.

'Dear God,' said John, under his breath.

Spibey stood back, his hands across his chest. 'If I were a Papist, I should be crossing myself a thousand times,' he whispered, though there was no one to overhear them.

The thing, the creature, had been exposed when a large clump of peat had fallen from the side of the cutting. A strange, distorted face peered out from the bank, and a face it was. Though squashed, flattened and lopsided, it had once been human. The eyes were closed, the nose pushed to the right, almost pressed flat against the cheek, and the thin lips were stretched over brown, stained teeth. In his curiosity John forgot his pain and leaned forward, touching the face, itself the colour of the bog which surrounded it.

'It's like leather,' he said, leaning further and pulling more clumps of peat from the body. 'Look, Sir Moreton.' He pointed with his muddy fingers. 'The face is a man's, or was a man's, see, this is his shoulder here.' He rubbed away more of the soil. 'I can feel the bone and in places it pierces the skin. It's as if the flesh underneath has gone.'

'Sucked out by the devil himself,' said Spibey, taking a cautious step towards John. 'Oh, take care, Master Carne. We're not dealing with minor imps or demons here.'

'Maybe, maybe not. Could this be some poor person fallen into the Moss and drowned, then covered with mud and peat?'

The magistrate was now by his side. 'No one knows how long it takes for the Moss to form. This thing is what?' He looked up. 'Five feet below the surface. Was a grave dug? Why is there so little corruption of the skin?'

'I don't think it's a man, though.' John continued pulling sods from the body. 'See what we have here—'

Spibey jumped backwards. 'It has paps on it. A woman!' He leaned forward and examined the flat leathery sacks that had once been breasts, now stuck against the chest, where the outline of every rib could be seen through taut skin.

The men worked together, but the more they revealed, the worse the scene became. A stake of wood had been thrust through her back; it'd burst from her belly, and out of the slit they saw a tiny skull protruding.

'This isn't devilry,' gasped John. 'Sir Moreton, this is murder. The killing of a woman and her unborn child. Killed most foully and then buried here, in this bleak place. Surely this woman, great with child, would have been missed. Someone, somewhere must be worrying over her.'

Suddenly Spibey seemed to lose his confidence. 'What are we

to do, John?' he said, chewing at his fingernails, distractedly pushing back his hat and surprising his assistant with the informal use of his name.

'We must investigate, Sir Moreton. We must ask questions in the villages hereabouts. Someone must have known her. And yet.' He looked up to the top of the gully. 'There's no sign that a pit has been dug for her. The peat seems undisturbed. Nevertheless, we know a crime has been committed. At the very least we must have her, and the child, removed from the Moss and brought back to Wem for burial.'

'But should we?' asked Spibey, anxiously, still gnawing at his thumbnail. 'I still smell devilry here. What if she's no Christian? What if we bring a demon back?'

'Sir Moreton,' said John evenly, trying to soothe the magistrate. 'You're a godly man. So, if you decide to take this woman back to Wem, to try and find out what happened to her, then we both know, as you are a godly man, this is God's will.'

'Do you think so?' He seemed to regain his confidence. 'Yes, you're right, I am a godly man; I should have faith. You see the devilish atmosphere in this place caused me to doubt my own Saviour. I'll get my men to dig the woman out.' He pulled the front of his coat straight and settled his hat even more firmly on his head. 'I still hold, those paps may have suckled a familiar or two. She may yet be denied the churchyard.'

'Let us endeavour to discover the truth.'

It wasn't just his leg but his whole body that screamed in pain as John pushed open the door to The Dial that evening. Once firmly closed behind him he staggered to the table and leaned over it. His left, damaged, leg began to vibrate uncontrollably, which made his entire body shake. 'No, no, no!' he cried as the pain, now magnified by cramps in both his calves, caused him to collapse, half onto, half off the chair. He heard Zipporah clatter down the stairs.

'Husband, John, what ails you?' She rushed over and pulled him fully into the chair, pushing a cushion behind him.

'I had to ride,' he gasped.

'You shouldn't have done that.'

'No, no, no!' he shouted again, as he tried first to straighten, then to bend his legs, either movement causing more pain than he thought he could bear. 'I hate being a cripple! I hate this. No, no, no!'

She thrust a tankard of strong ale into his hand. 'Drink,' she said, grabbing a large jug from the sideboard. 'I'll go to the tavern and get claret. It will help. Listen out for the children, will you? They've been fractious today. Call up to them if they cry.'

'Do not leave this house,' he ordered, but she'd already gone.

Every blanket, fleece, cloak and coat in the house was piled upon the bed. Between John's knees was a warming bottle and Zipporah had heated his wine and added some herbs and spices. At last the trembling subsided and the pain in his leg dulled. She pulled up the bolster behind him and he sipped more of the wine.

'Thank you,' he said with feeling.

'Your wounds are not as well healed as you think; you shouldn't have ridden. Preferably not at all, but certainly not so long. And the state of your clothes.' She indicated his jacket and breeches hanging from the rafters. 'If they ever dry, they'll need a good brushing. And look at your filthy hands, have you been rolling in mud? Anyway, I'll bring some salve and rub your leg. Now the pain is less intense it will relax you.'

She returned shortly and gently pulled back the covers. John still winced slightly at the sight of his left leg. The skin, once smooth, was pitted, the muscles unnaturally bunched in places.

The flesh was mottled, sallow yet marbled red and white. In some places the scars were hard, raised and purple. They were all closed, though. It had taken a long time, but the ripped skin had reunited and his wounds no longer wept.

'This will take away cramps,' she said, working the greasy ointment into his knotted flesh. Her hands were strong, her long fingers nimble as they kneaded. He couldn't help it, he let out a low moan, and it wasn't of pain.

'Enough!' She slapped his leg, swiftly extracted the warming bottle and pushed the covers off. 'You're hot enough now; the ill humour has sweated out.' She turned to leave.

He didn't want her to go. 'Don't you want to know what I saw today, while I was rolling in the mud?' he said, hoping her natural curiosity would bring her back.

She hesitated and turned in the doorway to look at him. 'Were you really rolling in the mud?'

He raised his eyebrows.

'Hmm … let me sing the children to sleep, then I'll come back with a candle, but if you don't interest me, I'll blow it out. Are you hungry?'

He lay back and smiled, she'd be interested all right. 'Some bread and cheese, anytime.'

He heard her moving around as the last light faded from the sky, then her beautiful soft voice sang the rhymes that calmed her children. He smiled and took another sip of wine, humming along with her tunes.

It was dark, except for the dim glow of a candle when he awoke. Zipporah was next to him, in her nightclothes but sitting up, her prayer book in her hand.

'I let you slumber,' she said, closing the book and pushing it under the bolster. 'Pain exhausts; sleep revives.' She slipped out of the bed and lit the candle by his side and indicated the tray of bread and cheese on the table next to him.

'Will you have some?' said John.

She nodded.

'Then put the platter between us and refill our mugs with wine,' he said.

She did that and then got back into bed and they ate companionably as John told her the events of his day. He was right; she was interested.

'Sir Moreton surprised me,' he said as he drew near the end of his tale. 'The body of the woman shocked him. Of course, for it was grisly, but for a moment he was so shaken, he didn't know what to do. He even called me by my Christian name, as if asking my advice.'

'A vile and violent crime has been committed, for sure. Do you think the woman was alive when the stake pierced her?'

John shuddered. 'I hadn't let my imagination go so far. I don't think we have any way of telling. Pray to God that she wasn't. Her face was distorted, but I think from being squashed in the bog, it was impossible to say if it showed distress.'

'And we can assume why it happened. She was got with child, either unmarried or the child not her husband's. If it was the latter, he took revenge. I suppose I should be grateful that my brother simply cast me out of our home.'

John's hand tentatively reached across the platter to her.

'No, sir.' Now she shuddered and shook her head.

'I only meant to soothe you.'

He saw her lips twitch, the shadows exaggerated in the candlelight. She pulled her knees up to her chin and twisted to look at him. 'May I tell you something of my childhood that may interest you?'

He shuffled himself higher in the bed. 'Of course.'

'When I was young, maybe ten or a little less, my father had his first parish in Wilmslow, in Cheshire. Close by was a place called Lindow Moss.'

'A moss like our own?' John couldn't help interrupting.

'I imagine so. I never saw it myself, but apparently it was a place of great bleakness, inhabited by creatures to be found nowhere else. Imps, fairies, elves, demons, so they said. "They" being the sort of people who believe the fantastical above the rational. One night there was a great commotion outside our parsonage. Some of the peat cutters were demanding to see Father. They had with them a hand cart, upon which lay the remains of a man, just from the waist down. Nothing above that. Around his nether regions was wrapped a cloth of plaid. He soon became known as "Scotch Bottom".'

John couldn't help chuckling. 'Scotch Bottom, poor fellow. I take it he was a man?'

'Oh, yes. My father had him put in the crypt of the church. It was cool there, as once he was out of the Moss, his flesh swiftly began to corrupt. Randall and I, my brother being full of good humour and mischievousness in those days, couldn't resist sneaking in and we just *had* to lift his tartan skirt. It, you know what I mean, had shrivelled to the size of your little finger, but he was once a man.'

'Tell me, can you remember what the skin was like, on all of poor Scotch Bottom, I mean not just his...'

'Brown, tanned like leather. Yes, it was like soft leather to the touch. I know I was young, but I'll never forget it.'

'He sounds, in condition, very like the woman from our Moss. What happened to Scotch Bottom? Was his identity ever discovered?'

'As I said, once out of the Moss, he began to moulder. Some people felt that, knowing nothing of him, he shouldn't be allowed burial in the churchyard. But my father –' she smiled at the memory of the man John knew she loved more than any '– declared he had the finest Christian legs and he was laid to rest with due solemnity.'

'Your father was a good man, Zipporah. Goodman by name, good man by nature.'

'Indeed he was.' She looked down and picked at the covers of the bed. 'I'll tell you what my father really thought,' she said eventually, lowering her voice, even though there was no one else to hear them. 'He was never convinced he was a man of our time. He went to the Moss to see how deeply he'd been buried and when he saw that he'd been retrieved from the lowest levels of digging, it made him wonder if Scotch Bottom were some ancient Druid, from the time of the Romans, or beyond.'

'Yet he buried him as a Christian.'

'Father said it was for God to judge, not man.'

John nodded, swallowing the last of his drink. 'Yes, he would have thought that.' He looked at his wife, so beautiful by daylight, so alluring by candlelight. Her shiny hair peeped from the edge of her nightcap, her long lashes made shadows on her smooth cheeks. She removed the platter between them and returned to bed.

He edged closer to her. 'Zipporah, I love you. Let me love you.'

Her smile, together with the soft chuckle as she turned to look at him bordered on malevolence. 'I spiced your wine with more than cinnamon and cloves, husband. You'll sleep.'

Chapter Three

John is involved in a strange investigation on the Moss. It made me remember the discovery of poor old Scotch Bottom. That in turn led to thoughts of my father. My dear, blessed father.

I was about God's business —
But that is a story I can never tell.

Journal of Zipporah Carne

John slept well and awoke the next morning feeling surprisingly refreshed and relatively free from pain. As he clumsily struggled down the stairs, Zipporah, who was already by the hearth, looked up at him. Her eyes were red-rimmed.

She must have seen his concerned expression. 'The twins kept me up most of the night. Did you not hear them? I suppose all the commotion unsettled them.'

'Perhaps you should take your own potions; they work, I assure you.'

'What and leave them to cry unattended?' She tutted under her breath. 'By the way, you owe the landlord of the Lion for the claret.'

'I'll settle with him. Were you all right when you went to get the wine? I mean nobody bothered you, or anything.'

She shook her head. 'There are better whores than me at the Lion.'

Now it was his turn to tut under his breath. 'Why do you say such things? Anyway, Sir Moreton has arranged for the Moss body to be brought back to Wem today. When they get here, will you come and look at her with me and see if she has any similarities with Scotch Bottom?'

She regarded at him quizzically. 'I can't leave the children, nor can I be with Sir Moreton.'

'It'll only be for a couple of minutes. We'll go when Sir Moreton isn't around. You say I keep you prisoner here; now I'm giving you the opportunity to get out and you refuse it.'

'I can't see how I can help.' She narrowed her eyes. 'Or is it to make me grateful to you, when I see how other whores are treated.'

Her words bit deep into him. 'No, that isn't the reason and never could be,' he snapped. He felt rage rise within him. Rage and bitterness, a deep hurt, deeper than any pain he could ever sustain on a battlefield, that she could even think him capable of such a thought. He shouted across the room to her. 'Stay inside, then. Stay here with your stupid babies.' He pulled open the door and stepped out before he said anything else.

'Your breakfast, John—'

He slammed the door behind him.

As on the first day he and Spibey prayed in the panelled study before they began their work.

'So, how do you fare, Master Carne?' asked the magistrate once they'd finished. 'I think the ride pained you.' He didn't look too well himself: dark rings shadowed his eyes and his complexion seemed greyer and more lined than usual.

'I'll not pretend I didn't have some discomfort, but I'm recovered now. How are you? If you don't mind me saying so, you look a little unwell.'

'It's nothing, nothing,' said Spibey hastily. 'My daughter is with child. She's very young and her husband hasn't been back home for two nights. She's all a-quiver over it. Oh, I've no doubt he's stayed away somewhere on business. But I'm having Margaret brought back to Wem; I don't want to leave her alone. She's so very precious to me.'

'Does she live a long way away?'

'At Whixall Grange, which I know is only a few miles from here, but in her condition I daren't risk leaving her.'

'Of course not. I'm sure her husband will return soon. Do you know where he was going?'

'About his estates, checking on his tenants. He has a lot of land. There's no need to worry.'

'I'm sure there isn't.' John thought it best to return to business. 'So, the woman's body will be delivered here today. Do you think we should make some enquiries as to whom she might be, or rather, was? I've been giving some thought to that.'

'As have I, Master Carne. And where do your contemplations take you?'

'I wondered if we should be asking in the villages close to the Moss, if there's a young woman gone missing. I'm assuming that, as she was with child, she was young. I think we must also assume she was either unwed, or the child was not her husband's.'

Spibey nodded. 'Some of the lines we think along are going in the same direction, but we must not discount that most wicked of crimes.'

John raised his eyebrows. 'Worse than murder?'

'Sacrifice, human sacrifice.'

'But whatever the reason for her killing, she must be missed by somebody.'

'And you're right, we must ask questions from the settlements around the Moss.' Spibey paused. 'But not today, John. We'll have a quieter day today, and tomorrow's Sunday, so we'll start our investigations fresh on Monday.'

'You've obviously had no reports of a missing woman.'

'None.' He leaned forward. 'Remember, Master Carne, some of these out of the way villages are strange, close-knit communities, wedded to the superstitions of the past. They may not tell the truth willingly. This is an opportunity not only to solve a crime but to break their pagan ways and bring them to our true religion.'

'Indeed so, Sir Moreton. There is one other thing, though. Some people think that such bodies, found in bogs and mosses, hail from times long before our own. All memory of this woman and the child she carried may be gone.'

'No, that's not true,' said Spibey with a dismissive wave of the hand. 'There is a slight distortion to the body, and it's been discoloured by the Moss, that's plain to see. But the tightness of the skin, the lack of corruption makes me think that this murder, this act, whatever it may be, is recent. And the more I think about it the more I believe devilry will be behind it.'

'Hmm,' said John, not wanting to encourage the magistrate's thoughts in that direction. 'I find it hard to believe that even in the isolated places by the Moss people would behave so.'

'It is to your credit that you cannot imagine such blasphemy, but it's part of my duty to think that way, so that I may protect as many as possible from evil.'

'If such misguided folk do exist, and they think they can appease their gods by sacrifice or whatever, they must certainly be stopped. And yet, I find it hard to believe that anyone would hold to so stupid a religion.'

Spibey let out a mirthless little laugh. 'Master Carne, you may have fought battles but you know little of the world. Such people do exist. Maybe they are possessed or they have chosen to follow the Evil One hoping for gain.' He paused. 'Tell me, from your experience what does a soldier need in order to win a war?'

In truth John's military career amounted to little more than a couple of skirmishes followed by his own personal disaster at Edgehill. He thought it was better that Spibey believed he was more experienced than he actually was. 'A good commander, certainly,' he said, thinking frantically. 'Weapons, of course.'

'Go on, go on,' urged Spibey as if John was saying something profound.

'Um, armour—'

'Ah ha!' exclaimed Spibey. 'In the battle you now find yourself, Master Carne, you have the best commander ever, Our Lord Jesus Christ, and the most effective weapon, the Scriptures – the word of God.' He flipped open his Bible. '"... *take unto you the whole armour of God, that you may be able to withstand the evil day.*" And as you know St Paul recommends the breastplate of righteousness and the shield of faith. We have everything we need here.' He slammed the book shut tight and thumped its cover. 'Everything we need to defeat the evil that surrounds us. Now, let us set down our findings.'

So, the magistrate dictated his report and John wrote. Afterwards Spibey found a plan of the area. It was roughly drawn, but at least gave some idea of the places they needed to visit. The magistrate then graciously asked John to share a meal with him. Together they enjoyed some slices of well-cooked mutton, covered in a bland but not unpleasant sauce, none of the ingredients of which John could identify. This was accompanied by some bread and cheese and two small honeyed almond sweetmeats. They'd just finished when they heard the rattle of a cart entering the courtyard, and at that moment Spibey's servant knocked on the door and came in.

'Sir Moreton,' he said, his bushy upswept eyebrows knotted into a frown. 'The men have arrived back from the Moss, much shaken. The thing, sir, I hardly know what to call it, is apparently even worse than was thought. Would you come and see them, sir.'

'Of course, Crowther. Tell my men to take the remains to the wine cellar. Make sure no one goes in there without my permission.'

'I don't think anyone will want to do that, Sir Moreton, but I'll make your wishes known throughout your household.' Crowther bowed and hurried out of the study.

By the time Spibey and John got to the wine cellar the carters were heaving a sacking covered lump onto a trestle table. Light streamed through the open door and candles and lanterns were also being lit, casting trembling shadows on the whitewashed walls.

'I've done a little research,' said John. 'Part of a body was found in Cheshire, some years ago. Once released from the Moss, decay became swift. This is a good cool place, the rot may be delayed.'

'That's interesting. What happened to that person? Was their identity discovered?'

'I believe not. Only the legs were found. The local parson declared them Christian appendages and they were buried in the churchyard.'

'Hmm, indeed,' said Spibey. 'Pull the covers off, then,' he ordered the men, who stood shiftily by the trestle.

'It's a bad thing, Sir Moreton,' said one of them. 'I don't wish to be here. Even the turf cutters, who are used to strange findings, will have nothing to do with this.'

'Pluck up, man,' chided Spibey. 'You have the Lord's protection. Fear not, even though you walk in the valley of the shadow of death.'

The man pulled hard on the brim of his hat, which he twisted in his hands. 'I don't fear, Sir Moreton, I trust in the Lord. But this isn't right. I and my family have worked for you many years and hope to continue to do so, but this task, sir, I plead with you, never give me such again.'

'Oh, very well, be gone,' snapped Spibey. 'Is it so hard to bring a bundle but five miles?'

John took his knife to the ropes which tied the covering. He pulled back the sheeting, then he stood and stared. 'Oh dear God, Lord Almighty.' He crossed himself and cared not if Spibey saw him.

The magistrate was slacked-jawed and speechless, until he took a deep, shuddering sigh. 'Abomination,' he stuttered, almost inaudibly.

John had regained the ability to move and stepped closer. 'No wonder your men wanted nothing of this,' he said.

'Be careful,' Spibey whispered hastily.

John held a candle close to the remains. Most of the soil and peat had been washed off. The woman lay, as she had in the ground, slightly to one side, her whole head, topped with straggly curled hair, now visible. The tiny white skull still protruded slightly from the ripped flesh of her abdomen where the stake had pierced through, but she and her child were not alone. The cruel javelin ripped into another body below hers, that of a man, his arms and legs twisted beneath her. His head had fallen to one side; the flesh, like hers, was tanned as leather. His jaw had fallen open, as if in a final scream of agony and despair, his teeth visible through the stretched lips.

'The eyes,' said Spibey, his voice actually trembled.

John was near enough to smell the beginnings of the sickly odour of death about them now, which would soon become a gagging stench. He held his candle next to the man's face: the eyes were sealed, the lids stitched shut by long thorns that pierced them. 'He saw what he should not have seen,' said John.

'I think we can assume he did more than look,' said Spibey. 'No Christian, not even the most depraved idolatrous Papist could do this.'

'True,' said John.

'Then at last, you agree with me, there is devilry here?'

'Or something that happened long ago, before anyone had knowledge of the Lord.'

'No, no, no,' said Spibey. 'How many times do I have to tell you? It's impossible a body could last so long. The Papists believed that the corpses of their saints were incorruptible, but all the relics were found to be fakes. A man dies and returns to the soil, dust to dust. Somebody, somewhere knows about this, Master Carne. And we must find out who they are and bring them to justice. But it grows late; the light fades. We'll be refreshed by our Sabbath and begin our investigations the day after tomorrow.'

As John limped home, he reflected on his employment with Spibey. It was, if somewhat strange, better than he expected. Although dour, and proud of it, the magistrate was possessed of a sharp intellect, and though his ideas verged on the extreme, his motives seemed honest and well meaning.

John saw The Dial in the distance and remembered that he and Zipporah had argued that morning. He briefly wondered what her mood might be – always a virtually impossible task – when he heard a familiar voice call over the clip-clopping of a horse that was keeping pace with him. He turned round. 'Dick!' he exclaimed. 'Dick! Good to see you.'

Richard Carne leapt nimbly from his mount and embraced his brother warmly. 'You're not looking too bad at all, John,' he said, holding him at arm's length. 'Not too bad for a cripple, and a lot better than the last time I saw you.'

'What brings you to Wem?' asked John.

Dick laughed. 'You of course, amongst other things. Have you some ale in the house?'

'What do you think?' John grinned.

Having reached The Dial, Dick took his horse to the small stable at the back.

John noticed the shutters to the children's room being closed. Zipporah must have seen them.

Dick wasn't long with the horse, and once inside, John poured them both some ale. 'I'm afraid she won't come down,' he said.

'I'll say nothing, John. You made your bed, and for some reason you wanted Zipporah Goodman in it.' He sighed, looked around, moved close to his brother, and lowered his voice. 'Yet, it doesn't have to be like this. Leave her. No one will think the worse of you. That's all that stands between you and reconciliation with our father. He'll forgive you all that Parliamentary nonsense, now you're no longer in the army. Just get rid of the whore and he'll take you back.'

John turned away.

'Oh, how you're missed at home. There was a lightness, a reasonableness about the place, which has gone since you left.'

John lit a taper from the fire and held it over the bowl of his pipe. He sucked hard on the stem until the tobacco glowed, then he exhaled and sent a plume of thick bluish smoke into the air. 'I can't tempt you?' he asked his brother, indicating his pipe rack.

Dick shook his head vehemently. 'Can't stand the stuff and you know it.'

'Take a seat,' said John, motioning his brother to the chair beside his. 'Firstly, Dick, I object to the way you refer to my wife. Secondly, I won't return, not to please you and not to please father, until you can accept Zipporah and myself as we are. Father paid for my education, now he objects because I think for myself. Personal differences aside, it's not just that I support Parliament, I cannot support this king, who's a bad ruler and whose powers should be curtailed.'

'It doesn't matter who the king is. This one will die and be replaced by another. It's the continuity that matters and the stability it gives us. Would you be ruled by the rabble? That's what it'll come to if Parliament wins.'

John shook his head. 'All Parliament wants to do is make the king act responsibly. He shouldn't call and then dismiss Parliaments on a whim, just because he can. That doesn't give the country stability.'

Dick refilled their mugs. 'Too many principles, John, and where has that got you? Look around, this cottage was meant for a workman.'

'It's enough for us. We live well here, and we're grateful to you and Hattie for it.'

The Dial had formed part of Dick's wife's dowry. It enabled him to help John without their father finding out. Dick smiled. 'I wouldn't see my own brother homeless, would I? Even if he's too stubborn and pig-headed to see sense.'

'I can always rely on you, Dick, I know that. So what does bring you to Wem, other than us?'

Dick looked a little shamefaced. 'You're right – not that you wouldn't be a good enough reason – but I'm actually on my way to Whitchurch. Hattie's confinement cannot be far off and she insists that Molly Kade is present, so I'm to collect her and take her back to Shrewsbury.'

'It's sensible. I know that if it hadn't been for Molly, Zipporah would surely have died.'

'And on my way I thought I'd better come and see you before the garrison seals up Wem as tight as a drum. You know the royalists will try and have it off them?'

'Let's hope not, but militarily I suppose they'll have to. Likewise Parliament must eventually try to take Shrewsbury.' He sighed. 'You'll stay the night? I'll see if Zipporah will come down, but even if she doesn't I can smell there's food in the pot.'

'Of course I'll stay. I'll have no trouble sleeping on your couch, and while you forbid me to say anything unfavourable about your wife, no one, not even her severest enemy can accuse her of being a bad cook. We'll eat and drink and talk about the happy times, and put the world to rights in our own way.'

John smiled. 'And I'll tell you of my new employment. Assistant to Sir Moreton Spibey, witchfinder of Wem.'

Zipporah was sitting at the top of the stairs, like a sentry outside the twins' bedroom.

'He's happy to sleep downstairs, so you don't have to move anything,' whispered John. 'Come down. It is only my brother; you've nothing to fear from him.'

Her eyes flashed and for once she looked frightened rather than wilful. 'I know I should be grateful. I'm grateful for this house, which I do love, and never consider it a mean dwelling. But I will not go downstairs.'

'If you'd just let him get to know you, he'd soon lose all his ridiculous preconceptions.'

She shook her head vehemently.

How she exasperated him sometimes. 'Then stay here, but you'll have no food.'

'As long as my babes aren't disturbed, I don't care.' She shrugged and looked away.

'Your blessed darlings won't be bothered by either of us. Good night, madam. May I warn you, those who listen at doorways, or the tops of staircases, may not hear any good spoken of themselves.'

'So,' said Dick, wiping his mouth and trying to hide a belch with a cough. 'Sir Moreton Spibey, indeed. I'd heard he was a man godlier than most, and everything you've told me confirms that.'

'He doesn't approve of tobacco, of singing, nor I suspect, happiness in any form, and yet, though it is early days, we seem to work together well enough.'

'I'm surprised though, John. You were never a man to see imps or elves around every corner.'

'Nor do I. And I see it as my duty to look for the rational explanation when Sir Moreton sees only the supernatural. I don't believe the devil needs that much help. We're both soldiers, Dick. We know the evil men can do, on their own volition, without any prompting from Satan.'

Dick rubbed his hand along his stubbly chin. 'How I miss your common sense. Father constantly rants over the price of everything. He cannot get the right sort of wine and all the rest of it; you know him. Master Pym and the whole of Parliament should be strung up. And you, you should be strung higher than any, except that he blames your wife for turning your head against the royalist cause.'

'Ha,' snorted John. 'You describe my father as he ever was. As for Zipporah, her father supported the king, for all I know, so does she. It's only her brother who's become so godly.'

'What I keep trying to tell you, dear brother, is that without Zipporah, father, with some resistance, of course, would allow you back.'

'That's enough! I'm full of food and ale. I know your trick: you think I'm mellow enough to agree to anything you say, but I'll never listen to your argument. It doesn't matter how many times you say it.' He leant back in his chair. 'Let's not fall out. I'm married to Zipporah till death parts us, and even if I was minded to cast her aside, which I assure you I'm not, where would she go, what would happen to her?'

'She's a good looking woman, so I've heard. She'd find another sap to keep her.'

John breathed deeply, stood up and went to the sideboard to get fresh tobacco for his pipe.

'Think about it. She's a millstone about your neck.'

'You've said more than enough.' His voice was tight with suppressed anger. 'This is your house, Dick, so I can't tell you to mind your tongue. I'll just say this, and that'll be the end of it: I love Zipporah, and have done for a very long time. Perhaps I'll never know what happened to her. All I do know is I found her alone, homeless, sleeping in a ditch, great with child and with nothing but the clothes she stood up in. I'll never let her go back to that.'

'Hmm, well, if you ever change your mind—'

'We're not enemies and never shall be, but we must agree to accept our differences.' He didn't refill his pipe and put the tobacco back into the pot. 'Sleep well.'

Despite his threat, he took a bowl of food up to Zipporah. She was in her nightclothes but still at the top of the stairs. Once she knew Dick had retired for the night she followed John to their room and sat on the edge of the bed, eating hungrily.

'Your brother talks a lot of sense,' she said, scraping out the last morsels, and licking the spoon. 'I am a millstone about your neck. You should return to your family. You do no good here.'

'I've done enough talking for one night,' he said, splashing water on his face before pulling off his clothes, wriggling into his nightshirt and getting into bed. She climbed in next to him.

Why did she share his bed? he wondered. Why didn't she sleep with her children? There was plenty of room for her there. Instead he had to endure the nightly pleasure and torture of lying close enough to touch, to kiss, to caress but never being allowed to do so. Was it sheer cruelty on her behalf, or something else? She immediately fell asleep. He wasn't sure if he should be flattered or insulted that she never feared that being so close to him, he would, one day, lose control and force himself upon her. But what would be the point of that? A brief moment of satisfaction for him and the life they had together, imperfect though it was, ruined forever with no chance of improvement. So, he must continue to control himself. He shivered; it was cold. Perhaps warmth was the only reason she slept with him. He pulled the covers up to his chin and felt her body relax even further.

He remembered their first meeting. It wasn't cold then. It was full summer and the world glowed with warmth.

Chapter Four

Has this war made monsters of men, or merely allowed the beast that was already in them to emerge? My babes cry. I cry for them. Will they ever know the happiness I once enjoyed?

Journal of Zipporah Carne

John's mind wandered back to the hot summer's day that now seemed such a long time ago. His university friend, Randall Goodman, asked if John would like to spend a few weeks with him and his family in Cheshire. The countryside was beautiful and full of sport, he said. John was happy to accept.

'I'd better warn you about my sister,' said Randall, as they approached Nantwich.

'I've got sisters of my own. I can cope with yours.'

'I doubt that yours are anything like mine. She's a sharp-tongued shrew. It's so shaming and she gets worse every day. It's so unbecoming for one of her sex. Some of the problems are caused by my father. He says the Scriptures are clear on the matter: men and woman are loved equally by God. That I *may* accept. However, he also thinks they have equality of thought and reason, which I cannot countenance. Due to my father's indulgence, Zipporah has grown wild. She not only says what she thinks, she actually expects people, *men*, to listen.'

John smiled complacently. 'Then, Randall, I shall attend to her closely. If she errs, I'll make sure she's corrected.'

'Ha! Your words show that you've never met her. You'd do better to ignore her.'

What his friend should have warned him, was that the moment John set eyes upon her, and saw the luminance of her beauty, and once he'd heard her silky clear voice, talking with both vivacity and sense, he'd known immediately that he loved her and that no other woman would ever touch his heart.

John turned in his bed, his back towards his wife. He willed himself to sleep and not remember the past, but his reverie would not leave him.

Was she beautiful? To him, of course, but if you examined her features dispassionately what would you see? Her hazel eyes were bright; they twinkled with intelligence, honesty and intellect, yet fringed as they were with long lashes, they could also appear dreamy and sensual. Her lips were maybe a little too thin, but they twisted into a smile that could change from happiness, to affection, or to something crueller, in an instant. She was clever and never tried to hide it. No silly girlish giggles or simpering from Zipporah, though her sense of humour was strong. She was her own person; you accepted her as she was, or not at all. Acceptance wasn't hard for John. Despite her present antipathy to him he'd always felt that the very moment their eyes had locked, some indestructible bond had formed between them.

His time in Cheshire had been as perfect as anything in this imperfect world could be. He enjoyed the long rides and hunting with Randall, but found himself increasingly looking forward to the evenings when the family would share a meal and talk together, sometimes of serious matters, other times of frivolous topics.

He remembered one of the more serious evenings. The main meal was finished, and they had glasses of spiced wine in front of them. The scent of cinnamon and ginger lay heavy in the air. In the centre of the table was a platter of cheese and fruit. A solid Cheshire, together with small tart strawberries, large juicy plums and sweet cherries, interspersed with candied orange and lemon peel. Parson Goodman knew and appreciated the finer things in life and never failed to praise the Lord for them. In his imagination, John could smell the richness of the evening, the aroma from the food and drink mingling with the wood smoke of the small fire which glowed just enough to keep the evening chill at bay.

John was talking. 'My father told me that when his grandfather read the Bible for the first time, he cried.'

'Ah yes,' said Parson Goodman, a rounded, smiling man, with what was left of his hair curling wispily around his temples. 'I can imagine he would. Tears of joy at being able to read our Saviour's words himself.'

John saw the sides of Zipporah's mouth twitch, as if she knew what he was going to say.

'On the contrary,' John said. 'He cried because everything he'd believed in was swept away.'

'Was your great-grandfather senile or a Papist?' asked Randall, with a little snigger.

'Certainly not the former,' said John, ignoring the insult to his family. 'He was brought up in an age when there was a saint for every occasion, like a friend to talk to. And if he hadn't time to sort out his sins in this life, then at least he had Purgatory to save him from the eternal flames.'

Randall began to choke. 'He sounds a dyed-in-the-wool Papist to me.'

'There was a time when we were all dyed-in-the-wool Papists, as you like to call them,' said the parson, ever keen to pour oil on troubled waters.

'Papist or not, the Bible saddened, not uplifted him,' said John.

'Then, with respect, my friend, I suggest he'd not read the book in the right spirit,' said Randall.

John hadn't noticed it at the time, but now, with hindsight, he realised Randall had, even then, already begun his journey towards bigotry and extremism.

'Shame on you, Randall,' Zipporah said, refilling her glass and passing the jug around the table. 'John is our guest and yet you think nothing of belittling his family.'

Randall's face reddened. 'I'll not desist from speaking out just out of politeness. Better to voice a few home truths than let a man fall into error.'

'I don't think John or his kinsmen have fallen into error,' she persisted. 'They simply don't agree with *you*.'

'Actually,' said John, holding up his hands, 'I don't think I expressed an opinion at all. I was simply remarking how it was before individual study of the Bible was as usual as it is today.' He looked at the parson. 'I do believe, though, that left alone with the Good Book – ' he sneaked an admiring glance at Zipporah '– a man or woman could get themselves into a muddle without a pastor to guide them.'

'I'm very glad you think that, young man,' said the parson nodding rather smugly.

'A man in a clerical outfit can sin and mislead as greatly as any in working clothes. The Pope in all his vain finery being such a man,' said Randall.

Zipporah pulled a face and snorted. 'Then why do you train for the church, brother?'

'What?' demanded Randall. 'I'm not training to join the

Church in Rome. I'm at university to study the Scriptures, all the better to guide the people of this parish once I take over the living.'

She smiled innocently. 'I was merely thinking that the Pope in Rome, if he knew of you, would have exactly the same opinion of you, as you of him. Except he could never accuse you of bodily vanity, since you've become so plain recently. Although of spiritual vanity, dear brother, I feel he could accuse you and be vindicated.'

John busied himself cutting some cheese and asked if anyone wanted anything else, or if he should poke the fire, both to give Randall a chance to calm down, and to stop himself from laughing out loud at Zipporah's audacity. Whether or not his friend knew it, Randall's problem with his sister was that she was by far the cleverer of the two.

'How dare you—' started Randall.

'Now, now,' said the parson. 'All she's saying is that two people can hold a very different view, yet still profess belief in the Almighty.'

'Then one will be wrong.'

'And they will both say that of the other,' said Zipporah.

Randall leapt to his feet. 'Stop this woman now, father. You've spoiled her. You've let her form her own opinions, and worse, you've never discouraged her from speaking them aloud. You must keep her quiet and stop her teaching in that ridiculous school of yours. I don't want people thinking my own sister is a Papist.'

'I'm no Papist!' she protested.

As their argument continued, all John could see was the brightness of her eyes and the way her cheeks dimpled as she spoke. She could argue her point as well as any man. She'd make a formidable lawyer. Better than he would. Randall tried and tried again to trick her, to overwhelm her with quotations, but she held her ground.

'It matters not,' said Randall, eventually. 'Every sign about you, sister, indicates to me that you are destined for damnation. Your fate is already decided.'

The parson jumped to his feet and thumped the table. 'I'll have no Calvinism preached in my house, son. Godly as you are, Randall, you cross a boundary when you assume to know the will of the Almighty.'

'That *was* harsh of you, Randall,' said John.

Randall's face was pinched with rage. 'As I said before, I'll not still my tongue out of politeness. Zipporah is damned, bear that in mind, my friend. I don't want her pulling you into the pit with her.'

Parson Goodman now rapped the table with his knife. 'No more of this!' he shouted.

John was relieved that ended the argument. They finished the evening with a jolly game of cards, just three of them, as Randall sat in the corner with his Bible and glowered. Later though, John was to see this as the beginning of the ruination of Zipporah. Randall's words would take away all hope, which was a damnable thing in itself.

John heard a creak from the staircase. Through the window he could see it was hardly dawn, only the faintest light tinted the sky. He crept out of the bedroom. Dick was on the landing.

'I was coming to bid you goodbye. I have to be away before some godly sort drags me to church, and that will be the day gone.'

Dick turned and they descended the stairs together.

'Do you need any food for your journey?'

'No, I've already helped myself to some bread and cheese. All I need to do is get to Whitchurch today, then I can take Molly back with me tomorrow. You be careful, eh, brother. You're not fully fit you know, and we'll have hard times ahead, mark my word.'

'Take care yourself, Dick.' The two men embraced warmly. 'I hope we'll meet again soon.'

'Let's hope.'

John retired back to bed, only awaking when it was fully light. He loved Sundays. More to the point he loved Sunday mornings and it wasn't because they attended church, although indirectly it was. Zipporah wore her best dress on Sunday morning; it laced at the back and, as they employed no servant, his job was to tighten it.

'Your brother was away early,' she said as she tied the skirt about her waist and twisted it around.

'He was keen to be at Whitchurch before being forced to attend service here.'

'I'm not surprised. A man could ride to Whitchurch and back in the time it takes our reverend to preach a sermon. Though the ride to Whitchurch would, I venture, be of greater pleasure and certainly higher spiritual value.' She sighed. 'Why is it, John, that I, a woman destined for damnation, must attend church?'

'We all must. It's the law. And I don't believe you are destined for damnation. Anyway, if you didn't go to church, I'd never see you in this beautiful dress. Pass me the bodice.'

'It's faded,' she said, holding her arms in the air and letting him guide the stiffened material over her head. Once in position his hands were allowed to smooth the fabric and pull the opening at the back closer. As always he took his time. His hand reached to the front. He was close to her breasts, yet he was careful not to stray too near. He straightened the shoulders and pulled a little at the laces.

'You need not be so precise,' she said.

'I'll not let you go out creased,' he said, once again flattening the garment, which was by now, smoother than the shell of an egg. Then gently, starting from the bottom, he neatly tightened the laces. He couldn't stop his hand briefly wandering to the creamy curve of her neck. She swept it away.

'There are no laces there, husband.'

'Just tidying your hair.'

'Lace the dress. You're slow today.'

He was always slow. He felt her warmth. His head dipped. He wanted nothing but to gently kiss her shoulder, to grasp her slender waist and to hold her as tightly as he could without crushing her ribs. He stood closer. His hands snaked about her middle. She must have felt his breath on her skin, but she didn't resist.

Then her elbow jabbed him in the stomach. 'It's the bells. Hurry or we'll be late. Your fingers fumble today. If we must make our appearance at church, let me be fully dressed.'

He swiftly finished lacing the bodice.

She peeped into the children's room. 'I hate to leave them.'

'We have to go. You know they'll be all right, they cannot get out of their cradle.'

John's mind wandered during the sermon. He had plenty of time, as the new rector, Andrew Parsons, was a man in love with the sound of his own monotone voice, and liked to preach for hours at a time.

The previous incumbent was a joyful, kind man. He'd married John and Zipporah five months ago. She was heavy with another man's child, her eyes darting with fear, while John was pale, sweating with fever and hardly able to stand. However, the rector had done the wedding properly, by both the law and the church, and wished them every happiness, as if he really meant it.

He wondered again, who was the man that defiled his wife? He knew this was an unworthy thought to have in a church, but if he ever found him, he'd do some damage to the fellow, which would at least make him feel better, if nothing else.

He looked around the congregation. As always he and Zipporah sat at the back. Up at the front he saw Spibey. There was a young woman sitting by him, maybe it was his daughter. Crowther and his family sat just along from John and Zipporah, and the man did have the decency to nod his head to them. Farmer Laycock wriggled in the right-hand pew, and next to him the landlord of the Crown sat with his head bowed, and a soft rumbling snore was occasionally audible.

The wind howled outside. Was the Almighty himself growing restless with this endless preaching? John was no longer sleepy but incensed by the self-righteous droning of Parsons. It occurred to him that Randall would thoroughly enjoy such a sermon.

At last it was over, and he was sure he wasn't the only one who was relieved to be able to shake their numb limbs back into life.

As usual no one acknowledged them as they left the church. They waited in the chilly churchyard. John motioned to Zipporah to stay where she was, while he sought out the rector.

'It's a terrible affliction that affects the people of Wem,' said John, his anger now so great his lips trembled as he spoke.

Parsons made a move to walk away, but John gripped his sleeve. 'Do you not think it strange, a whole town, every man and woman, deaf as a post?'

The rector looked sharply at him. 'It's Master Carne, isn't it? I've no trouble with *you*, sir.'

'And I have no trouble with *you*, rector, except my worry for you and my fellow townspeople.'

The rector raised his pitch-black eyebrows, huge arcs completely at odds with his swept back white hair.

John continued. 'Did I not hear in one of the readings of Scripture today, that Jesus himself warned against standing in judgment against the woman taken in adultery, a whore. Yet everyone in this parish seems ready to cast the first stone at my wife.'

Parsons' normally bland features hardened and he took a step closer to John. 'I believe you are employed by Sir Moreton.'

John swallowed hard. His anger, stoked by the length of time he'd had to dwell upon it, had made him reckless. Reckless enough to risk Zipporah. He raged inwardly at himself now, for it was nothing but hurt pride that made him speak that way.

'Do you speak thus to Sir Moreton?' said Parsons.

'I do not, sir. Nor should I have done to you,' he said with a brief nod.

'If every whore in every town were treated with forgiveness and given a place in society, why, the land would be riddled with harlotry. You should listen to my sermons with greater diligence and spend less time trying to interpret the Scriptures for yourself.'

John was desperate to counter that. He'd presumed all the scholars who'd suffered, even been martyred, to get the Bible translated into English, did so to allow exactly such interpretation, but he merely nodded again and walked away.

Zipporah was standing by the lychgate, where he left her, her head held high, her eyes staring at everyone who passed her by, though none would meet her gaze. Farmer Laycock practically ran past them, his face turned away.

'I'm going to get a torch and burn this vile town to the ground,' said John softly.

She looked at him and frowned. 'Why?'

'Because of the way they treat you. Everyone knows old Laycock will poke any woman who can't run away quick enough and probably even his own ewes, if all else fails. Yet he's considered to be a pillar of this rotten community.'

She laughed softly. 'You're in a strange mood today. Look behind you, I believe you're wanted. I'll see you back at home.'

'Wait for me, don't walk on your own.'

'It's but two minutes. You could be a long time, and I want to get back to my babes.'

The tall young man who hovered behind John, and who did have the decency to touch the edge of his hat as Zipporah left, introduced himself as Isaac Wellings, steward to Thomas Perks.

Wellings must have seen the question in John's expression. 'Master Perks is Sir Moreton's son-in-law.'

'Ah, yes, of course. Has he returned from his travels yet?'

'No, sir, that is why Sir Moreton would like to see you, just you, though, not the lady you were with. Perhaps he wishes to talk of serious matters and would not wish to upset her.'

John smiled. 'You're definitely not from around here. That lady is my wife and neither Sir Moreton nor anyone else will talk to her because they think she's a whore.' Zipporah was right: he must be in a strange mood to talk so openly.

Wellings shuffled his feet in an obviously embarrassed way. 'Well, I thought she looked nice.'

John pulled his coat straight. 'No, she's not nice.' He laughed as he limped across the churchyard towards Spibey.

'All our priorities must change, Master Carne,' Spibey said, with no preamble, taking John by the sleeve and pulling him out of earshot of the young woman whom he had sat with in church. 'There's still no sign of Tom Perks. He was last seen on Thursday. Where can he be?'

'Does Master Wellings, the steward, have a list of all the tenants Master Perks was due to visit? You did say that was the business he was about.' John looked over to Wellings, who was talking quietly with the young woman.

'Yes. Wellings may be young but he's efficient. He's either visited them himself, or sent a reliable messenger. No one has seen him. I wasn't that worried at first, but now I feel something is most amiss.'

'Master Perks must have had a horse. Has that been found wandering?'

Spibey's already pasty face grew even greyer. 'No, no, I've heard nothing. Of course, oh dear, does that mean horse thieves?'

That made a change from witches and devilry, thought John.

'I'll go to the garrison and ask around. If they've found any horses, they'll have kept them for themselves,' said John.

'Not today, Master Carne. I don't care what others say, but I believe we must keep the Sabbath holy. I want to see you first thing in the morning.'

John touched the edge of his hat, nodded to Spibey and then turned to the young woman.

'My daughter, Margaret,' said Spibey.

John acknowledged her.

Spibey stood close to him and lowered his voice. 'With her husband gone, though hopefully not for long, I asked Wellings to bring her to me.'

'That was sensible,' said John. He could think of nothing else to say and limped back to The Dial, unable to shift a sense of unease.

Chapter Five

As John entered the house, Zipporah looked up from the pastry she was rolling, 'If you intend to take your brother's advice and leave me, please let me know in advance, so I'll not make any food that's wasted.'

'Eh?' He took off his cloak and best jacket. Then he recalled the conversation he'd had with Dick the night before. He'd forgotten the whole episode, his mind now preoccupied with the disappearance of Thomas Perks. He pulled on his comfortable working jacket, with its patched elbows and darned pockets and selected his favourite pipe.

'You heard everything I said to Dick. You know I'm here for good. What are you angling for? Compliments?'

She shrugged and changed the subject. 'What did that pleasant young man outside the church want?'

'That man, who, I agree, does seem pleasant, was Isaac Wellings, steward to Thomas Perks. This Perks, as I think I've mentioned, is the son-in-law to Sir Moreton. He's been missing for these past three nights. Wellings thought you looked nice, by the way. I put him right on that score.'

She pulled a sneery face and slammed two mugs of steaming ale on the table and sat opposite him.

'You see, that proves my point.' He smiled, then pretended to snarl at her. 'Now, as I told you, I only saw Master Perks the once, but I'd reckon he was well into his sixth, if not seventh, decade. Hard to think of him married to a pretty little sprig like Margaret.'

She took a tentative sip of the hot liquid. 'No doubt she coveted his money. His lust and vanity craved her flesh.'

'Spibey is a rich man.'

'Money is never happier than when it's with more money.'

He laughed. 'How very true. Now, if it was young Margaret who'd run away I'd be less surprised.'

'When your belly gets that big, you can't run anywhere, believe me.' She paused and sighed wistfully. 'This Master Wellings sounds an uncommonly decent fellow. He had a handsome look about him, too.'

He grinned at her. She might not be nice, but in the right mood, as she was now, she was the best of company. 'On an extremely brief acquaintance he seems both sensible and polite. Anyway, the upshot of all this is that I'm to be at Sir Moreton's at cock crow tomorrow, and all other investigations are to be put to one side until Master Perks's whereabouts are discovered.'

'I hope you're up to it. Sir Moreton seems little bothered if he ruins you with all this activity.'

'I did put myself forward for the job and I'm feeling stronger every day.'

'So the fate of the woman on the Moss is no longer important.'

'Not as much now. But I forget, you don't know the rest of it.' He outlined the most recent revelations, that the woman and her child had not been alone.

'Barbaric,' she said when he finished telling her of the man found beneath the woman. 'I've a meal to finish preparing, I'll think about this strange discovery while I work.'

It wasn't until they'd eaten their dinner that she made further comments. 'In a way, Sir Moreton might be right. A whole village could be behind such a crime, or justice as they would see it. They never need tell anyone what ritual they performed, or whatever they think it is. The thorns, though, that's ghastly. It couldn't have been done when the man was alive.'

John agreed.

'The babe was innocent. That's the worst crime. The child suffered for the acts of the parents,' she said with a sad sigh.

John tapped his chin thoughtfully with the stem of his pipe. 'And yet it's always the children that are punished. Even if the child had lived, the stain of illegitimacy would always be there.'

'So wrong,' she said under her breath.

He reached across the table, and for one brief moment she allowed him to hold her hand before she pulled away.

'Zipporah, please tell me what happened. I'll be sympathetic. I'll not judge you.'

'I've told you, it'll never be spoken of.' She stood up jerkily and began to tidy the table. As always, the minute it seemed there might be some closeness between them, she retreated into her shell, busying herself with menial tasks.

He had another idea. 'There's something I'd like you to do.' He stood and scraped the remains on his plate into the pig bucket.

'What?' she sounded suspicious.

'I'd like you to look at the bodies.'

'How can I? Anyway, I won't.'

'I'd like you to. You see things differently from me. You might notice something that's escaped my attention.'

'You're not listening, John. *How* can I see them?'

'All we have to do is wait for the bell for evening service. Sir Moreton and his household will all be at church. We can slip into the courtyard around the back. The door there is never locked.'

'What about my children?'

'I doubt we'll be more than half an hour. They manage without you for longer than that when we go to church.'

She bit her bottom lip, a sure sign she was interested. 'The light will fade soon.'

'Then we'll take lanterns.'

'I'm not happy about this, John.'

———

Suffering no more than a couple of nettle stings, for the path they used was overgrown and tangled with weeds, they arrived at the rear of Spibey's house. John opened a narrow gate and they walked through into a walled courtyard. Although the sun was about to set, the sky was still light. John pushed open the door to the cellar and lit their lanterns with his strike-a-light.

By the time they descended the steps, Zipporah was waving her hand in front of her face. 'It is the same stench as Scotch Bottom. I remember it now.' She paused when the remains came into view. As she knew what to expect, she wasn't as shocked as John had been.

'It's a vile crime, for sure,' she said, leaning forward with her lamp at arm's length in front of her. 'Do you think it was the stake that killed them?'

'We must assume so.'

'Or was it a way of keeping them together forever? Nailed to the ground, no longer able to love each other in this life, nor to rise from the dead.'

John wiped his forehead. 'It's hard to believe that people can be so vindictive. How could anyone think that to do such a thing is right?'

'Stop being so rational, John. Imagine you lived all your life in a small community, close to the Moss. Close to a place everyone believes is evil. What if, over the years, the inhabitants have developed rituals that they performed to stop the evil from the Moss engulfing them all? It doesn't matter that there is no evil in the first place, the fact that you're not affected by it only means that you are completely certain that it's your rituals, your magic, that's keeping you and your family safe. Am I explaining myself clearly?'

'Frighteningly so. Sometimes I forget you have such a powerful intellect.'

'It's not intellect. It's simply the ability to think yourself into another person's mind. And I'm probably wrong. I expect the woman's husband came home and found her up to no good with thorny face. That would be enough to give him serious doubts about the paternity of the child and, enraged by what he saw, he killed them both.'

'And he got away with it? Did no one, not even her family demand justice?'

She laughed. 'When a woman sins, the last people who will aid her are her family.'

He sighed sadly, for she spoke the truth. 'What a world we live in.'

'Now, if thorny face's family had complained, that might have been different.' She bent lower. 'Bring your lantern closer. What's this?'

Even with the extra light he couldn't see.

'Look.' She pointed at the man's shoulder. 'Although the skin is darkened by the Moss, here and here, it looks even darker, in a great swirl. This man was decorated.'

He saw it now. 'A gypsy. That could explain everything. Their ways are so strange compared to ours.'

'And when did you last encounter a gypsy?'

'Never. But you see, Zipporah, you *did* notice more than I did.'

'And it didn't help at all.'

'Once we've found Master Perks, I'll try and get Sir Moreton back on this case. He seems to know more than most about pagans and the like. Perhaps the painting on the skin will prove to be significant—'

There was a sudden, strange creaking noise, followed by a snap and the bodies on the trestle table suddenly twisted and jerked, the stake broke and the woman collapsed to the side of her lover. Zipporah yelped, clasped on to John and then put her hand to her mouth. 'What did we say, about the dead rising?'

John's heart beat fast. Despite the horror in front of them, Zipporah's touch sent a tingle of pleasure through him. Then he noticed the skin on the woman's hip had split, showing white bone through. 'No, they're not rising. Think of a wet stick, when it dries, it twists. As the water in their bodies returns to the air, their very flesh is shrinking.'

She stepped away from him. 'Do you think so?'

He felt empty now she no longer touched him. 'I'm sure of it.'

She laughed softly and without mirth. 'We need your rationality to temper my imagination.'

'Oh, no,' groaned John.

'What?'

'They've shown us more of their torture.'

The movement exposed the front of the man. His manhood, shrivelled as Zipporah had described Scotch Bottom's, was pierced with thorns.

That was enough to make Zipporah grab her husband's arm once more. 'He can never see her again; he can never have her again, never love her again.'

'And was most certainly dead when this was done,' said John, 'for no man would allow this without—'

Once again, Zipporah yelped, and this time she dropped her lantern as a low moan, definitely that of a man, echoed through the cellar followed by an unpleasant gurgle. Then all was quiet. She and John quickly untangled themselves for they had grasped each other that time.

'So, the sensible John Carne *is* frightened of ghosts,' she said, retrieving her light, which was still aflame.

'No, but it's time to go, because the sensible John Carne thinks that there's someone else around and I don't want us to be discovered.'

It was cold once night fell. As neither wished to stay up or read, they retired to bed early that night, all the better to save on candles and wood. But sleep did not come easily to John. His mind buzzed with countless thoughts, and none of them could be marshalled into any order. He slipped an arm around his sleeping wife and rested his head on her shoulder. She made no move. Now he would relax.

He was back at the parsonage house in Cheshire and his stay with Randall and his family was coming to an end. As the time for him to depart drew nearer, he became increasingly anxious. He didn't want to leave Zipporah and, more than that, he didn't want to leave her with nothing said. At the very least, if they reached some understanding, his sadness at going would be tempered by the knowledge that she would, eventually, be his.

He'd spoken to Zipporah's father the night before, and he couldn't have been happier at the thought of having John as a son-in-law. So, full of confidence, he enticed her with the offer of a walk through a nearby orchard. Their conversation, as always, buzzed happily along. He didn't care that she was cleverer than him, or could best him in any debate; it would simply spur him to read more books and hone his rhetorical skills when he went back to university.

'Would you consider becoming Mistress Carne?' he blurted clumsily, unable to contain himself any longer.

She laughed. 'You mean marry someone by the name of Carne?'

'Exactly.' He took both her hands in his and pulled her close to him. 'I mean, will you marry a man by the name of John Carne? In fact, me, to be precise?'

'I do like precision.'

'And I like you. I love you. From the first day I saw you, I loved you, and it's not just some fancy. You're my life, Zipporah, without you I'm hollow, nothing—'

She jerked her hands from his and looked away. 'Too much, sir,' she snapped.

'It's not too much: it's the way I feel. And if you're bothered about the practicalities, and I know ladies can be, then let me assure you that I'm from a good family and your father approves of my approaches to you. I'm training to become a lawyer, and I'll be a good one; your position is assured—'

She held up her hand, still looking away from him. 'Stop, John, don't embarrass yourself further.'

'I'm not embarrassed.' He stepped towards her, still confident, but she wouldn't look at him. 'Zipporah, don't you feel anything for me? Marry me and I'll make sure you have all the books you need. I know you love to read and study. We'll visit your father often. I'll not curb you in any way. And, let me assure you of this, most certainly, no woman in this whole country will be so loved and cherished in bed, as you will be in mine.'

She span around. 'Now you really do go too far.'

'I'm sorry, I meant no offence. All I'm trying to say is this is no marriage of convenience and I'll be a good husband to you.'

Her lips turned down, as if something completely disgusting stood before her, rather than a man professing undying, full bloodied love. 'Be quiet, John,' she said, softly, but with steel in her voice. 'I'll not marry you, sir. I never will.'

He watched her stride away. He wished she would turn and run enthusiastically back to his embrace. In a more considered thought, he wouldn't mind if she took a little time to decide. Never had he thought she would refuse him so completely. He ran after her. 'Mistress, mistress,' he called, catching up with her and blocking her way. 'Don't be so hasty, take your time, simply think about what I said.'

'Don't ever repeat your offer to me. I shan't change my mind. I know you to be a decent man; you'll not push yourself where you're not wanted. Thank you for the walk. For the most part it was pleasurable.'

He looked on as her tall, determined figure marched back to the parsonage, her chestnut hair billowing, until he could bear to look no more. Then he walked and walked, he had no idea where, trying to work out how a summer of nothing but happiness had disappeared as quickly as the swifts left the sky. All he could hear was her saying, 'I'll not marry you, sir. I never will.'

'You vile man!'

He felt a sharp pain in his shoulder and awoke with a start.

She pushed him again. 'You try to take advantage of me while I sleep.'

'Stop it.' He rubbed his eyes. 'How can a man asleep take advantage of a woman asleep? Take a grip of your senses, Zipporah.'

'Vile man! Your arm was around me.'

He sat up. 'And you're a vile woman. Though at least you've awoken me in good time to await upon Sir Moreton at dawn.'

She slipped out of the bed and pulled open the shutters.

'What did I do all those years ago?' he snapped. 'I've only ever treated you with respect and yet you hated me then and you hate me now.'

She was vigorously tightening the bodice of her everyday dress, which fastened at the front. 'I never hated you, John. You are you, and that is enough.'

He sat on the edge of the bed. Everyone around him urged him to leave this dreadful woman. Could they all be wrong? Why did he persist, when in all honesty, she'd told him at the start there was no hope. But that was the point: he always felt there was. No matter how she spurned him, that hope would never die.

It was a hope that had only ever been fuelled by his own rationality. Why, despite all her protestations of indifference, did she keep their house so well? Why did she clean and mend his clothes and cook him such tasty meals? Why did she share his bed and, when she was asleep, for it was not the first time he'd done it, did she allow him to wrap his arm around her and hold her tight? And why, when she forgot herself, did they talk, and their minds met as his never did with anyone else's? And why, when the Moss bodies frightened her, did she cling to him?

Clothed and ready for the day, he looked through to the nursery as the door was ajar. She sat next to the cradle, her foot rocking it gently as she sang.

'Zipporah—'

She briefly put her finger to her lips before continuing her song, her smile for the babies was full of love and happiness.

'Do you think the discovery of the bodies on the Moss and the disappearance of Master Perks can be related?' asked John of a bleary-eyed Spibey.

'How can that be?' He was just finishing dressing, tying the cord to his collar, and by the blotchy look of his face had given himself a rough and ready shave.

'I don't know. It's simply that the bodies were found, then Master Perks disappeared.' John was trying to persuade Spibey to look at the bodies again, hoping to point out the new discoveries to the magistrate, without admitting he'd seen them the evening before. 'Also, I wondered if you had spoken to the rector. We cannot leave those remains indefinitely in your cellar, they must be buried somewhere.'

'There's so much going on, Master Carne,' said Spibey, wringing his hands distractedly.

'Perhaps, if I may suggest, we might check on the Moss bodies first. It will take but a minute. And while we're there, you might dictate to me a list of the investigations, in their priority. Master Perks will of course be our main concern until he's found.'

'You do like your writing, Master Carne.'

'I like to have things ordered. It's what you employ me for.' John desperately hoped that employment would last. At least while he worked for Spibey, he knew what the man was doing and could hopefully moderate some of his excesses. The last thing he wanted was for the magistrate to instigate a witch hunt. No woman considered even slightly outside accepted society would be safe then, and that very much included Zipporah.

Chapter Six

John and Spibey stepped down into the cellar. For a while their lanterns barely pierced the gloom. Once their eyes adjusted they saw that the bodies had shifted again. More slits had opened up in the flesh and the woman's arms were splayed back.

That was enough to thoroughly unnerve Spibey. 'The devil has moved his creatures,' he said.

John explained his theory, that the distortion was caused by the drying process. He suggested that the covering should be dampened and placed back over the bodies when they were not being examined. 'It's imperative that we dispose of them somehow and soon,' he said.

'I agree,' said Spibey, squinting at the remains and then gasping when he noticed what had happened to the man's private parts. 'Oh, to think that this evil has happened in our own county, 'tis shameful.'

John was pleased to be able to 'discover' the possible decoration of the man, which took Spibey's mind off the worse desecration.

'Gypsies, Master Carne. This could be our answer. They are

very different from us, and there are plenty of them in Wales, I believe. Is *she* one of them, though, or did they steal one of our own maids?'

'We know she was no maid,' John reminded him.

Together they also remarked that the nails of both the man and woman were neatly cut and the hands uncalloused.

'That's even more intriguing,' said John. 'A lonely village somewhere might manage to perpetrate such a crime against one of their own and escape detection. People of quality rarely disappear without being missed. As we know in the case of Master Perks.'

The light at the open doorway dimmed as a figure stopped at the top of the steps, then slowly descended.

'Father,' said a soft voice.

John turned to see Margaret Perks, her round pretty features showing both apprehension and curiosity, her heavily pregnant body at odds with her childlike face.

'Daughter, leave this place!' cried Spibey, rushing over to her. 'Don't expose your unborn child to such evil.'

But she pushed past him, curiosity clearly overcoming any other feelings. Her tongue softly licked her lips as fascination got the better of her and caused a strange smile to spread across her face. 'Appalling,' she said softly, as she held a candle close to the bodies.

'Mistress Perks,' said John. 'This is no place for you. Your father is right, you shouldn't be here.'

'What hatred there must have been,' she continued. 'Not only to kill, but to maim, so to destroy forever the passion they felt.'

'We don't know how or why this happened to them,' said John.

'Oh, I think we do,' she said with a chuckle.

'Please, Margaret,' said Spibey, grasping her shoulders. 'I'll not allow you to stay here a moment longer.'

She shrugged him off. 'You're my father, not my husband. You no longer have the right to tell me what to do.'

'Please, listen to your father,' said John. He felt disturbed by Margaret's attitude, although he couldn't work out why. 'We've finished here now and are about to go and look for your husband.'

'Oh, he'll turn up. No doubt he grew tired of my fat belly and has gone to console himself elsewhere. That's what men do, isn't it?'

Her strange mixture of young innocence and worldly knowledge was disconcerting.

She stared at John. 'Except for you, Master Carne, who keeps faithful to his whore of a wife.'

'Margaret,' warned Spibey. 'We don't talk of such things. I insist you leave this place now. You need to go back to your apartment and rest.'

She looked up at him. She was so small, so defenceless and yet so intimidating. 'You've no idea, have you, father? How can I rest while your less than godly grandchild jigs in my belly? Oh, yes, father, this child likes to dance.'

Spibey's hands shot to his mouth and he began chewing his fingernails. 'Stop this, Margaret,' he spluttered, before turning to John. 'It's her condition, Master Carne, she knows not what she says.'

'I heard nothing,' said John.

'I remember your wife,' said Margaret to him. 'Father made me attend Parson Goodman's academy for young women. Mistress Goodman, as she then was, tried her best with me, but I was no scholar. I remember she told me she'd have an easier time teaching her poultry to read and write than me! I hope it wasn't my fault she took to opening her legs to any and all.'

John remained rigid, shocked that such vileness could emerge from such an innocent looking mouth. Spibey's face was now the colour of the blood trickling down one of his mangled, bitten thumbs. For a terrible moment John thought the man might suffer a seizure. In the end the magistrate found his voice.

'We do *not* mention Master Carne's wife.'

John was still fighting back the anger that rose inside him. Whatever had happened to Zipporah he was more than sure that opening her legs to any and all had not been part of it. He turned away, breathing heavily. He must not lose his position with the witchfinder. No matter what cost to his pride, or anything else, he must accept these insults to his wife, absorb them and disregard them.

'Mistress Perks! Mistress Perks!' called a voice from the courtyard above.

'Master Wellings, she's here,' Spibey shouted up, guiding Margaret towards the stairs.

'Oh, there you are.' The young man jumped down the steps two at a time. 'We feared you were lost, too.'

Margaret seemed offended. 'I stir one yard from my room and the household is in uproar. But I'm tired, so I'll take your arm, Master Wellings, if you'll escort me to my chamber.'

'Your maid awaits you above,' said Wellings. He cast a glance at the bodies from the Moss and his lips curled with distaste. 'Mistress Perks, you should not have come here and looked upon such vileness. It cannot be good for you. It cannot be good for your babe.' His hand gripped hers and he lead her out of the cellar.

'Master Carne,' said Spibey, twisting his mouth, and indeed his whole body, most awkwardly.

John waved his hand. 'No, Sir Moreton, say nothing, that's for the best.'

Crowther was waiting in the courtyard when they emerged from the cellar. 'I have a message for you, Sir Moreton, but I wouldn't come down. Not with that thing—'

'If only everyone else was so sensible,' said Spibey.

Crowther continued. 'A travelling peddler called. He wouldn't stay, nor leave his name or his next destination. He was insistent, though. He said he'd heard, at the tavern last night, that evidence of the dark arts had been found at the Moss and that you are a man keen to rid the county of devilry. He told me that when he was out and about selling his goods, he became aware of a witch. She lives just outside Hornspike. This woman burned and then ate her cat, in the form of a cake, which was later seen flying through the sky. The cat, not the cake.'

'Hornspike, have either of you heard of this place?' asked John, biting his lips to stop himself laughing, as the thought of either a cat or especially a cake flying, amused him greatly.

'It's an insignificant hamlet, close to the Moss and not far from Whixall,' said Crowther.

'Master Perks lives at Whixall,' said Spibey, his cheeks returning to a more normal hue. 'Now we know where we have to go.'

As Crowther had told them, Hornspike, they soon discovered, was indeed a tiny hamlet. In fact it was little more than a scattered collection of a farmhouse, four cottages and two hovels.

John found the journey less painful than his last ride. He was learning to shift his weight in the saddle in order to save his damaged thigh.

They pulled up their horses by the farmhouse, where a new top storey was being added and the work looked close to completion. Two men, who'd been positioning a wooden ladder against the scaffolding, stopped their work and came over.

Spibey introduced himself, puffing out his chest as he did so. 'I've had reports of a witch living hereabouts. Tell us where she is and we'll rid your village of her evil.'

The two men, who now stood before their horses, looked at each other and shrugged.

'May I?' John asked Spibey, who nodded.

'I'm assistant to Sir Moreton and have some questions. Firstly, Master Thomas Perks, have you heard of him?'

'Indeed,' said the older of the men. 'From Whixall Grange. He owns this land. I'm a proud tenant of his.'

'Is this your house?' asked Spibey. 'You're improving it mightily.'

'Technically, it's Master Perks's property, but he's a fair man. If I grow rich, then he grows rich. He doesn't begrudge me, nor I him.'

'When was the last time you saw him?' said Spibey.

The men shrugged again, and once more the elder spoke. 'A couple of weeks ago maybe, he was just passing through. He leaves us to our business, just as his father before him left my father before me to his own affairs. He may have other tenants that cause him grief, but not the Simmonds of Hornspike.'

'It's a grand house you're making yourself,' sniffed Spibey, obviously affronted that a mere tenant farmer could have a house almost as big as his own.

'It's a growing house, to accommodate my growing family.'

'Concerning Master Perks,' said John. 'He's not been seen by anyone for the past four nights, if you do hear anything of him, please let us, or someone at Whixall Grange, know.'

Master Simmonds shrugged again. 'He's gentry. They come and go as they please.'

'That they do,' said Spibey. 'But Master Perks is in his seventieth year or more, so we have some worries. Now about this witch—'

'May I ask one more question?' interrupted John. 'Has a woman, I'm presuming not that old, gone from here? I mean, disappeared? She was with child at the time, the birth not far off. There may have been some scandal.'

The men looked at each other again, frowning. Simmonds spoke once more. 'We maybe don't keep to the pretty ways of the town, but we look after our women here. We see to it that they and their children are cared for.'

'What sort of an answer is that?' demanded Spibey.

'An honest one.'

'So, you look after your women here, do you?' said Spibey. 'What about the one who burned her cat alive and then ate it? That cat was seen flying through the air the same night. Do you look after her and hide her from the law?'

John felt uncomfortable. He wasn't sure that it was exactly the same story Crowther told, but it made the men laugh.

'That's Baccy. Crazy old crone. She's got cats, but they don't fly. And she's no witch.'

'Baccy?' said Spibey.

'Baccy Blanchard. We call her that because she loves her pipe. Her real name's Rebecca. She lives just outside the village, along there.' Simmonds pointed to a narrow lane. 'She's a funny one, all right, thinks herself a class above us. But, like I said, no witch.'

'Just follow that track,' said the younger man. 'At the end you'll find Baccy, but don't expect any sense from her.'

'She's bewitched them,' said Spibey as they nudged their horses forward. His lips were tightly pursed, an expression John now recognised as signifying great disapproval.

The lane was lined with hedgerows and there was a small copse ahead. Though still cold, a weak sun was battling to pierce the clouds. A battle John was sure it would lose. Winters seemed to be harder and longer since this wretched war had began.

The house at the end of the lane was timber framed. Old fashioned, while at the same time well maintained. It had its own neatly kept grounds. The main door was ajar, and by the time John slithered untidily from his mount, Spibey was banging the hard handle of his whip on the frame. John limped up and stood respectfully behind him.

'Jim, is that you? Come in,' called a woman's voice from inside. 'Take your boots off if they're dirty and close the door, it's chilly.'

'I'm Sir Moreton Spibey, Justice of the Peace, from Wem,' he shouted. 'I'm coming in, Mistress Blanchard.'

'Then *you* can take your boots off and close the door,' said the voice, closer now. And then, the small body from which it emanated, stood before them.

If John had ever thought about witches, and he never did, then they would be as they were described in childhood stories: bent old women with warts and cackly laughs. Baccy Blanchard didn't live up to that description. She might, at most, be ten years older than him. She was well dressed, her cuffs and collar decorated subtly with lace, and her greying, fair hair was neatly tied under a crisp white cap. Apart from the stubby pipe which jutted from the corner of her mouth, the only odd-looking thing about her was the fat and fluffy black and white cat she held in her arms. Its amber eyes looked lazily at Spibey, before it yawned and with a quick twist of its body leapt from Baccy's embrace and scuttled back into the house.

'Hmm,' she said, cocking her head to one side and narrowing her pale blue eyes. She took the pipe from her mouth. 'Master Pipkin doesn't like you and I'm inclined to agree with his judgement. Who did you say you were?'

John had to look away, in case either of them saw the curl he couldn't help appearing on his lips. He wondered if Spibey had met his match.

'I am Sir Moreton Spibey, magistrate, from Wem, and I'm coming into your hovel, woman, whether you like it or not. Come, Master Carne.'

John looked down at his shoes, which were dusty rather than muddy, so he rubbed the foot of his good leg against the calf of his bad one, which was as much as he could do, and followed Spibey in.

'You insulting man, this is no hovel, Sir Molten Spikey, or whoever you are,' said Baccy, pulling viciously on her pipe and blowing a cloud of smoke Spibey's way, causing him to cough and splutter.

John was really biting his lip now.

'This is a well-built house. I've paid good money to keep it sound. Does this roof leak? No. Does my chimney smoke? No, it does not. Can you say the same for your house, Master Spikey? I doubt many people can. Painted every year this house is, inside and out, whether it needs it or not. And look at my new floor, waxed and polished wood. It shouldn't have your heavy boots upon it.'

'Madam, I'm not here to discuss the maintenance of your home. I am here on greater matters.'

'Really, well, you can sit at my table, but I'll offer you no refreshment.'

'Nor would I accept any,' said Spibey, pulling a plain but well-made oak chair from under the table.

John was about to do the same, but she came over and poked him in the chest. 'Not you. You're laughing at me, that's rude. You can stand. Who are you, anyway?'

'John Carne, assistant to Sir Moreton. I'm fine standing, thank you.'

She took a seat to the side of Spibey and a tabby, even fatter than the black and white cat, jumped on her knee.

'Madam, give me your attention,' said Spibey, looking warily at the cat. 'I'm here on most serious business. I investigate those who use the dark arts. Those who cavort with the devil. Those who commune with imps and demons to further their own ambitions and to stifle the works of God.'

'Rather you than me.' She stroked the cat. 'What do you think, Colonel Jojo? He's a big noisy man, isn't he? Thumping in here wearing his big black boots and his big black hat, staring at us with his beady, black eyes.'

John had to turn around. He held his breath for a while until he was sure he wouldn't laugh out loud. He tried to concentrate on anything but the woman, and looked around the room. As Baccy said, her house was well kept, if somewhat untidy. Some dirty pots and pans lay by the fireplace and the black and white cat was licking one of the plates. The cauldron was set to one side of the fire, and wood was neatly stacked to the other. All the furniture was solid and well made. Most curiously there was a set of shelves filled with books and more of them were laid over the table. He picked one up, it was a brand-new edition.

'Put that down! Books are for gentle people, not brutes like you,' she shouted.

John obeyed. 'You're a fortunate woman to have access to all the most up to date titles,' he said.

'Yes, books,' said Spibey, squinting suspiciously. 'Where is the man you keep here?'

'There's no man. I live alone,' said Baccy.

'You can't expect me to believe you read all these volumes.'

'No, that's right, I just like the colour of the covers,' replied Baccy with a supercilious sneer.

'That's more like the truth of it. If there's no man here, who is Jim that you call for? Is he your apprentice in sorcery, or another of your familiars?' He looked down to where the black and white cat was now hunching before him, ready to leap upon his knee. 'Away, away,' he muttered, pushing the cat from him.

Baccy didn't seem to have noticed. She shook her head and tapped the stem of her pipe on her bottom teeth. Then she leaned forward. 'Jim's a boy from the village who does jobs for me. I don't do the chores myself; I'm a lady. Jim's sister cooks for me, just the once a day. It's enough, I don't eat much. Not that any of this is your business, whether you're a magistrate or not.'

It didn't seem that Baccy was guilty of the sin of gluttony, thought John, just before a cramping seizure made his leg jolt and he cried out in pain. He held up his hand. 'Please, excuse me, I have an old injury. I'll be better if I can move around.'

'Feel free, move about as you will, or can. Sorry I'm not a

proper witch or I'd have some potion to ease you. All I have is wine, but it's of good quality, so I'll not waste it on you.'

'What kind of witch are you, madam?' asked Spibey. 'If not a proper one?'

'No sort at all.' She pushed the cat from her lap and went to the grate, where she knocked out her pipe, and put it into a rack, next to several others. 'What have they been saying about me in the village? They take my money quickly enough when I need something doing.'

Spibey stood up. 'Look at the evidence. You live here alone with only these fat cats for company.'

'They're not fat; they're well fed.'

'Today they look like fat cats, what were they yesterday? Weasels? Tomorrow what will they be? Bats? Toads? How many more hide about this house?'

Baccy merely shrugged.

John stood close to Spibey. 'She's odd, that's for sure,' he whispered, 'but a witch? She seems to have committed no crime.'

'As always, your innocence does you credit, Master Carne. But these people hide their sins well. We need to take her back to Wem. If she doesn't confess quickly, we'll examine her for signs. The devil will have left his mark on her for sure.' Spibey smiled triumphantly. John found that somewhat disconcerting. 'We have our witch, Master Carne! We have her!'

Chapter Seven

If John found the encounter between Baccy and his master amusing at first, he certainly didn't now. He felt chilled to the marrow. Spibey had made up his mind. Baccy was a witch, and if she didn't admit it he'd subject her to some unspeakable 'inspection' until a harmless mole or wart convicted her. Or would the magistrate use trial by water? Float and you're guilty, drown and you're innocent. Just the sort of justice Spibey would probably relish. John rubbed his hand across his face.

'If you've not the stomach for this, Master Carne, I'd best get another assistant,' snapped Spibey.

'It's all right, Sir Moreton, stomach I have,' lied John. 'It's my leg which lets me down.'

'Of course, of course.' Spibey turned to Baccy. 'Mistress Rebecca, known as Baccy Blanchard. You are arrested and ordered to return with me to Wem, to be put to questioning on suspicion of witchcraft. The accusations against you are grave, in that you have communed with the devil by way of these familiars, known as Master Pipkin and General Jojo.'

'He's only a colonel,' she laughed, but John saw fear creeping behind her confident expression. 'You're not serious, are you? I'm just a harmless old woman who happens, by force of circumstance, to live alone. I've committed no crime. There's no point taking me to Wem, or anywhere else. I can't tell you anything.'

'So you say,' said Spibey. 'Once I start my prodding, you'll remember all sorts of things I'm sure.'

John's uneasiness grew. 'Mistress,' he said, as gently as he could. 'Sir Moreton has the authority. Come with us willingly. If you are innocent, then you've nothing to fear.' How he wished that would be true.

She took a step back, and crossed her hands over her chest. 'I haven't done anything. I'm not interesting. I stay in this house and do very little. You must be able to see I'm no witch.'

As far as John could tell, that was true, but he knew Spibey would not be stopped. 'Come with us now, Mistress Blanchard.' He held out his hand.

Both men jumped as she began to shriek. 'My babies, my babies! I'll not leave my babies. You can kill me first, but I'll not leave my babies.'

Spibey looked confused. 'Do you think she has children hidden here, to feast upon?'

'No, no, I think she means the cats, sir,' said John hastily.

'A-ha! You see how the devil panics when confronted,' gloated Spibey.

'I don't care what you do to me, but don't leave my babies. You, sir.' She looked at John, her face bright red, tears bursting from her eyes. 'Take my babies, look after them, I don't care what you do to me, but care for my babies.'

Spibey looked triumphant and seemed to be enjoying himself. 'They look like cats but they are her babies, spawned by her unnatural carnal relationship with Satan. Perhaps we should send for more men and bind her with chains.'

'I don't care, I don't care,' screamed Baccy pulling off her cap. She ran to the fireplace and banged her fists on the mantel shelf.

'I'm all alone; there's no one to help me.' Her words degenerated into random screams.

John saw a basket by the fireside, it was full of twigs and kindling. He emptied it, and managed with hardly any effort, as the animals seemed naturally friendly, to squeeze the cats into the wickerwork and secure the lid on them.

'My babies,' she screamed again, rushing towards him and pummelling his chest with her fists.

He staggered back a little, before regaining his balance. Though she was small, her anger gave her strength. 'Mistress Blanchard, I'm taking your babies into safe keeping. I implore you, stop this.' He snatched her wrist with his free hand and at last she sagged and continued to sob. Tears dripped off the end of her nose and onto the polished wooden floor.

'Master Carne, what are you about?' demanded Spibey, stomping over to them, and taking Baccy's other arm.

'Evidence, Sir Moreton,' he said. 'I'll keep these animals in my own home, that way, if they do turn into weasels, or frogs, or whatever, we shall have the incontrovertible proof.'

Spibey's eyes widened. 'Indeed we shall, Master Carne. I was just about to suggest the same. What a good assistant you're proving to be.'

John leaned over to Baccy, let go of her arm and spoke softly. 'Did you hear that, Mistress Blanchard? I personally undertake to look after your cats.'

She looked up at him, but he couldn't be sure if she'd understood what he had said. She was quiet though, and wiped her face with her sleeve. 'Very well, I'll come to Wem with you, but it'll do none of you any good.'

'She threatens us,' said Spibey.

'I don't think so,' said John, though he silently agreed with her. Very little good was likely to come of this.

Once outside, Spibey instructed John to tie Baccy's hands to a rope, which was in turn attached to John's saddle. 'Make sure those knots hold,' said the magistrate.

John grunted as he scrambled onto the pony.

Spibey rode ahead, his back straight, his chin jutting, proud of his day's work. John balanced the cat basket in front of him, and occasionally looked behind at Baccy, who followed, dragging her feet. 'You're only making it worse for yourself,' he said. 'You'll end up with ruined shoes and aching legs.'

'As if you care,' she snapped back, but the next time he looked she was walking more sensibly.

The sergeant at Wem's small gaol was surprised to see them. 'Plenty of room at the moment,' he said cheerfully. 'We'll make the little lady comfortable.'

'Thank you,' said John. 'Mistress Blanchard is being held pending questioning by Sir Moreton, so she should be treated with respect.'

'I respect all ladies, sir,' said the gaoler.

'Good to hear it. Now, Baccy –' he turned to the prisoner ' – I'll be back later with some food.'

'Just bread, cheese and an apple, I don't eat much,' she muttered, before flopping down on the bench. All her spirit appeared to have left her, but John suspected she was exhausted, for she seemed unaccustomed to exercise. The rope had been used more as a support than a restraint by the end of their journey.

'I'll bring you whatever my wife has prepared. There'll be plenty,' said John.

Baccy shrugged again and rubbed her legs, then looked up at him. 'Married, eh? I hope your wife's suitably grateful.'

'I don't know what you mean,' said John.

Baccy shook her head and lay down. 'You don't look in the mirror often then, Master Carne.'

John turned to the gaoler and took his leave, but the man followed him.

'It's a grim discovery on the Moss, I hear,' he said. 'A man and woman sewn together in the act of congress. How could that have happened?'

John had neither the energy nor the desire to add anything to the already distorted rumours. 'It's a vile thing indeed,' he replied.

———

Spibey was in his panelled study together with Isaac Wellings. 'We've been waiting for you,' said the magistrate as John walked in. 'Is the witch secure?'

'She's too tired to get out her broomstick,' said John, instantly wishing he'd not attempted any form of humour with Spibey, whose ever present frown furrowed deeper into his forehead.

'There's nothing in the cell she can use for her spells, is there?' said Spibey.

'No, save for the bench, table and a bucket, it is bare. Master Wellings, may I ask if there has been any news of your master?'

The steward shook his head.

'I've had men looking all over the county and there's nothing,' said Spibey. 'This is truly most mysterious and suspicious.'

'Hmm,' said John, noncommittally, putting the quivering basket on the floor. He hoped to be able to take his leave soon, so he could pass the increasingly agitated cats into Zipporah's care.

'And', continued Spibey, 'you and I, Master Carne, are among the last to see him.'

'Yes, I remember. On the day I had my appointment, my interview, with you. We merely passed in the hallway. I doubt I'd recognise him again. How long was he with you that day, Sir Moreton?'

'Barely half an hour. He didn't even take refreshment with me. He was keen to be about his business.'

'I should have insisted I went with him,' said Wellings. 'But he would be independent.'

There was a loud squeal and the basket almost tipped over. 'Sir Moreton, may I ask you a favour?' said John. 'I need to take these cats, creatures, whatever they may be, back to my house now, before they rip each other apart.'

Wellings's previously troubled expression lightened somewhat.

'They belong to the witch I have in custody,' explained Spibey. 'Now it's my opinion, and I doubt I'll be proved wrong, she'll be found responsible for this outrage we discovered on the Moss—'

'We need some evidence,' interjected John.

Spibey waved a dismissive hand. 'It'll be found. Why, she may even be responsible for whatever has happened to dear old Tom.'

'How can that be?' said Wellings.

'Off with you, then, John,' said Spibey. 'And mind those things, those familiars. If they cause any trouble or look as if they're going to change, destroy them. I'll take a sworn affidavit from you as to what happened.'

'And if you have no need for me, Sir Moreton, I'll go,' said Wellings.

Spibey dismissed him with a wave.

'I'll take care,' said John, picking up the basket. 'There's just one other thing, concerning Master Perks. I do still fear that he's fallen from his horse in some isolated place. We all know horses; they will either make their way home, or find another horse. We need to discover if anyone has seen it.'

'Or it's been found by a horse thief while wandering. But I catch your drift, Master Carne. If we could find it, it would at least be something. Now take those creatures away.'

John didn't get very far, as the door swung open and a flustered Crowther barely had time to announce Farmer Laycock, who pushed him aside and burst into the room.

'What's going on, Spibey!' said Laycock. 'I hear you've got a witch locked up. The people aren't happy. They say she's been flying over Hornspike, sweeping up all the cats, now the place is awash with vermin.'

John's lips twitched.

Laycock stared at him. 'I don't find this funny.'

'Nor do I, and it's not true.'

'It doesn't matter whether it's true or not. The people are rattled. So, Spibey, what are you going to do about it?'

John noticed Spibey's chins wobble, a sure sign he was flustered.

'The due process of the law must be followed,' said John.

'I'm talking to the magistrate, not you,' said Laycock. 'I'm telling you, Spibey, it's getting ugly out there. It's bad for business, get rid of the woman, I don't care how.'

Spibey pulled himself upright. 'The witch will be examined and when found guilty, hung. This is God's work.'

'She'll only be hung *if* she's found guilty,' said John.

'You should come to the gaol and see what's happening,' said Laycock.

'My assistant will attend to it.' Spibey waved his hands in John's direction.

'You're the magistrate, come and speak to the mob,' said Laycock.

'Mob?' Spibey looked decidedly shaky.

'They won't listen to me. It's you they look up to, Sir Moreton,' said John.

'We'll do this together then,' said Spibey, though with little conviction.

'That you will,' said Laycock, guiding a hesitant Spibey through the door.

John would hardly call the group of people outside the gaol a mob. There was no more than ten of them, and though muttering and shifting about uneasily, they hadn't reached the baying stage.

'I was expecting the Jones brothers to till my fields today,' said Laycock. 'Now they say they're too frightened to leave Wem in case the witch escapes and eats their children.'

'Ah,' said John. Now he understood why Laycock was so upset.

The group moved towards them and Spibey stepped behind John.

A tall man shouted. 'Hang the witch, Sir Moreton. We don't want her casting evil spells over Wem.'

'She can't hurt you from behind bars,' said John. 'And there must be a fair trial.'

'She's sucked the life from every cat in Hornspike.'

John held up the basket. 'I have two fat healthy cats from Hornspike here.'

The small crowd fell back. 'Familiars,' John heard someone say.

'Just cats, I assure you.'

'Help us, Sir Moreton, only you can save us,' said a voice from the back.

There was a murmur of agreement. By now the gathering had almost doubled in size.

Spibey stepped out from behind John. 'Godly people of Wem, my good and gentle townsfolk. As your magistrate, when a crime is reported I act. The witch will be examined and hung. You'll all be there to see justice done. Now, be back about your business. Trust me, I know what I'm doing.'

The tall man wasn't satisfied. 'And what about the bodies you found on the Moss. Stitched together whilst in congress. Are they part of the coven?'

'It's all part of my investigation,' said Spibey. 'You do no good here. Now, go to your homes, or to work.'

There was some grumbling, but apart from a few diehards the group began to disperse, whilst Laycock harangued the Jones brothers.

Spibey bit his nails. 'Should I release her and let them do as they will? In the unlikely event she's innocent, God will protect her, won't he?' he said to John.

John spoke firmly. 'No, sir. You are the law, not the mob. People look up to you and expect you to do God's will.'

'You're right, you're right.'

The basket jerked about in John's hand. 'I really need to get these cats home.'

Spibey nodded.

'We must tread carefully. Justice must be seen to be done,' said John, but Spibey had already turned and was scuttling back to Noble Street.

John felt hollow as he walked back to The Dial.

'It's ridiculous,' said John to Zipporah. 'This Baccy woman's a bit eccentric but no witch, I'd swear it. As for the old man, the poor fellow has simply fallen from his horse. Let's hope some kind person has taken him in and is looking after him.'

Her eyes widened and she tugged his sleeve. 'Oh, no, no, no.' She pointed across the room. 'John, that cat is dropping a turd in my house. Stop it!'

John leapt to his feet, something he should never do. It caused a thunderbolt of pain to sear up his side. 'Ah, argh!' he cried, clutching his thigh and shouting at the discomfort, rather than the cat.

Master Pipkin, the perpetrator, made a show of hiding the evidence by scraping his paws on the stone floor a few times. Then slinked back to the place by the fire, that he and Colonel Jojo had already made their own.

Zipporah ran to the door and opened it wide, pulling and pushing it to and fro. 'The stench! Sir Moreton is right, they are pure evil. What's the witch been feeding them? John, I want the cats and the turd out, not necessarily in that order.'

'My leg,' he protested.

'Husband, now! You brought them here. They're your responsibility.'

When she spoke like that he knew it was better that he acted, no matter what agony he might be in.

The excrement was easily disposed of, and she'd soon mopped the floor clean. The cats, he explained, had to stay.

She raised her hands. 'You're mad, bringing them here.'

'No, I'm trying to save an innocent woman from being convicted simply by Sir Moreton's prejudices. Not to mention the superstitions of the people. There was a nasty little group outside the gaol. At least Spibey persuaded them to leave.' The corners of his mouth turned down. 'I'd hate to see a lynching.'

She shuddered. 'The poor woman must be released.'

'If I can convince Sir Moreton, these are simply cats, not familiars, it might, possibly, help persuade him she's no witch.'

'They *are* cats. They look like cats; they eat like cats; they shit like cats. From everything you've told me today, Sir Moreton Spibey is nothing but a bully. I expect he looks like a bully, acts like a bully and doubtless he shits like a bully—'

Now John held up his hands. 'Stop it,' he laughed, rubbing his eyes. 'The thought of Sir Moreton on his heaving stool is more than I can bear.'

'Well, you know what I mean. He's all big and brave when it comes to arresting an old woman and two fat cats. Now tell me, how difficult is that? When it comes to organising a search for his Methuselah of a son-in-law, what happens? "Oh, help me, John, it's witches." He's pathetic.'

He was still chuckling, he couldn't help it. His love for her burned. With pink cheeks and sparkling eyes, her beauty – of mind, body and spirit – was radiant.

'It wasn't quite like that,' he protested. 'But, yes, you're right: Sir Moreton did show himself as something of a bully today.'

'Don't laugh at me, John.'

'I'm not laughing *at* you, but when you're like this, I adore you more than ever.'

She pushed his shoulders. 'You mock me.'

He tapped her, playfully. 'I do not. Am I allowed no pleasure?'

'None at all. This is a godly house.'

He laughed even louder.

'John Carne, stop it! I was not making a joke. I want your soul to be saved.'

He pulled his features straight. 'Very well, I'll remain serious. I've had a warning today, though. Sir Moreton has shown his true nature. At heart he *is* a narrow-minded bully, one that may not be averse to using violence on a poor defenceless woman.'

'Then on that point I'll have to agree with him. I'd give her a tanning if she was here, the trouble those things are causing me.' She gestured to the sleeping cats.

John had to hide his grin. 'I hardly dare ask, then, if you'll make up a plate of food for her.'

'Of course! Keep the witch alive! Don't worry about the extra effort you put your already overworked wife to!'

His shoulders quivered with his badly suppressed mirth.

'Do *not* laugh, John. I forbid laughter.'

John stopped at the gaol on his way to Spibey's the next morning. The guard seemed rather more reserved than he'd been the night before.

'Are you sure?' he asked before letting John into the cell

through the arched door made of steel bars. 'She's a witch, you'd do well to remember that, sir.'

'Nothing's proved yet,' said John.

Baccy herself seemed happy enough. She handed him the now empty bowl from the night before. 'My compliments to your wife. She's a good cook. How are my babies?'

'In the care of my wife, who is as good a carer as she is a cook.' He gave her a folded napkin. 'Just some bread and cheese for your breakfast.'

'And an apple, I hope.' She peeped inside. 'Yes, there's an apple.'

He reached into his pocket. 'And, if you promise not to tell Sir Moreton, I've brought you this.' It was a pipe, filled with tobacco.

'I'll enjoy that first. I thank you, sir.' She lit it from the candle in the sconce on the wall.

'Have you had as comfortable a night as possible?' he asked, thinking what a stupid thing it was to say but wanting to make her understand he was on her side.

'It was going well,' she said, puffing contentedly, sending a plume of smoke into the cold air. 'I had someone to talk to, which made a nice change.'

'And exactly who did you think you were talking to?'

'The sergeant, there was no one else here. It's a quiet town, don't you think? I didn't even have a drunk to share him with. Anyway, we enjoyed a good gossip. He told me about these bodies found on the Moss. All nailed together with thorns. What a thing.'

'What a "thing" indeed. Have you ever heard of such a "thing" before, Baccy?'

'Of course not, nor has anyone else.'

'Do you have any idea what sort of person might have done this?'

'From the sound of it, someone with a lot of time and a lot of thorns. Stitching two bodies together by such means must be most difficult.'

John wondered if he should tell her that the bodies weren't sewn together at all, and see if her face registered anything, but decided against it. 'What else did you and the sergeant speak of?'

'Oh, this and that. He shared a jug of ale with me. He didn't come in, though; he passed it through the bars. I wouldn't want him to get into any trouble.'

'What did you really say to him, Baccy?'

She fiddled with the material of her skirt. 'Are you sure about my babies? Are they crying for me?'

'They make some irritating mewling noises; whether it is for you or not I cannot say. So, you and the sergeant were sharing a drink and a bit of gossip, and then something happened that made him afraid of you. Made him believe you're a witch.'

She wriggled slightly. 'I suppose I got bit silly. I'm used to fine wine, not rough ale. It's been such a long time. I said if he wanted to come in and get friendly, I was more than amenable. It was a genuine offer; I wasn't trying to escape.'

'And that frightened him? Why?'

She shrugged. 'I don't know. I was insulted. I'm not that old, but too old to incite lust it seems. I don't suppose I can entice you? If your wife's got any sense she grabs you the moment you walk through the door.'

John swallowed hard. 'I need to ask some more questions about the accusations made against you.'

She put down the pipe and picked up the apple. 'And I'd like to know by whom. The people of Hornspike are mostly in-bred idiots, but they've got the sense to know I keep some of them in well-paid, easy work.' She bit into the fruit.

'Sir Moreton was informed that you burned one of your cats, or familiars, and baked a cake with the ashes, then ate it.'

'I've never baked a cake in my life, out of any ingredients.'

'So, is there some basis to this story?'

She wrinkled her pert and not unattractive face, took another bite, chewed noisily and swallowed. 'If I'm hung for a witch, will you keep my babies and look after them?'

'Baccy, this is a bit more important than your cats.'

She thumped the bench with her fist. 'Nothing is more important than my babies.'

'Yes, yes,' said John hastily, hoping to prevent a return to the hysteria of the day before.

She yawned. 'I'm tired, I've had enough. Just promise me you'll keep Pipkin and Jojo.'

John nodded, hoping this wouldn't be enough to make her give up and confess to anything. That would only encourage Spibey into making more baseless arrests. 'Don't hang yourself yet, Baccy. I'm not convinced you're a witch. Come on, something happened with the cat, I can see it in your face. Tell me.'

'I suppose you'll try to be understanding?'

'I'll do my best to be sympathetic, I promise.' He hoped he would. What if she told him something that would only confirm that she was a witch? Would he tell Spibey?

Chapter Eight

B accy shuffled uneasily on the bench. 'Not that I'm bothered if anyone understands me or not.'

John adopted what he hoped was an expression of sincere interest.

Baccy continued, 'It started with Princess Poppy; she's Master Pipkin's mother, well, was. She died and I buried her most respectfully in my garden, but wild animals show no respect, and the next morning...' The corners of her mouth turned down and she paused to wipe a tear from her eye. 'They'd dug her up. She was in pieces, all over the place. My Princess, my first baby, all matted bloody hair. I couldn't stand it. Master Carne, imagine if your own child was dismembered and scattered around, how would you like it?'

'Not at all. It's not a thought to dwell upon. However, please continue with your story, distressing though I realise it is. How did you recover from this tragedy?'

'I recovered because I'm strong. I have to be. When my second child, Sir Pokey, died I didn't risk an interment. I'd read that the ancient Vikings burned their warriors on a pyre, sending them straight to heaven.' She sniffed loudly. 'So when Pokey's time came I dispatched him to Valhalla, the traditional way.'

'Be careful, Baccy, the Vikings were pagans. Will you swear that you're a true Christian?'

'Will you?'

'I would so swear, because I have faith in the Lord.'

'I believe in Him too, and I *hate* Him.'

John took a deep breath, looked around and held up his hand. 'I strongly advise you to think before you say any more,' he whispered.

She shrugged and re-lit the pipe. 'I don't care. You may as well know the truth. Over the years I've asked the Lord many questions and not received a single decent answer to any. Why did He make my husband desire men rather than me? Why did He not let me conceive, to at least have the consolation of children? Why has He let me be old and despised, well before my time? None of this is my fault. God is cruel. Look around. If you haven't worked that out for yourself, then you're a fool, Master Carne.'

He didn't want to get into a theological argument with her. 'So, you have a husband, Mistress Blanchard, and he keeps you. He sends you fine wine and money, doesn't he?'

She looked at him but didn't answer.

'The wine in your cask was of the best quality. Your house is well kept; your garments are made of excellent fabrics, and you have many books. Someone is paying for that.'

'Guilt is paying. I'm thirsty.'

John called for the gaoler, who brought some more ale. Then she continued her tale. Though disappointed by remaining childless, she had thought her marriage happy until she found her husband engaging lewdly with a man she believed to be simply his best friend. After this discovery, the husband and his lover removed themselves to London, where they lived, ostensibly as two bachelors.

'London is a most Puritan place,' said John.

'My husband is a most Puritan man. They can be the worst. The thing is, I was prepared to accept his passions for another, as long as I kept my reputation. But he's gone and everyone knows why. So I'm left alone, neither a respectable wife, nor a respected widow, who'd be free to marry again if the chance arose. He says he thinks of me as a friend, but what place does a friend have in society? My husband used me ill, Master Carne, and God is cruel that He let this happen to me.'

'Your husband, if what you say is true, has indeed been unfair. But whether God or the devil caused this, I cannot say.' He reached out and took her hand. 'Baccy, I don't believe you're a witch, and I'll tell Sir Moreton that's my opinion.'

She pushed him away and looked stubborn. 'I don't care, just promise to look after my babies.'

If she hung it would be his fault as much as Spibey's. He stood. 'Mistress, if your cats cannot be returned to your care, I will have them.' He had a real motivation to keep Baccy alive now, for he dare not face Zipporah with the news that Pipkin and Jojo had a permanent position in their home. He nodded to her. 'I'll leave you to your breakfast, mistress.'

As he left the gaol, John approached a small group of townspeople talking to the gaoler. He heard the words 'witch', 'flying cats' and 'unnatural lusts', being bandied about. He felt anger and frustration building inside him. Baccy was already condemned as far as these good people of Wem were concerned.

'She's just a confused old woman,' he said.

'Can you not see the devil at work, Master Carne,' said one. The others nodded in agreement.

It was no use, their minds were made up. He headed to Noble Street. Spibey had no idea of the evil he'd unleashed in the name of fighting sin.

Later that morning John recounted a somewhat edited version of his earlier conversation with Baccy to Spibey.

'Better we'd interrogated her together. What if you'd been bewitched?'

'There was no chance of that, and the sergeant was in attendance at all times. I was preparing the ground for you, so to speak, Sir Moreton. There's no need for you to waste time with the preliminaries.'

Spibey nodded. 'I know you try to assist me in all ways. Now, the creatures, the imps, did they change at all, overnight?'

'They did not,' said John with a wry smile. 'Though I think my wife might have wished they had.' He stopped as he saw Spibey's face cloud. 'Sorry. It was simply that they're not clean animals and my – we keep a clean house.'

'Oh,' said Spibey, flatly. 'They definitely remained cats? Behaved as cats? They never flew about the place?'

'They ate, slept and shitted as cats, to be blunt,' said John quoting Zipporah. He didn't give Spibey time for further comment. 'Mistress Blanchard has a husband, it transpires. He lives in London, but makes sure his wife wants for nothing. I believe him to be a godly man, and not without means.'

Spibey frowned and looked confused. John hoped that, bully as he was, now there was a man involved, no matter how distantly, he might think again.

'The accusation has been made against this woman, I have to investigate.' muttered Spibey. He turned to John. 'I think I should examine her myself. If she doesn't admit to witchcraft, she may have some of the signs about her. Oh, yes, Master Carne, I can see from your face how distasteful this is to you, but the devil will use our decency to try and blind us.' He narrowed his eyes. 'Do you suggest there is an estrangement between this man and his wife? Is he trying to escape her witchery?'

'Their estrangement is for personal reasons.'

'Come, Carne,' said Spibey harshly. 'Do not dissemble. It does your character no credit.'

John sighed. Baccy seemed quite open about the whole thing; she would probably have told Spibey anyway. 'Master Blanchard lives in London with a friend, an old friend, a man who is more than simply a friend, if you understand my meaning.'

The magistrate juddered from head to toe and leapt to his feet. 'Then the husband's no better than his witch of a wife. Can you not see? Evil has infected this couple, both of them.'

John groaned inwardly. He'd tried to help Baccy but everything he said just seemed to make things worse. The way Spibey's desire for 'righteous' justice was going, there'd be a hanging before the day was out, evidence or no evidence. But Spibey was illogical and bigoted; surely he could outwit him.

'Sir Moreton,' he said softly, wondering if he should say anything, but unwilling to leave things as they were. 'Why do people follow Satan and not Our Lord?' He swallowed quickly. 'Isn't it so that they may prosper in this world, though they know they have forfeited salvation in the next? And yet, what has Mistress Blanchard got to show for any sorcery? She lives alone, eating, at her own admission, very little. She never travels; she has no position in society. She's merely tolerated and reliant upon youngsters in the village to do her chores. Surely there's nothing here worthy of risking a soul?'

'Why do you persist in trying to protect this woman? What she gains is the knowledge that she and her infernal master are stealing souls from the Lord.'

It was time to keep quiet. There was no point trying to engage Spibey in rational argument. John might as well resign there and then. Except he couldn't. He'd have to learn to sit back and accept the loss of the likes of Baccy Blanchard, if that's what it took to keep his employment, which, for numerous reasons, he couldn't afford to lose. It put him in a highly uncomfortable position, though.

Any further discussion was curtailed by the arrival of Crowther. 'Excuse my interruption, Sir Moreton, but I have two men from Hornspike in the hall below. Apparently, a rather distasteful discovery's been made there.'

Spibey's expression was triumphant. 'Hornspike, Master Carne! How can so much evil reside in so small a place?' He actually smiled. No, it was more. It was a wide, malevolent grin, exposing his large, crooked teeth and almost splitting his face in two. 'Come, let us hear about this evil for ourselves.'

The messengers were Simmonds, the farmer from Hornspike, accompanied by his son. Simmonds told them a body had been found hanging from a rowan tree, at a place called Low Meadow.

'A suicide or a lynching?' Spibey asked.

The man was definite. 'No lynching, sir, and I would venture it was no suicide, either. I recognised the body. It's Thomas Perks, my landlord.'

Spibey nearly fell to the ground, so completely did his legs buckle. John and Crowther managed to grasp his arms and guide him to a chair, where he spent a while, quaking from head to toe. His skin became a dirty grey colour, his lips reddish-blue and tight across his teeth. John poured a good portion of wine and, though Spibey slobbered a lot of it, his revival swiftly began. Colour poured back to his cheeks, which became almost livid, and the tremors stopped.

'My dearest Margaret,' he whispered under his breath, before giving Crowther strict instructions that the news would go no further, and especially not to the young widow. 'I must tell her myself,' he said. 'But first, we go to Hornspike, to see this abomination for ourselves and to ensure Tom is brought back here with respect.'

Spibey's horses were soon saddled, and he and John accompanied Simmonds and his son back to Hornspike.

'He definitely wasn't there yesterday,' the farmer assured Spibey. 'I check my sheep every day, and yesterday me and my boy moved them from Short Furlong down to Low Meadow. That and setting right any holes in the hedges took us most of the day. If there'd been a man hanging we'd have seen him, wouldn't we, Jim?' Simmonds looked over his shoulder.

The younger man nodded. He rode next to John.

'Are you the "Jim" who helps Mistress Blanchard?' John asked quietly, pulling his cape more tightly round his neck. The sun hadn't even turned up on the battlefield that day. Dark, dank clouds claimed absolute victory.

He nodded. 'She's an odd one, but all right. Well, I thought she was all right, if you know what I mean. Now it seems she's a witch.'

'She's not been tried yet, never mind found guilty,' said John. 'But if you can think of anything that might help either prove or disprove the accusations made against her, let me know.'

The youth nodded again. 'She talks to herself a lot, does Baccy. But then, so does my ma. She says it's the only way she can have a decent conversation in our house, on account of the house being full of men.'

They rode a little further before Jim spoke again. 'Who told you Mistress Blanchard was a witch?'

'A travelling peddler reported it. He wasn't sure enough of his accusations to stay around and make them in person. He simply passed a message to Sir Moreton.'

Jim's lips twisted uncomfortably.

John guessed he wanted to say more. 'Did you tell the peddler that Baccy was a witch?' he asked.

'I never said that, sir,' said the youth. 'But we were laughing together and I told him that Baccy burnt her cat on a fire and then sprinkled the ashes on a cake and ate it.'

'Did you add the bit about the cat flying through the air later that night?'

Jim looked at him wide-eyed. 'I did not, sir. How could the cat fly? It was dead and burned. I wish I'd said nothing.'

'Sometimes it's better to keep one's own counsel,' said John, not unkindly.

They were quiet for a while, then the two men in front urged their horses into a trot and they did likewise.

'At least the justice seems to have recovered,' said Jim, a little breathlessly and changing the topic. 'He took the news very badly, sir, didn't he?'

'Yes,' replied John. 'He did.'

And so they arrived at Low Meadow, which, as the name suggested, lay in a hollow. A small stream, the water tanned brown like that on the Moss, ran through it.

'How far are we from the Moss?' asked John.

Simmonds pointed. 'Just past those trees, sir.' Then he turned to Spibey. 'You can see it, I mean him, sir?'

The magistrate nodded. John too, could see, in the distance, what appeared to be a length of cloth hanging from a tree.

'I'll warn you,' said Simmonds, just before they reached Perks. 'It's not simply a hanging. The body has been … interfered with. The lips have been pinned together with thorns.'

They pulled their mounts to a halt. Spibey's hands trembled, as he held his reins tight. 'Abomination, vile abomination. The witch will pay, for it must be her.'

'Let me examine the evidence, and then we'll bring his body to the ground,' said John as smoothly as he could. It wasn't looking good for Baccy. The fact that she'd been locked up in Wem gaol all night might be the only evidence in her favour at the moment.

'We touched nothing,' said Simmonds.

As Spibey seemed momentarily struck dumb, John answered for him. 'And that was very much the right thing to do. We needed to see the body of Master Perks just as he was found. Tell me, sir, when did you finally leave Low Meadow yesterday?'

'At dusk.'

'And what time did you return this morning.'

'After milking. It was full light.'

One of Simmonds' shepherds, who'd been guarding the body, was clearly pleased to be relieved of his duty.

Spibey asked him if he'd seen any imps or demons.

'No, sir,' said the man. 'But them crows over there look interested. I'm surprised he's still got his eyes. A dead lamb will lose theirs within the hour.' He looked up at Simmonds. 'I reckon I've done my duty, master.'

'Yes, thank you,' he replied. 'You may go.'

John looked at the rowan tree and its gruesome fruit. Perks hung limply, only a slight breeze swayed him. He was clothed as a man on a long journey in cold weather would be. His hat was still on his head, his coat buttoned and a heavy cloak hung from his shoulders. The same clothes he'd been wearing when he'd visited Spibey. Which, John reasoned, was only to be expected as he hadn't been seen at his home after that day. His face was grey with the pallor of death but looked quite peaceful, apart from the thorns pulling the thin lips together.

'I assume you have a cart?' John asked Simmonds.

'I'll bring it,' said the man, and he rode off.

John nudged his mount closer to the body. He reached up to the man's shoulder. The rowan was not tall, and it was only the fact that Perks was such a tiny man, that stopped his feet grazing the ground. The rope around his neck was of a common sort that would be used by any farmer. How John wished this could have been the work of an imp or vile demon. Instead, he realised, this was a cold bloodied act of one person to another. To fight, to kill, on the battlefield was one thing. To do this, to murder a defenceless old man and then mutilate him, was something else. And why? What message was the murderer trying to convey? Was it a warning, or simply an act of spite? He looked around. Was this place, this field significant? Crows were wheeling overhead, cawing with anticipation at the thought of the feast below. They reminded him of the onlookers outside the gaol, gorging on Baccy's misfortune. John swallowed down bile. He returned his attention to the body and gently swung it around. He pulled out his pocketbook, licked the end of his lead, and began to write.

'What's that you're doing?' asked Spibey.

'Taking notes, Sir Moreton. There's something not right about this.'

'It's all very wrong, that's obvious. You don't need paper and a pencil to work that out.'

'No, I'm not talking morally. I mean that it's wrong. I don't think Master Perks died by hanging.'

Spibey's fingers went up to his lips. 'What? What? What are you suggesting? The man swings from a tree; it's plain, he's hanged. Don't try and get fanciful with me, Master Carne.' His voice sounded strangled by panic again.

'I'm sorry,' said John. 'Perhaps it isn't right for you to investigate the murder of your own son-in-law. I can see the distress it's causing you.'

'No, no, I'm strong. I'm the very person who must do it. Tell me, what do you see?'

John guided his pony next to Spibey's horse, knowing the magistrate would feel more secure looking down at him. 'I think that Master Perks was killed and then strung up. When a man dies from hanging his face bloats, the tongue swells and lolls, the eyes pop—'

'You're my assistant, remember that. Yet you presume to tell me that a man most definitely strung up, indeed, hanging here before us, did not die by the noose about his neck?'

'The last thing I want to do is step above my position, but I feel I must tell you what I see.'

Spibey's face twisted. 'You do overstep. *I'll* find out what happened, then you'll write the report *I* dictate.'

'Very well, sir,' said John, but he continued with his own jottings. If his ever-increasing understanding of Spibey's character was correct, once his panic subsided the magistrate would become more amenable to rational investigation.

The body swung again in the breeze. The rope creaked, John heard a soft snap of wood. The branch was weak. He didn't want Perks to fall to the ground, like a rotten apple.

'Get him down, quick man!' shouted Spibey.

With relief John saw the cart trundling into view as it bumped along the meadow. The farmer parked it beneath the tree, and he and his son most respectfully cut Perks down. They laid the body on some sack cloth and covered it with a sheet.

'Do you want us to take him to your house at Wem, or back to his home?'

'My house,' said Spibey. 'I'll make all the arrangements. Let us pray.'

The men dipped their heads.

'We pray for vengeance,' said Spibey. 'For the vengeance of the Lord to come down swiftly upon the perpetrators of this unholy crime. And we pray that we may be the instruments of His vengeance.'

There was silence, then Spibey raised his head. The farmer and his son saw this as a signal to shake the reins and the cart bounced off.

Back at Wem, Reverend Parsons was keen to assure Spibey that, although undoubtedly the victim of witchcraft, Master Perks would be ensured a Christian burial. Not so the Moss bodies.

'Evil and pagan through and through,' he said. 'I'll not have them within a mile of my churchyard.'

'See to it, Carne,' said Spibey. Despite his grief, he was keen to play the decisive master in front of the clergyman.

'I will,' said John. 'But I don't know where they can be interred. I've little enough land of my own, and all well within a mile of the church.'

'I've an odd patch, just off the road to Ellesmere,' said Spibey.

'We call it the Spare Field; Crowther knows of it. Get him to send some men to dig a pit, and make sure those beasts are thrown into it.'

'They stench of hell and corruption,' said Parsons. 'I'm surprised your whole household hasn't become infected with evil.'

'A less godly establishment would certainly have fallen to the devil, but I see to it that we all wrap ourselves in the Scriptures,' said Spibey piously.

'Of course you do, Moreton.'

Keen though he was to examine Perks's body, John realised he wasn't required, and took his leave.

'I'll send for you when I need you again,' said Spibey dismissively, which made John wonder if once he'd disposed of the bodies his time as the witchfinder's assistant would be over.

Crowther knew of the land Spibey mentioned.

'It's a small field, but there's plenty of room for your purpose. I'll get a few of the men on to it straight away. We all want to see those bodies gone, so they'll have the hole ready for first light tomorrow. Do you want me to arrange the cart?'

'Yes, thank you, Crowther. You've been very helpful. I'll be here at dawn.'

John limped morosely back to The Dial. Nothing was working out as he hoped. He thought he'd have an easy job, helping Spibey with his administration. Now he was embroiled in a murder investigation, where the culprit, verdict and punishment had already been decided. The pain in his leg was nothing compared to the ache in his heart.

Chapter Nine

John stopped dead in front of the door to the Dial. A message was written across it in chalk. "Do not enter". His heart jumped around in his chest. What was going on? He ran round to the back of the house, where they had a relatively small but adequate patch of land for their hens and pig.

Zipporah was by the sty, weaving some willow twigs. 'You didn't go in, did you?' she called. 'I've got them locked inside, until I've finished this.'

'What?'

'The cats.' She looked up from her weaving. 'I can't keep them in the house, pissing and the rest of it. They won't catch food for themselves and will only accept the tenderest morsels of meat. There's nought left but gristle for you tonight, husband. You can blame your favourite witch's familiars for that.'

He looked down. She'd fixed some planks to the end of the sty, and the willow mesh must be for the top. 'Good work, Zipporah, you're wasted as a wife. Your talent is obviously for carpentry and basketry.'

She shrugged. 'It could have been even better if I'd taken my time, but they're not worth the effort. I knew they had to live outside when I found them both in the babies' cradle; fortunately my darlings weren't in it at the time.' She twisted in another twig. 'That's not all. The monsters will only drink milk heated to a certain temperature, too hot they run away, too cold and I must scold it for them again.'

John laughed. 'You've cheered me up.'

She snorted. 'So it seems my discomfort gives you pleasure.' She placed the lid on top of the small enclosure. 'Perfect fit.'

'Neat weaving, but why not use some more planks of wood?'

'I'm not cruel, it would be pitch-black inside if I did. Hold it steady while I lash it in place. What are you doing home at this time, anyway?'

'I think Sir Moreton may have dispensed with my services.'

'Good. I'll take in washing and sewing. It would be a more honourable employment than working for that man.'

'There's been some truly terrible developments. The way things are going, we may end up with the cats forever.'

She squinted her eyes at him. 'Let's get the beasts incarcerated, then tell me.'

Despite their usual languor, Master Pipkin and Colonel Jojo put up a spirited fight before they were caught and re-homed in their cage. Once inside they were soon mollified with some lukewarm milk and a kidney plucked from that evening's pie. Zipporah had, of course, been joking when she said only gristle remained for their meal.

When they finally got back indoors, John sank into a chair and rubbed his leg. 'Some of your salve is needed. How these cramps grip me!'

'Do you want me to apply it?'

Of course he did but there was no point. 'No, best I do it myself, lest your lusts are inflamed by the comely turn of my thigh.' He pushed down his britches.

She looked down dispassionately at his ruined leg, and handed him an earthenware ointment pot. 'You're doing a lot more riding and walking than you're used to. I'm not surprised you're pained. Now, tell me of the developments you mentioned earlier.'

'Ah yes. Thomas Perks, has been found. Dead. Hanging from a tree in Hornspike.'

'What!' She pulled up a chair next to him. 'And Hornspike, isn't that where Baccy comes from? Here, let me.' She pushed his hands away and began applying the salve herself. She was better at it, and he immediately felt the benefit. He recounted the details of their discoveries, together with Spibey's dismissals of his theories, such as they were.

She remained thoughtful as she finished massaging John's leg. Then she served them both a slice of pie, smiling ruefully at the kidney shaped space.

'So, you don't believe it was the hanging that killed Perks?'

He shook his head. 'This is delicious,' he said.

'So, the man was killed elsewhere, by witches or whatever, and then, rather than dispose of the body secretly, it was hung in a place where it was sure to be found.'

He swallowed a mouthful of ale. 'I suppose the farmer and his workers are the only ones likely to pass that way, and there was no attempt made to hide the body at all. The business with the thorns is the strangest thing. There must be some connection with the bodies on the Moss. We presume the man on the Moss was punished for what he saw, so his eyes were sealed.'

'More pie?'

He nodded.

'And,' she said, pushing his plate back to him, 'he was punished for what he did. Don't forget the other place where the thorns were found.'

John nodded. 'Perks's mouth was sealed. Are we to assume he said, or was about to say something?'

She got a small wooden tray from the sideboard and put a generous slice of pie and an apple on it, before wrapping it in a cloth. 'For the witch, when you've finished here. See if she's surprised to hear that Perks is dead. Have you asked her if she knows of any missing pregnant girls with painted lovers?'

'If I'm no longer working for Sir Moreton, there's not much point. I'll feed her, of course, but I doubt I'll be involved in any further investigations.'

'You will. Spibey has many faults, but being a fool isn't one of them. He panics when you notice something he should have seen for himself, but he'll want you back.'

When he finished his food and ale she handed him the package, and briefly, their fingers touched.

'Dearest Zipporah.' He leaned forward, imagining a closeness between them.

She pushed him away, of course. 'Go and feed your witch!' But she was smiling as she spoke.

———

'Huh, I'd hoped you'd come to tell me I'm to be hung, at least something would be happening,' said Baccy, churlishly pulling some crust off the pie and nibbling it. She was sulky.

Her words, so carelessly uttered, carved a hollow pit in John's stomach. 'Be careful what you wish for. If Sir Moreton has his way, you'll hang sooner rather than later, trial or no trial.'

'I've had enough. I welcome death. Now I know my babies will be cared for, I'm happy to go. How are the darlings?'

'My wife's giving them very close attention.'

Her pinched expression relaxed, and she gurgled happily. She took a larger bite from the pastry.

'Is the gaoler talking to you?' he asked.

'Not a word.' She wiped her mouth with her hand.

She couldn't know that Perks had been found, then, even if she knew he was dead. He wouldn't mention it for now. Instead, he asked if there'd been any young women gone missing recently.

'The woman found on the Moss was great-bellied with child,' he said.

She shrugged, wiped her mouth with her hand again and filled her mug from the jug of ale he'd brought her. 'I have to rely on that grinning idiot Jim and his doltish sister for information, so I know very little. Women get with child all the time. I haven't heard of one going missing. You could have brought more pie. That was hardly sufficient.'

Zipporah had cut a more than adequate piece. Baccy was obviously greedier than she pretended to be. 'You've still got your apple.' He sighed. 'I'll make sure I bring bigger portions next time. The man found in the Moss, there's a possibility that his skin may have been painted.'

Her face puckered and she picked her teeth. 'Strange, I've never seen such a man.' She paused, sucked her fingers and leaned forward. 'Now, Louisa Hines, she went missing, well, it would be maybe ten or so years ago, I suppose. They said she was with child, by the squire himself, but no one believed it. After all, Perks had had three wives by then and no issue, so we presumed there was no ink in his nib.'

Perks! John didn't move and tried to keep his expression neutral. 'Would that be Thomas Perks of Whixall?'

'That's the one. Runty little fellow, but his wealth made him popular.'

'The present Mistress Perks is about to deliver his heir.'

'So, there you go. Never listen to gossip. Have you brought me some tobacco?'

He had. 'Did anyone look for this Louisa Hines when she went missing?'

'There was quite a search, but I suppose in the end we all presumed Perks wasn't the father, and she'd run away with another lover.' She puffed her pipe and raised an eyebrow. 'Perhaps he was a gypsy.'

'Were there gypsies around at the time?'

'Not that I recollect. It was years ago, Master Carne. Anyway, you can go now. I'm tired. Can get me a new gaoler? This one's no good since he's stopped talking.'

Welcome or not, John thought he should at least report back to Spibey. The magistrate was about to go and dine at the rectory with Reverend Parsons, but granted John a few minutes of his precious time.

'You've got to learn,' he said sternly, 'that you're my assistant. I lead and you follow. In private, I don't mind if you air your opinions, but when others are present, especially if they're from the lower orders, then you must let me take precedence. Do you understand?'

'I do. I can only apologise. As you so rightly said, I've only been your assistant a short while, and I freely admit, I do have much to learn.'

Spibey motioned him to sit down and took his usual seat behind the desk. John presumed this gesture meant that his apology had been accepted.

'May I ask how your daughter has taken the news of her husband's death?' said John.

'It's difficult to say. She simply sits and says nothing. I'm not sure she fully understands.'

'I'm so sorry. When is the baby due?'

'Not for at least two months, but this shock, who knows what effect it may have?' Spibey shuffled awkwardly in his chair. 'I believe the midwife, Molly Kade, is the best in the county,' he said, staring blankly at the tabletop.

'She's very competent. She's with my brother in Shrewsbury at the moment, attending to his wife.'

'That's good,' said Spibey, at last looking at John.

'I'll write to my brother and ask if he'll send her to you, once she's no longer needed by them.'

'Would you do that? I feel that once the true horror of the situation is understood by my poor Margaret, the baby may come sooner rather than later. Bring the letter to me and I'll arrange a messenger.'

John nodded in assent. 'The real reason for my visit this evening is to inform you what I've learned from Mistress Blanchard. As far as I can tell, she knows nothing about Master Perks's death. Concerning the woman found in the Moss, she recalled that about ten years ago, a young woman by the name of Louisa Hines went missing, thought to be pregnant.' He paused, swallowed and then decided to continue. 'The father of the child was rumoured to be Master Perks.' He held his breath wondering how Spibey would react to this.

'What nonsense,' spluttered the magistrate. 'Everyone knows that Tom – well, the squire had no children when he married my Margaret.'

'As I said, the disappearance happened many years ago. I believe Master Perks had already been three times widowed. He'd not be the only lonely man to take solace outside the marriage bed. Please excuse me for talking so, but I'd like to discover his murderer just as much as you.'

Spibey held up his hand. 'We all want to see justice done. But to suggest that Tom Perks "sought solace" as you so politely put it is ridiculous. You didn't know him, Master Carne. He was godly, and I urge you not to mention any of this scurrilous gossip outside this room. Gossip fed to you by a vengeful witch.'

'I'm simply repeating what she told me for your information. Whatever she may or may not be, she certainly didn't hang Master Perks at Low Meadow, as she was safely in gaol all night.'

Spibey wriggled. 'She's involved. She must be. It's not impossible for a witch to be in two places at once.'

'I bow to your greater knowledge. I don't think she's much of a witch, though. May I share one more thought with you, which of course you may dismiss?'

Spibey stood. 'Share it with me tomorrow. I'm already late for my appointment at the rectory. I'll see you at first light, Master Carne.'

'I'm to dispose of the Moss bodies at first light.'

'Of course, well, as soon as you can after that.'

———————

Back at The Dial, Zipporah was not engaged in any of her normal occupations: such as looking after her babies, cooking, washing, sewing, or tending to her various wines, pickles and preserves. Not to mention the tilling and animal care that occupied her outside. Instead, she was sitting at the table, pen and ink in front of her, staring at some papers. John thought for a moment she was updating her journal, which she did every day and kept most private, the covers tied tightly with leather straps when not in use. On this occasion, the papers before her were loose.

'I'm glad you've got the writing box out,' he said, sitting opposite her. 'I need to send a letter to my brother.'

She didn't look up. 'There's plenty of spare pens, help yourself.'

He quickly wrote the request for Molly Kade to be returned to Wem, and put it in his pocket ready for the next day. He leaned across the table. She'd drawn vertical lines to divide her pages into columns. 'What are you doing, your accounts?'

'Trying to make sense of things. Every column is a day of the week. It begins on Thursday, when you first went to see Sir Moreton. Here's when you went to the Moss.' She tapped the paper. 'Sunday is a narrow column, because we only went to church and then sneaked a look at the bodies.'

He went round the table, sat next to her, and looked down at her jottings.

'If I can get everything organised, perhaps it'll become clearer.'

'And you do like to be organised.'

She shot him a swift glance.

'I'm not mocking, believe me,' he said and lit his pipe.

She was so absorbed in her thoughts, he noticed, that she didn't wince or criticise him for his proximity.

'So, Thursday is the last report we have of Master Perks being seen by anyone. Has his horse been found?' She was writing 'T Perks' halfway down the page.

'No, and that bothers me. Why has no one reported seeing it?'

'Because they've kept it for themselves. Or it died, or it fell in the Moss. But you're right, John, it's strange nothing has been seen of it. It seems that Perks rode away from Sir Moreton's house and, that was it – he vanished.'

John nodded. 'I'll ask Crowther if he saw Master Perks leave, and if he did, which way he headed. Baccy Blanchard told me of a woman who disappeared some ten years ago, who was rumoured to be with child by Perks.'

'You think she could be the woman in the Moss?'

'I don't know. It's a long time ago, even if the Moss does preserve. But by then Perks had been widowed three times and still had no heirs. Don't you think in those circumstances he'd simply have married the woman? Even if her morals were loose.'

She nodded. 'If the child was his, almost certainly, provided she wasn't already married.'

'Sir Moreton seemed, briefly, to suggest that Perks was thought to be incapable of fathering children, though he quickly changed the subject. Baccy wasn't so reticent; she said he had no ink in his nib.'

'And I've none in mine.' She chuckled, dipped her pen in the pot, then made some more notes at the bottom of the page. 'Do we know when Sir Moreton was informed about the Moss bodies?'

'I presume it was later on the Thursday, or very early Friday, for we set off to see them as soon as I arrived for my first day's work.'

'There must be some link between them and Perks. The thing with the thorns is too similar.'

He poured them both a mug of ale. 'I agree there is some connection, but I cannot go as far as thinking it's devilry.'

'I don't think it can be completely discounted. *You* may not believe, but others do.'

He smiled. As her sharp mind buzzed, his body awoke. He watched as she took a sip of ale, her finger running across her mouth afterwards. She blinked her long eyelashes as she scanned her notes, looking for connections, for order, for organisation. Her tongue softly moistened her pink lips; her concentration was complete. He needed to touch her. He needed to love her.

'Excuse me, I'm going outside,' was all he could say.

'Did you have a look at the cats?' she asked when he came back.

'No, I only went to ease myself.'

'I'll see to them later.' She looked at the paper again. 'I do wonder if the bodies on the Moss were killed by the stake that pierced them.'

John raised his eyebrows. 'You don't think being impaled by a pike is sufficient to kill?'

'I suppose so. But the thorns, they must have been done once they were dead. You couldn't do such a thing to a living person; they'd put up too much of a struggle.'

'They need not be dead. They could be drunk, drugged, or in some sort of religious trance if pagan ritual is involved.'

She sighed heavily. 'Why do you have to think of everything?'

He refilled their mugs. 'I don't think of everything, but I do like the way you're trying to work things out.'

'Who hung Tom Perks and why?' She looked up at the ceiling.

'Why wasn't it simply enough to kill him and dispose of the body? It would be so easy with an old man like that, riding alone, to make it look like an accident. Now foul play is a certainty.'

'Correct. There's hatred behind this act.'

'Or magic. How can we know how far someone is prepared to go to try and change their fortune? If they know themselves to be damned already, and some of us do, why should they not dabble with the devil?'

He briefly reached out and squeezed her hand, then quickly withdrew it before she snatched her own away. 'Zipporah, how many times do I have to tell you? Just because your brother says your soul is lost, it's not true. Randall is not God. Nor should he presume to be. You're beautiful, in soul and body. If you're damned, then I'll be damned with you. For without you, there will be no heaven for me—'

She suddenly threw down her pen, tiny ink blobs splattered over the tabletop. The legs of her chair grated on the stone floor as she pushed it away from the table. Her hands landed hard on his shoulders. 'No, sir, never, ever say that. I'll not lead you to hell. I will not! Leave me, cast me out. Don't breathe the air I breathe.' She grabbed her journal, held it close to her chest and clattered up the stairs.

John stretched his arms across the table and laid his head on them. What could he do? Why did she so constantly rebuff him? Despite all his love, why did she find him so obnoxious?

His arms were tingling when he finally lifted his head. All light had faded. He lit a candle, and placed it next to Zipporah's chart. For a time, they'd become so absorbed in the puzzle they'd been able to put their troubles behind them. He put the pages side by side. Thursday to Tuesday. Not quite a week and yet so much had happened. He stared at the sheets covered with her spiky writing. There must be something there, yet neither of them could see it. The dim candle flickered in a draught. He needed his bed.

She was fast asleep, sniffling slightly into the bolster. His leg, his back and his head all ached. He peeled off his clothes, shivering slightly, and pulled on his nightshirt. He lay on his back. She turned over and rested her head on his shoulder and then, and he wondered if he was dreaming, her arm snaked across his chest and lay heavily there. Complete exhaustion seeped through him, and to his shame he felt hot tears pricking his eyes. Would he never sleep? he wondered, just as darkness enveloped him.

Chapter Ten

So much evil in the world. John showed me the grim remains from the
Moss. At times I was so distressed I held him. To my shame it gave me
comfort. Then some poor eccentric crone is arrested. Can I in some way
help John to set her free? John is a good man. If this war had not
intervened I would have… Could I even now? But I cannot allow myself
to think like this. He must never know what happened. For my babes, I
will remain strong.

Journal of Zipporah Carne

Thick fog enveloped the house when John looked through
the shutters the next morning. Zipporah was already
downstairs, poring over her charts. He peered over her shoulder,
and saw a new spidery diagram linking Perks, Louisa Hines and
the Moss bodies. Down the side she had written 'M Spibey', 'B
Blanchard' and 'J Carne'.

'That's good, I see you've got me down as a suspect,' he said,
trying to keep his tone light.

'You're certainly a witness. There's porridge in the bowl.' She pointed to the fireplace. 'You're burying the Moss bodies today aren't you? Try and have one more look at them, see if there's any evidence of the cause of death, other than by the stake.'

'I'll see what I can do. Also, I really must, somehow, persuade Sir Moreton to let Baccy go. Though, how I'm to do that, I don't know.'

'You'll have to hope he's so wrapped up in Perks's murder he'll forget about her. You should try and see the squire's body too. If he wasn't killed by the hanging, then what did kill him?'

He was trying really hard to be patient, but what had been so appealing the night before, now seemed irritating. He reached for a ladle and dipped it into the porridge.

'And there's another thing, you'll need to talk to Perks's servants, they always know more than they let on—'

He bad-temperedly threw the ladle back into the bowl with a clatter. 'Enough, woman! *I* am assistant to Sir Moreton Spibey, not you.'

She jerked back a little in her chair.

'Good!' he snarled. 'Are you feeling upset and confused? I hope you are, because that's how you make me feel most of the time.'

'My, my, we're a little chippy this morning.'

'And how can you be surprised by that? How could I not be? Married to a wife who is no wife at all. Who does nothing but boss and mither her husband, and shows me not the slightest bit of kindness.'

She leapt to her feet and banged her hands on the table. 'At last we agree on one thing, I *am* no wife to you, John Carne, nor ever shall be. Please cast me aside. I tried to remove myself from you before, but you stopped me.' She swiftly turned and yelped. 'The porridge, you've made me burn the porridge.' She snatched the pan from the fire, threw it on the table, and dashed up the stairs.

John sighed. He managed to skim some un-charred porridge

off the top for his breakfast, poor Baccy would have to make do with the rest.

He couldn't leave the house without speaking to Zipporah again, though. She was in the nursery.

'All nice and clean again, George,' she said, wrapping the baby in a blanket and holding him close to her chest.

John stood in the doorway. 'I've got to go. You'll be here when I get back, won't you?'

'Where else would I be?' She returned George to the cradle and brought out Arabella, kissing the child's forehead. 'Oh, my baby. Let me change you. Which one of your pretty dresses will you wear today?'

'No matter what I say, no matter if I shout at you, I don't want to be rid of you Zipporah. You understand that don't you? You won't do anything, will you?'

She briefly looked up. 'No, sir, you'll not find me hanging from the rafters. That was before I had my beautiful babies.' She nuzzled against the child. 'Mummy's not going to leave you.' She turned and looked at him. 'I'm a damned whore and a bad wife, but I keep my promises.' She returned her attention to Arabella. 'Mummy's always going to be here for you and Georgie. Yes, she is, even if she has to live with that nasty man.'

He kicked the door jamb so hard the whole room vibrated.

She chuckled malevolently as he winced in pain.

He clutched his thigh. 'Holy Christ Almighty, Mary Mother of God and every saint in heaven!'

She giggled. 'Don't let Sir Moreton catch you in such Papist profanity.'

'I'm not surprised you've had a tiff with your wife, she's burnt the porridge,' said Baccy.

John's patience was running thin. 'I don't have time to stay. I'll bring you something else later.' He paused. 'It was my fault it burned, but how did you know we'd argued? Did you see it in your crystal ball?'

'No, in your demeanour. Your eyes are dull, your step more halting, your shoulders hunched.'

'My leg aches, that's all. I've got to go.'

'Back to your wife I hope. You might as well make up now, don't be sore all day, for you're sure to be friends again tonight.'

'You don't know as much as you think, Baccy. It's an arranged marriage. There's no feeling between us.'

She laughed out loud. 'None at all, save that you love her more than your own life.'

He jerked his arms in the air and roared. 'Spare me this! I've a mind to tell Sir Moreton I've seen you and my wife kissing the devil's arse and let him do his worst to you both.'

'My, but you're even handsomer when your angry.'

John practically flung his arms around Crowther, who was waiting for him in the courtyard. 'At last, a man! I can hope for some sensible conversation now. I've been much bossed by women this morning and it's not yet fully light.'

Crowther laughed, sending his magnificent bushy eyebrows dancing about his forehead. 'Can't live with them, can't live without them. As for light, I don't think we'll see much of that today. It seems appropriate sort of weather to be seeing off those two lost souls, doesn't it, sir? Shrouded in mist and shrouded in mystery.'

'Master Crowther, there's something of the poet about you. See, I'm calmer already. Are the lost souls ready to go?'

'They're on the cart. The groom is just finishing saddling the horses; the workmen who'll bury the bodies left some time ago.'

'While I think about it, I need to ask you a question. Do you remember the day I first came here? When Master Perks was waiting to see Sir Moreton?'

'I do. That was the last time we saw him. He wasn't best pleased to be kept waiting. Not that I'll speak ill of the dead, but Master Perks was not a patient man.'

'When he left, which way did he go?'

'I never saw him leave. I presumed Sir Moreton had seen him out. Or perhaps they went to the Lion Tavern together.'

'The Lion, why?'

'That was one of the reasons Master Perks was so testy: he said he was eating at the Lion before he set off on his travels, and he was hungry.'

'So, did he have his horse with him?'

'No, he was on foot. I presume the horse was at the Lion.'

'So what *has* happened to it?' John said quietly to himself.

Crowther, John soon discovered was, when away from his master, most amiable company. Despite the solemnness of their duty, they rode happily the short distance to Spare Field.

The fog had thinned a little by the time they got there, and the day became brighter as the watery sun shone dimly through the mist. They passed Spibey's workmen on the way, who hailed them cheerily.

'Sir Moreton had to pay them extra for this,' explained Crowther.

While they waited for the men to catch up with them, John took one last opportunity to look at the bodies. As he peeled back the sacking he saw Crowther turn away.

'If you don't mind, Master Carne, I find them troubling.'

'As do we all, but I have to make one last investigation. If there's anything that can help us discover who these people were and how they died, I must look for it.'

The time for burial was overdue. They were fluffy with mould, and in some places, where the skin had broken, a black and stinking substance oozed. Gagging at the sight and smell of them, he'd all but given up on making any further discoveries, when he noticed something that looked like a piece of twine at the back of the man's neck. He pulled his knife from his pocket and used it to smooth the rotten flesh away from the ligature. He saw a knot, drawn tight. A neatly twisted cord was hidden in a groove it had cut in the flesh. The woman's neck was straight and stretched. If she'd been strangled it had been done by hand.

'Anything?' asked Crowther.

'I'm not sure,' said John, 'but you can turn around. They are covered. Oh damn—'

'Master Carne, what is it?' said Crowther anxiously, swivelling round.

'Nothing,' said John with a laugh, 'I just trod in a pile of horse dung.' Then he frowned. 'Does Sir Moreton keep horses in this field?'

Crowther shrugged. 'Maybe. I expect the men who dug the grave yesterday brought a cart with them.'

'Of course. I keep wondering what happened to Master Perks's mount, that's all. I wondered for a moment if it had been left here.'

Now it was Crowther's turn to frown. 'I don't see how the squire's mare could have ended up at Spare Field.'

'She couldn't have done, but where is she?'

———

Spibey's men were quiet as they respectfully lowered the bodies into the pit. That done, they stood still and turned to John. He realised he was expected to say something.

'Gentlemen,' he said, 'I don't think we're allowed to pray for these people, but if any of you wish to bow your heads and give some thought to them, then I don't think Sir Moreton would be displeased.'

They all looked down, and despite his words, John composed a prayer in his head, asking for the Lord's mercy and forgiveness, not just for the man and woman, but for all people. Then he prayed that their souls would rest forever in heaven. Exactly the sort of intercession, which, if murmured aloud, would have him dismissed from Spibey's employ.

Leaving the cart to bring the men back, once the pit had been filled in, John and Crowther rode swiftly back to Wem. John learned on the way that Tom Perks had been a surprising choice of husband for Spibey's daughter.

'Margaret's so young and spirited. She led her father a merry dance; she wasn't naturally solemn and godly like her parents,' said Crowther.

'I must say,' said John, 'when I briefly conversed with Mistress Perks the other day I found her somewhat outspoken.'

'Well, that's a word for it.' Crowther grinned. 'When she came back from London she seemed changed. It's a very godly place, London, so I'm told. Next thing, she was married to Squire Perks. Even stranger, she seemed happy with the situation. Believe me, if young Mistress Margaret didn't like something, we all knew about it.'

'Though it would seem he got the better part of the bargain,' said John. 'I thought Sir Moreton had other children, yet he only ever mentions Margaret. I presume the others are away, or have they died?'

'That's the great tragedy,' replied Crowther. 'Mistress Spibey had many children before Margaret, all boys but none saw their first birthday.'

'A tragedy indeed,' said John, with feeling. 'How did Mistress Spibey remain sane, suffering such loss?'

'She was as godly as my master. They took it as a testing. They prayed harder and looked deep into their souls to see how they had offended the Lord. Then Margaret was born, but Mistress Spibey lost her life in the effort.'

John was silent for a while. 'Thank you for telling me that,

Crowther. Now I understand why Sir Moreton is so protective of his daughter.'

'We were surprised he made no objection to the marriage to Squire Perks. Perhaps he thought an older man might steady her.'

'I know she spent some time at a school in Nantwich,' said John.

Crowther allowed himself a rather soft chuckle. 'Parson Goodman's school, yes, I remember that well. Oh there was much screaming about the house when Sir Moreton decided upon that course of action. From time to time, you see, Margaret's high spirits caused my master such concern that he tried to correct her.'

'My wife is Parson Goodman's daughter,' said John. 'She remembers Mistress Perks well, mainly for her high spirits, as you call them.'

Crowther smiled. 'Yes, firstly he tried Nantwich, then some years later he sent her to London to stay with a cousin of the late Mistress Spibey. That cousin is a member of a church so godly that the congregation are often taken violently with the spirit. That leads them to hurl themselves about and jabber away in tongues.'

They passed through the sentry post at the town perimeter, then waited as a cart loaded with sharpened poles crossed in front of them. The horses heaved it up the earth rampart that was being built. Soldiers and townsmen quickly unloaded the cart, the poles being used to strengthen the barricades. Wem was a Parliamentary town. There were royalists troops in the county. An attack seemed likely.

'Never thought I'd see Wem come to this,' said Crowther under his breath. Then he looked at John. 'May I say one more thing, Master Carne, and I hope you don't take it the wrong way?'

'Of course, Crowther.'

'I see you and Mistress Carne in church every Sunday. Terrible things are said about your wife, but I'd like you to know, I don't believe any of them.'

'Master Crowther, please don't take *this* the wrong way, but I could kiss you.'

Spibey was waiting in the courtyard and seemed relieved that at least one of his problems had been resolved.

John decided to seize the moment while Spibey seemed relatively calm. 'Given that we must now put all our efforts into finding the killer of Master Perks, I've a suggestion to make concerning Mistress Blanchard.'

Spibey frowned. 'I'll not be soft on her.'

'This isn't soft, but I hope it will prove cunning. We've no idea who the Moss bodies were, but Squire Perks, that's a different sort of murder altogether, for he's a man of quality. A relation to you, no less. Baccy Blanchard is nothing. She knows no spells and she brews no potions. At the moment all we have against her is a fondness for two fat cats. Whoever did this dreadful thing to the squire is a greater malefactor than her and of the cleverer sort. I suggest we free Mistress Blanchard.' He heard Spibey gasp. 'Sir Moreton, there's no risk, I assure you. She'll not go anywhere, and the villagers at Hornspike will be sure to keep their eyes on her. Even half a step out of place and they'll let us know. Releasing her will send out a message. A message you'll not like. The message will be that Sir Moreton Spibey is soft on witches.'

Spibey's eyes narrowed and he pulled his lips tightly over his teeth. 'You're mistaken, Master Carne. We need to show that we're strong.'

'Please, sir.' John guided Spibey to the furthest corner of the courtyard. 'No one can hear us, let me explain. By appearing weak we shall be strong; it'll give us the upper hand. If we keep a pathetic specimen like Baccy, those more experienced in the dark arts will sink further down, not raising their heads. We may never find them. Let her go free and they'll laugh at us, but we must bear that, for they'll become overconfident; they'll flaunt their magic, and we shall find them. I admit that, at first, this plan will be a blow to our pride, but pride is a sin we must guard against.'

Spibey stood still, his misty breath snaking jerkily through his nostrils. He began to chew his thumbnail. 'You're sure that Baccy Blanchard hasn't the power to fly away from her cell?'

'I'm convinced she's no such powers. After all, if she could fly away, why would she fly back? If she had the ability, she would be long gone from your gaol. Also, as an added precaution, I kept her well fed and in drink. The guard says she sleeps most of the time.'

Spibey ran his hand across his mouth, and then rubbed his chin. 'Yesterday, didn't you suggest that Tom was dead before he was strung up. She could have killed him before we brought her here.'

Damn a clever employer, thought John. 'But we know the hanging wasn't done by her. We also know it must be an important part of their filthy ritual. These people are as slippery as eels. We must be slippery, too. As I said, we'll lose some face, but the final victory will be yours, Sir Moreton. Lull them into a false sense of security, let them show themselves. Then you pounce.'

Spibey let out a long breath. 'Your mind slithers in many directions, Master Carne.'

'I was training to be a lawyer, remember.'

'I hate to let the witch go. We should swim her first, at least.'

'We know exactly where she's going. You can rearrest her any time.' John twisted his lips. It wasn't going to work. Spibey had his suspect and he was loath to release her.

The magistrate was gnawing his nails again. 'You're right in one respect. The creature that did this vile thing to Tom is evil beyond anything we've ever seen, and you're also right, in that the Blanchard woman is verging on being a simpleton.' Spibey pushed up his hat, then pressed it firmly down again. 'Very well, you may let her go. Reluctantly I'll allow it. But if it turns out she was in even the tiniest way involved, I'll hold you entirely and personally responsible.'

John kept very still. 'I shall see to it, sir,' was all that he said.

Spibey slapped his hands together. 'And now I must ask you to come inside on yet another unpleasant task. We have yet to examine the sad mortal remains of Tom Perks, and it's our duty to do so. Let us see if his body provides any evidence.'

Chapter Eleven

P erks was laid out in one of Spibey's guest rooms. The magistrate pulled back the heavy curtains and opened one of the leaded windows to let in as much light as possible. He gently drew down the bedlinen. 'I feel disrespectful to my old friend, doing this,' he said.

'It would be more disrespectful not to try and discover what happened,' said John.

Perks was a tiny, wizened man, hardly more than five feet in height, and his body seemed verging on emaciation. Every rib showed clearly through the pale, wrinkled skin, and his legs and arms were twig like.

'Did he fast a lot?' asked John.

'Who knows what a man does in private? Whenever he dined here he ate well enough. He's always been a slight fellow.'

'As I said yesterday, a hanged man's features are changed.' John gently pulled down Perks's jaw. The marks where the thorns had pierced his lips were hardly visible amongst his wrinkles. 'Look here, there's not even the slightest swelling of the tongue, and only a light bruise on the neck where the rope was tied. His body has also lost all stiffness.' John sniffed. 'And decay has started.'

'How do you know these things?' whispered Spibey.

'I was a soldier. We lived with death. Let me move his head. See, the hair at the back is matted with blood. He was struck from behind. The act of a coward.'

'You think the blow killed him?'

'Look how frail he is. I'd not be surprised if the softest of taps would have seen him off to heaven.'

'Oh dear, dear,' muttered Spibey. 'Yet he always seemed so strong when he was alive. Dear me, dear me.' He wiped a tear from his face with a trembling hand.

'Sir Moreton, I'm still not convinced you should be conducting this case. You're distressed.'

'No, I must do this. Do you have any further observations?'

'Only that, as there's so little bruising to his lips, I think that the thorns must have been threaded after death.'

'Part of a ritual so evil, we cannot comprehend it?'

'That I can't answer.'

Spibey replaced the coverings and they turned their attention to Perks's clothes and the rope.

'This jacket is wet, far more than from dew alone.' John sniffed it, then rubbed his hand across the cloth. 'See these spots, they're like specks of peat. I wonder if he was killed on the Moss and then taken to Hornspike for his hanging.'

'The Moss,' breathed Spibey. 'A place like that, so heavy with malevolence, would be sure to attract witches.'

'I believe you said Master Perks resided at Whixall.'

'Whixall Grange, yes. It's a fine modern house. It's hardly been up five years; Tom was proud of it.'

'And it's close to the Moss?'

'Oh, yes.'

It was John's turn to let out a long sighing breath. 'We've much to think about.' He took his leave of Spibey, desperate to get Baccy released before the magistrate changed his mind.

'You're free to go,' said John, putting the cat basket down while he unlocked the cell.

'My babies,' Baccy cried, rushing out, lifting the lid and peeping in at them. 'They've lost weight!'

'Good, they'll be less heavy to carry. If you set out now you've plenty of time to get home before it's dark.'

'What, walk back?'

'Yes.'

'Can't you come with me and carry them?'

'I'm a cripple, I'd be even slower than you. And also, I expect Sir Moreton will need me this afternoon.'

'Why?'

'Because I'm his assistant.'

'You haven't made it up with Mistress Carne yet, have you?'

They walked to the main door. The gaoler cowered when John returned the key to him.

'You truly scared him,' said John to Baccy, once they were outside.

'He thought he'd catch witchcraft if he poked me. Still, it was his loss. If you don't make it up with your wife and you get the urge, you're always welcome to pay a visit to Baccy. But that's not likely, is it?'

'I told you, concerning Zipporah and me, you know nothing.' Some people walked by, staring at Baccy and muttering oaths or prayers under their breath. John took her arm. 'I'll accompany you as far as the town gate. You should be safe from there.'

Seemingly oblivious to any danger, she shrugged and returned to her theme. 'Zipporah. See, just saying her name gives you pleasure. What did you argue about? Nothing much at all I'll wager.'

'It's none of your damn business, except my wife believes she's damned, which is part of the problem.' Why did he tell her that?

She let out a sharp laugh. 'She probably is. You probably are. I almost certainly am. My husband definitely is, praise the Lord for one small mercy. It's such good practice for hell, this world, isn't it? I'm surprised more don't court the devil's favour in this life, since he claims so many of our souls in the end.'

Thankful that Spibey wasn't around to hear that outburst, John said no more and they continued in silence until they reached the gate.

John nodded to the sentry before turning to Baccy. 'I wish you a safe journey.'

She touched the brim of her hat. 'Well, I'll thank you for nothing, save your wife's victuals and the minimal care you've given my babies.'

He grabbed the front of her cloak. 'Mistress Blanchard, if I ever discover you really are a witch, I shall personally swim you, string you up and burn your entrails.'

'Always something to look forward to, isn't there?'

He pushed her away and watched her small lopsided figure tottering up the misty road. He couldn't help smiling, though, because in her own, strange way she'd lifted his spirits. And relieving Zipporah of the cats had led to a small rapprochement between him and his wife.

The sentry spat. 'They say she's a witch. There's no cats left in Hornspike for she's eaten them all. Next she'll start on the dogs, then it'll be children. The magistrate should've strung her up.'

John gripped the man's arm. '"They" say many things, Trooper. Most of them best disregarded. Do you not have some old lady in your family who sometimes speaks out of turn? That's all she is, an old, friendless woman who sometimes talks nonsense.'

The sentry shuffled, embarrassed. 'I'm sorry, Captain, I'm only saying what I've heard.'

'And now you've heard from me, that's wrong. Don't go repeating those rumours, eh, there's a good fellow.'

'No, Captain, no, I won't.' John heard the sentry stutter as he walked away. He simply prayed that Baccy got home safely and stayed there.

Spibey looked dreadful. His jowls had sunk even lower. The dark circles around his eyes had grown, and the creasy puffiness about them meant that he observed the world through two narrow slits. The tips of his fingers, as he rubbed his ravaged face, were raw and scabbed by the almost constant gnawing they endured.

'Has there been more bad news?' asked John.

'No, no. I've been with my Margaret. My poor little girl. She eats a little, sleeps a little, but she says nothing. Her face, normally so lively, is blank. She's too young to understand what widowhood is. She'd not even been a wife for a year.'

'It's hard for women. I think they feel so much more than we do.'

'You think? You're still young, Master Carne, real sorrow hasn't touched you.'

John remained silent for a while. 'Shall I leave you, to be with your daughter?' he said eventually.

'What else had you in mind?'

'I think we should go to Whixall Grange and talk to the people there. I'm happy to go alone, I'm armed, and I'll have no trouble getting back into town, even if it's dark. All the sentries know me.'

'Yes, of course. You think the answer lies at Whixall?'

'I think there are questions that need to be asked there.'

'I'll come with you. I am the magistrate, after all.' His features did brighten a little at the prospect of some activity. 'The witch has gone?'

John nodded. 'Though I warned her, if she turns out to be a real malefactor, I shall personally swim her, hang her and burn her entrails.'

Spibey actually smiled. 'My, but you are learning, Master Carne, you surely are.'

Baccy had made good progress. She was more than halfway to Hornspike when they passed her, taking a break, sitting on a tree stump and puffing on her pipe. John touched his hat. Spibey looked away and then began quoting the 23rd psalm, which he continued to do for the rest of the journey.

Squire Perks's staff were a subservient lot; they rarely raised their eyes. None mentioned their master with any affection, nor did there seem to be any hostility to him either, even of the hidden kind.

During the interviews, a familiar story began to emerge. From time to time it seemed Perks had fallen out with his neighbours, but only in the normal way of country squires. Arguments were fuelled by such small events as a fence post moved a foot onto his land, or a heifer wandering to a neighbouring field and claimed by the landowner. And all had been sorted out in the normal way of country squires, over ale, over food and with the occasional exchange of money.

Neither indulgent nor harsh with his tenants and servants, he was careful with his time, his words and his fortune. Even the arrival of a much younger wife had caused little comment, since it was only natural that such a man would crave an heir.

'I'm executor to Tom's will,' said Spibey, as they sat at Perks's table and took some refreshment.

'In the circumstances, that's good,' said John. 'Your daughter's child inherits a fine manor.'

'All I hope for now is that she's safely delivered.'

'Of course. There's one thing we haven't considered. This war rages all about us, did Master Perks have any political enemies? I presume, since you let your daughter marry him, he was for Parliament.'

'In truth, John, though he was a godly man, all he cared for was to make a profit. You know how these gentry are. Kings come and go, but their land, their way of life endures.'

Spibey must be tired; he was talking to John as an equal.

Spibey continued. 'So why was he killed? Is everyone here a witch do you think?' He poured himself another goblet of wine, which given his exhaustion, John wasn't sure was wise.

'See the evidence of your own eyes,' said John, moving the jug away from Spibey on the pretence of refilling his own cup. 'Everything here is wholesome. The milk isn't sour. Did we not hear the groom in the stables reciting Scripture as he curry-combed the horses? I've seen at least three Bibles. Everyone is dressed in a most seemly manner. Devilry cannot thrive here. On a practical note, I think you'll have to take the responsibility for the running of this place for some time.'

'Yes, I shall.'

John left Spibey looking through some of Perks's ledgers.

'You shouldn't have done that,' said the cook, when she saw John returning their plates to the kitchen.

'There's still more to be collected. I couldn't manage it all on account of my stick.'

'You shouldn't have managed any of it.'

'I want to speak to you myself. At some time or another, many people come through the kitchen in a big house. There's no magistrate here now, just me. If there's anything you can tell me that might help us discover what happened to your master, I promise I'll treat it in the strictest confidence.'

The cook shrugged. 'Truly, sir, there's little to tell. The squire didn't inspire great affection, but he was a good master and none of us wished ill upon him'

'And the squire and his young wife, was all well between them?'

'I work in the kitchen, not the bedroom, I'd have no way of knowing.'

'I see. And the mistress, she must have had little experience in looking after such a big house.'

'She spent most of her time in her rooms. She liked her books, I believe. She left most of the organisation to the housekeeper, and of course, anything outside the house is Master Wellings's responsibility.'

John considered the cook didn't know Margaret Perks at all if she thought she liked books. Unless the respectable Mistress Perks had changed radically from the former somewhat flighty Mistress Spibey. 'Master Wellings seems young to have such a position,' he said.

'His father was steward here, as was his father before him. All the Wellings boys have Whixall Grange in their blood. The family go right back to the times when it was a wooden hall with a thatched roof.'

'Born and bred, eh?' said John.

The cook paused. 'Actually, not the present steward. Young Master Wellings was born in the American Colonies, New England. His father had some fanciful notion to go abroad and make his fortune. It didn't work out, though. He was soon back here, in his rightful place.'

John sighed. 'There seems no motive for so vicious a crime.'

'Is it true, then, that my master's body was desecrated?'

He might as well tell her. 'Thorns had been thrust through his lips, to sew the top and bottom together.'

She flinched. 'No one here would have done that, sir. Now may I ask you another question?'

He nodded.

'We all fear what will happen to us, what with there being no heir.'

'Don't worry, I'm sure Sir Moreton will run things as efficiently as the squire would have done, until the child is of age.'

'Child?' The cook looked mystified.

'Mistress Perks is with child.'

The cook fell back onto the bench that ran alongside the central wooden table, and slapped her hands on her thighs. 'Glory be! The old squire managed it at last, bless him.'

John was surprised. 'You didn't know?'

'Well, I didn't, and you're right to presume I know most of what goes on here. Did the old squire know? How tragic if he died before he knew he'd have a son at last. Oh, it must be a son, sir.'

'I presume Master Perks knew. I've seen his wife, and she's a belly on her. You'd think, after all this time, he'd have trumpeted the news from the rooftops. Are you sure no one knew about the pregnancy?'

'Of course not, I said so, but praise the Lord indeed that we'll have an heir. And in the meantime, do you think Sir Moreton will be good to us?'

'He'll be a fine master.' Despite his many reservations as to Spibey's character, John was sure that he would run the estate fairly and efficiently.

'Come, follow me, there's someone you should see.' The cook led him down a short corridor to a spacious room, with a stone flagged floor and tiles on the wall. A large copper cauldron stood over some hot coals in the corner, and a small figure was stirring it with a long wooden ladle.

'Nanna Grey,' called the cook. 'NANNA GREY!' she shouted. 'She's deaf,' she explained to John.

The old woman looked round and gave them a friendly, albeit toothless, grin.

'Nanna, we're saved. This man is assistant to Sir Moreton of Wem, the young mistress's father. We're saved; she's with child. The Grange has an heir. Nothing will change, so you needn't worry: you'll be able to die here in peace.' She turned to John. 'I'll go and get us some drinks.'

'Pleased to meet you, Nanna,' said John deliberately, bowing a little. 'What are you making?'

The toothless smile spread across her face again. 'I don't make. I do the laundry. Always have done. Anyone pisses their pants at the Grange, I know about it.' She continued her stirring.

'Oh, I see. So if you know that, do you have any idea who killed the squire, and why?'

'You'll never find out who did it.'

'And why do you think that?'

'Because you never do.' Round and round went the wooden paddle.

The old woman had obviously lost her wits along with her teeth, but he continued to humour her. 'We never *will* find out, if no one tells us what they know.'

'I don't know anything.'

'Except who pisses their pants. Did you know that young Mistress Perks was with child?'

She looked up at him and chuckled. 'No one did.'

'So strange, Why would Master and Mistress Perks keep such important news to themselves?'

Nanna shrugged.

He remembered what Baccy had told him, and as old people were often better at recalling the past, not the present, he asked if she'd heard of Louisa Hines.

She stopped her paddling and squinted her eyes at him. 'Now how do you know about her?'

'I'd heard that the squire got her with child, but she left him.'

She rolled her head from side to side. 'Maybe that was the case. He'd had at least two wives, or was it three by then? Not only were they childless, but there was never even a miscarriage or a stillbirth.' She beckoned him closer, and he obliged, stooping to listen to her. 'People said he had trouble with his pecker, but you say the young mistress is with child. That's good. As for Louisa, we were never sure about her. They were a flighty pair.'

'The squire and Louisa?'

'No, those Hines sisters. Louisa and Rebecca. They had a competition between them as to who would be the next Mistress Perks. The master, I should say, was never an interesting man, save for his fortune, which made him fascinating to many a young woman. First he tried out the elder, Rebecca. She was strange, flying into rages one day, sweet as a kitten the next. We had hopes of Louisa, though. She'd no morals, but she knew how to behave in company. She'd have made as good a mistress as any.'

'So what happened?'

'No one knows. She went away and by then the sister had wed Sam Blanchard, so the master had to look around again for another wife.'

John turned, and sucked his teeth. That witch Baccy! Why hadn't she told him that Louisa was her sister? He didn't care if it was midnight, he'd stop at Hornspike on the way back and have a few strong words with her. He looked at the old woman. 'Thank you, Nanna. Be honest, do you know of anyone who'd want to kill Master Perks? I must know.'

She gripped his sleeve. 'Your master, the magistrate, he thinks devilry is involved, doesn't he? Don't discount that, young sir. The devil finds his way everywhere, never underestimate his fiendish influence. This is a strange land, and strange people inhabit it.'

'If you think of anything else, be sure to let me know, Nanna.'

'I'm exhausted, John,' said Spibey with unaccustomed honesty. 'I'm going to bed. Will you stay the night here?'

'I'd rather not.'

'It's getting dark.'

'It's not that late. I have a lantern; I'll easily find my way.'

'Well, I'd be grateful if you would go back. Call in on my Margaret and let her know I'm staying here. And tell Master Wellings I need him here tomorrow.'

John assured him he would. 'There's only one observation I have to make. It seems very strange that everyone is so surprised to hear that an heir is expected in the not-too-distant future. I should have thought such a long-awaited event would have been the talk of the manor.'

Spibey nodded. 'There's a reason for that. You know that my own dear wife bore many children before Margaret.'

'I've heard of the tragedies you endured, for which you have my sympathy.'

Spibey nodded sadly. 'From the moment she realised she was with child, Margaret was fearful. Fearful that the heir to Whixall would not survive, and that she would be blamed if anything went wrong. So she confined herself to her rooms, only Tom and I knew of her condition, and Wellings now, of course. We couldn't bear the thought that the weight of expectation laid upon her by the household would cause her any further distress, which might lead to a miscarriage.'

'That explains everything. You were doing your best to protect her.'

On reflection John considered it hadn't explained much at all. He stepped out into the cold early evening, wondering if staying the night at Whixall Grange might have been for the best. He needed to get back to Zipporah, though. And those strong words with Baccy needed to be said.

Chapter Twelve

'You should see the size of my blisters,' said Baccy as John walked, unannounced, into her house. She was sitting with her feet soaking in a crock of pitch coloured, foul smelling liquid. 'Come all the way in then and shut the door, it's draughty.'

'That stinks,' he said, pointing to the bowl. 'You'd do much better letting them dry out than soaking them.'

'That silly girl from the village made this for me, but you think you know better.'

'Just a soldier's knowledge. Even a cavalryman does a lot of walking.'

She lifted her feet out of the bowl and inspected them. Then she started to rub them with a cloth. 'Don't suppose you're here to ask about the condition of my old toes.'

Without being asked he poured them both a mug of that good wine and sat opposite her. Within moments Master Pipkin was on his lap, pummelling his thighs with his paws and purring ostentatiously. John grimaced, and pushed the cat off his knee. 'Why did you lie to me about Louisa Hines, you being a former Mistress Hines yourself?'

'I never lied. It didn't seem important that you knew if she was my sister or not.'

'What was the real story about you two and Master Perks?'

She stood up and passed him a pipe from the rack and put the tobacco caddy between them. As with her wine, it was of the best quality. She resumed her position, and after a bit of cooing Pipkin was persuaded to join her.

'It was always said that, though Tom had an eye for the girls, he could never get it up. All those wives and no children, there had to be something wrong, didn't there? At the time Louisa and I lived by the philosophy that, as good works couldn't save you, we may as well please ourselves and do as we liked, and take our chances with God's grace. We liked men, Master Carne.' She smiled wistfully. 'Oh, we did. And they liked us. We became experienced in pleasure, but the necessities of life are such that a woman must have a husband.

'Once the mourning period had passed after his last wife, I decided I'd have a go at Tom Perks. He was lustful, but his lust was never enough. I tried all my tricks, and believe me, Master Carne, I was skilful, still am, but never did we join. So I gave him to my sister. One day she returned from Whixall Grange triumphant. She'd roused Tom Perks and made a man of him. I wasn't bothered. The bugger Blanchard was sniffing around by then, and he had no trouble in that direction, so I settled for him, fool that I was.'

'And Louisa?'

'She told me she was with child. I assumed Perks would marry her. He'd be stupid not to. Then she was gone. We all searched. Everyone helped, but there was never even a hint of where she went. In my heart I knew her. She might have been carrying Tom's child, but if she found another man, more exciting, she'd have run off with him.'

'How advanced was her pregnancy?'

'It was never visible.'

'Did you remain friends with the squire? Did he ever mention Louisa to you?'

'I entered society as Mistress Blanchard. I met with Tom on many occasions and he never treated me as anything other than the respected wife of a neighbour. Do you think the body you found is that of my sister?'

'Probably not.'

'And now I hear that Tom is dead at last, and even then old age didn't carry him off. Have you discovered who did it yet?'

'Unless it was you and your devilish accomplices, no.'

She snorted.

'Keep yourself out of trouble then, mistress, and let those blisters dry and harden. They'll fall off when the skin beneath has healed.'

'Your silken words would charm any woman. Have you made up with your wife yet?'

John drained his mug and left.

Travelling in the dark didn't trouble him, though he conceded to himself that at a time of war it probably wasn't the most sensible thing to do. The clouds of the day had lifted and the sky was inky black, pierced with stars and a sliver of moon. The frost would be hard that night. He heard an owl hoot, then saw the bird itself, swooping low, its plumage silver against the silhouetted trees. He passed the Simmonds's house. He smelled the peaty aroma of smoke curling from the chimney. There was no lantern glow from inside. As farmers they'd be early to bed and early to rise. John thought of them all, snugly asleep, and felt a pang of sorrow, both for the family life he'd lost and the future family it seemed unlikely he would ever enjoy.

'Come on, Freddy,' he said with a sniff, though for once, sensing he was on his way home, the pony needed little encouragement to speed up.

John thought that Margaret Perks would probably be in bed by the time he knocked on the door of Spibey's house. Crowther surprised him by saying she was still up and took him through to the sitting room. Her face hardly changed expression when he entered. Nor did she show any interest when he told her that Spibey would stay the night at the Grange. 'You'll be safe here, with all your father's people about you.'

She sighed, then at last looked up at him. 'If your wife died, how would you feel, Master Carne?'

Even the suggestion made his stomach churn. He swallowed hard. 'I'd feel empty, mistress.'

'Would you be able to carry on?'

In reality he doubted it, but he had to put a brave face on for her. 'In time, of course, yes, I'd have to. I would, definitely.' He hoped that sounded positive enough.

'And if you met another, would you marry again?'

'After a suitable period had passed, especially if I was young, well, yes, of course, I would marry again. I know Zipporah would want me to find another.' She'd told him to do so enough times. 'This is a testing time for you, mistress, but you will recover and you'll have your babe to comfort you.'

'Ah, the babe,' she murmured. 'You'd better get back to your Zipporah. Is Master Wellings still here?'

'Yes, though your father will need him at Whixall tomorrow. Is there anything you need, Mistress Perks?'

'Send Master Wellings to me. He can take a message to my father.' Then her face resumed its previous blank expression.

John made a slight detour on the way back home, stopping off at The Lion. Inside he recognised the tall man who'd been outside the gaol, now snuck in a corner with his cronies holding forth about the mistake Spibey had made, releasing Baccy. John ignored him and spoke to the landlord, who couldn't remember the last time he saw Master Perks. As for the horses, he said, they were either tied up on the road, or put in the courtyard or stables behind, depending on the length of the visit. None of this helped John, at all, though he did purchase a flagon of claret as a precaution, as his leg was beginning to throb.

John saw yellow light glowing around the edges of the shutters at The Dial when he returned. As he opened the door, he heard Zipporah's laughter. She wasn't alone. He stepped inside, dreading what he'd see.

'Trooper Benbow!' exclaimed John, with relief.

The man sitting at the table, opposite Zipporah, jumped to his feet and crossed the room to take John in a tight embrace. John was forced to hold out his jug of wine and his wife quickly rescued it.

The younger man stood back. 'And it's Cornet Benbow, if you please.'

'Good to see you, Jack. There's nothing like a war to see a man promoted at speed.'

'All on my own merits, I'll have you know! Captain Carne, I can't tell you how good it is to see you.' Benbow simply had to take John into his arms once more, and from out of the corner of his eye, John could see that Zipporah was smiling broadly.

At last he was released.

'I beg your pardon,' said Benbow. 'Forgive me, but when I last saw you I'd not thought we'd meet again in this life.'

'I've heard more of your exploits from Cornet Benbow than I ever have from you, husband,' said Zipporah. 'Though whether you're brave or foolhardy, I've yet to decide. Anyway, I'll pour you both some of this claret and leave you to your men's talk.' Having dispensed the drinks she took a candle and disappeared through a door to the side of the chimney breast that led to the larder; where her cheeses, pickles, ales and wines were made and stored.

'Sit yourself down,' said Benbow, pushing a mug across the table. He leaned forward and whispered. 'This is a mean house for you, Captain, yet to share it with one such as Mistress Carne must make it a veritable palace.'

John hoped he was hiding his uneasiness as he took a seat and drank from his mug. Jack Benbow was an irrepressible, good-hearted man. From the pleasant look on his happy face, Zipporah had been sensible enough to say nothing that would arouse his suspicions. Though, while John was glad to see an old friend again, he'd have been happier if the encounter had taken place outside his home. 'So, how long have you been in Wem?' he asked.

'Got here yesterday, from Chester. I'd hardly got past the first sentry when I heard that Captain Carne was alive and well and living here. How did that happen?'

'My brother owns this house. When we married it seemed as good a place as any to live. At the time I had no income, so, though you may consider it mean, this house serves its purpose and is more than ample for the two of us.'

'That's not exactly what I was asking. If it's not an impolite question, how are you not dead? I mean, we pulled you away from the action, but already you were pale and lifeless. The surgeon confirmed it. He said there was no point trying to save you. I've spent a year mourning you, John. What happened?'

John lit his pipe, there was no reason why he shouldn't tell Benbow his story, or most of it. 'I remember hearing the surgeon say there was no point dulling his blade on a dead man, a decision which probably saved my life. I lay on the battlefield all night. I half remember it. It was so cold I felt no pain, not then. The next day local people came and took those of us who were still alive into their own homes. How my rescuers divined that I had a spark of life, I'll never know. But they nursed me through fevers and sickness, until gradually the flesh on my thigh began to heal. It'll never be as nature intended and I'll limp until the end of my days, but I have my leg, I can walk and for that I'm grateful.'

'And then?' asked Benbow, raising an eyebrow towards the larder door.

John knew he was really interested in Zipporah. 'Once I could get around on my crutches I made my way back to Shrewsbury. My father refused to see me, and still does. So I carried on to Cheshire, to the home of an old friend.'

'And? Come on, Captain, I've heard enough of the detail. How did you meet her?' He grinned impishly. 'And does she have a sister?'

John had to laugh. 'She's the sister of my friend. His *only* sister.'

'Damn! Still it does my heart good. After all you've been through, you've landed on your feet.'

'Well, one and a half of them, so to speak.'

Now Benbow laughed.

'Enough of me. What's been happening with you, Jack?'

'We travel around. We take a town here, and we lose a town there. Chester is secure, and if we can hold Wem, we'll eventually take Shrewsbury.' He looked up, then poured them both more wine. 'Do you ever think, Captain, that with a bit less hesitation and more determination we could have carried the day at Edgehill?'

'Of course, I often think that, as it's the truth, for both sides. As it was, neither army was determined, or experienced enough, and we're left with this mess. Still, I should imagine that's true of all wars.'

'Unless it's the mighty Romans of old: invading with precision, conquering without mercy,' said Benbow with a certain relish.

'We're fighting our own brothers. It's a different matter altogether.'

Zipporah returned from the larder. 'I know it's late but will you eat with us tonight, Cornet? It's only pigeon, with bread and cheese and some cake, but there's plenty and you're more than welcome.'

John wished she hadn't made the offer. Predictably, Benbow was more than happy to accept. Yet John wondered if he could take some advantage from the situation. As she busied herself around the fire and her cooking pots, he beckoned Benbow close. 'Do you see under my wife's cap? Her hair is short.'

'I did notice and wondered what might have happened.'

'We'd been married hardly a month before a fever gripped her, so strong an illness that I thought I'd be a widower before I'd become used to being a husband. As part of the treatment, her hair was cut to the roots.'

'Of course, everyone knows that can help.'

'What I'm trying to say, is that, as it gets colder, the soldiers from the garrison will be billeted in the town. Zipporah isn't well enough to take people in.'

'I see your point. Don't worry, I'll mention it to Colonel Mytton. You've hardly any room anyway. The Colonel's desirous to see you again. You must come to the camp.'

'Good, thank you, Jack. Zipporah is not as strong as she looks and I must do everything I can to protect her.'

'And I'll do everything I can to help you.'

Cornet Benbow wiped his lips. 'Mistress Carne, never say "it's only pigeon" again, that was the most delicious meal I've had in a long time, and I don't just live on army rations you know. And that cake, it simply melted in the mouth.'

'It's John's favourite, ginger and aniseed.'

'Right then, my friends,' said Benbow, pulling a pack of cards from his pocket. 'The shutters are closed; the godly people of Wem are all asleep or at their prayers; let's play cribbage.'

'We should not,' protested John, holding up his hands.

Benbow began to shuffle.

'We should not play cribbage,' said Zipporah, taking a seat next to John, 'as I'll be left out. How about puff and honours, Cornet? It's years since we've played. I'll trounce you both.'

'I don't think we can ignore such a challenge, do you, Captain?' said Benbow.

'She'll not trounce either of us, Jack.'

However, she did, amongst much laughter and good-natured banter.

Eventually the cards were put away. 'Oh, by the way, I was sent here with a message from the Colonel,' said Benbow carelessly. 'We've had such a jolly evening I almost forgot to pass it on. Colonel Mytton said he'd been asked by a man with a strange name, the magistrate that you work for…'

'Sir Moreton Spibey?' said John, wishing reality hadn't intruded upon this unexpectedly carefree evening.

'That's the fellow. He came to the camp asking if we'd found a horse wandering, we hadn't then, but we have now, By my own troop, in fact. Fully harnessed. A decent solid cob, nothing special, the sort any farmer hereabouts would have. Bay, white star. She's requisitioned for the army now, but you're welcome to come and identify her.'

'Was there anything to suggest who the owner might have been?'

'A book of accounts or something was found in one of the saddlebags, with the name Perkins, or some such written in it.'

'Tom Perks,' said John to himself.

'Duty discharged,' said Benbow. 'Lady and gentleman, I thank you for a most pleasant evening.' He bowed and left.

Zipporah hummed as she tidied up the table. 'Your friend's a nice man' she said, before picking up the tune again.

'You shouldn't have invited him in.'

She began to sing loudly, ignoring him.

He raised his voice. 'Listen to me. Jack's a good fellow, but you must be careful. Don't invite anyone into this house again without my permission.'

Her singing stopped and she stood in front of him, hands on hips. 'Don't play the Draconian husband with me, John. It doesn't suit you. And as you well know, Jack Benbow doesn't wait to be invited in. I could hardly throw him out, could I?'

'I'm simply being protective,' he said patiently. 'And you know why.'

Her face, which had been relaxed, began to harden. 'So you say. Or is the truth that you don't like me to enjoy myself? You're just as much a Puritan as Sir Moreton. No wonder he loves you so.'

'He doesn't love me, and your happiness is what I desire more than anything else in this world.'

She dismissed this last comment with a sharp blow of breath through her lips. 'Spibey does love you. Apparently when Colonel Mytton spoke to him, the magistrate couldn't speak highly enough of you. And Cornet Benbow is in thrall to you because of your bravery and the way you withstand your injuries without complaint. And I've no doubt that the infamous Baccy Blanchard toasts your name throughout the county as the man who saved her from the rope. Of course the reason all these people love you so, is because they don't have to live with you and put up with your petty prohibitions.'

'Enough, wife! We've had a good time, don't spoil it. You must realise that everything I do is to protect you ... and your children,' he added hastily. 'Nothing more and nothing less drives me. It would be something if you could appreciate that.'

'Well, someone has to be immune to your perfect charms.'

'Yes, but why does it have to be my wife?' he muttered bitterly under his breath.

She turned her back on him and stomped up the stairs. 'And don't you pretend for one minute that you care for my children,' she called from the landing. 'Since I know for a fact you cannot even bear to be in the same room as them.'

He sat down and drained the dregs of wine from his mug and let out the longest sigh. She hadn't told Jack about the babies though. He would have been sure to have mentioned it if she had. Deep down he knew she had good sense. Why was it though, that every minute of happiness he experienced with her had to be balanced by hours of ill will. He went to put his pipe back in the rack, and glimpsed her papers as he did so. He took them closer to the candle. There were lists of names with lines snaking between them, trying to make connections. He added some words to the bottom.

The woman, Louisa Hines, who went missing some years ago, is Baccy Blanchard's sister. Baccy tried to win Perks for herself but claims he was impotent. Louisa claimed to be with child by Perks.

Zipporah might not be talking to him, but she could think for him.

Chapter Thirteen

She was already poring over the notes when he came downstairs the next morning. 'There's porridge with cream and honey. Help yourself,' she said without looking up.

He did so and sat next to her.

'Thank you for this extra information. Exactly how long ago did Baccy's sister disappear?'

'Baccy said about ten years, but no one seems to remember for sure.'

'The Moss preserves, though. The woman in the bog must be her, don't you think?'

'I don't know. Baccy says her sister was not obviously with child when she went missing, while we know the woman in the bog must have been close to her time.'

'Still, it's a strange coincidence. And why was Perks presumed to be impotent? He simply had no children. That proves nothing.'

'Except Baccy says she couldn't rouse him.'

She curled her lips in disgust.

'She seems to have enjoyed a somewhat lively youth,' he said.

'And people call me a whore. I'm not sure I like the people you mix with. Bad enough she fornicated, or tried to, never mind discuss it with all and sundry.'

'This is the most delicious porridge,' he said, sneaking a glance at her. 'I was asking Baccy questions as part of my investigations. I'm not interested in her private life.'

She shook her head slightly. 'Did you get to see the Moss bodies and Perks?'

'Yes. Lord, was that only yesterday? I said prayers for the souls of the Moss bodies as we buried them. Was that wrong, do you think?'

She shook her head. 'Probably pointless, as their fate is decided, but not wrong. Anyway, did you discover anything else?'

'The man had a thin, tight ligature around his neck. It would have killed him.'

'A hanging of sorts, then.'

'The cord was too thin to support an actual hanging, but a strangling, yes. There was no evidence that the hanging killed Perks. He had a wound on the back of his head that could have seen him off.'

She sighed. 'Was the body hard or soft?'

'Soft. And another thing, his clothes were wet and had traces of peat on them, as if he had been on the Moss. Also, there was a shepherd guarding the body when we arrived at Hornspike. I didn't think anything of it at the time, but he said a dead lamb will lose its eyes to a crow in less than an hour.'

'But Perks's were intact.' She doodled on the paper while he helped himself to more porridge. She looked at him when he took his place next to her. 'Did you get to see −' she pointed down '− you know? Were there any thorns in it?'

'There was nothing.'

She twisted her lips. 'You realise what this means, don't you? She had a reason and I've no doubt she had the opportunity. Anyone can creep up behind and old man and break his head. Baccy Blanchard must be the killer of Thomas Perks.'

John didn't want to believe her but he had to admit, as she outlined her theories, that Zipporah made a good case for Baccy's guilt. She reasoned that Baccy, upon hearing of the discovery of the Moss bodies and especially of the condition of the woman, had assumed it was Louisa. After he'd been to see Sir Moreton, Perks went to Hornspike, where one of his tenants lived. Baccy saw the squire and challenged him. Eventually he admitted that he'd killed Louisa. Either he'd found out the child was not his, or the child was his, but she preferred another and wouldn't marry him. Whichever way, it meant he would be denied an heir, something that was important to him. That was why he murdered Louisa and her lover. On hearing this confession and in a moment of anger, Baccy struck Perks, killed him and hid his body on the Moss.

John thought about it for a while. 'If that's what happened, then why was his body brought back to Hornspike? We know Baccy didn't do that, as she was in the gaol at the time.'

'True enough, but she's a wealthy woman; she could have paid someone to do it. That'll be the chink in her armour. Her accomplice will have no personal feeling in this matter, and can be broken down by questioning or the offer of more money.'

'Steady, Zipporah, you're beginning to sound like Sir Moreton. You don't explain the thorns, either.'

'I can do. Baccy was simply avenging herself on Perks's body. Just as he'd taken revenge on her sister and her lover all those years ago. It sends out a message.'

'To whom, since you're the only person to have solved this mystery so far.'

She twisted her mouth. 'I've thought of that, too. The message is to the accomplices who helped Perks with the murder of Louisa. It tells them that she knows who they are and she's coming for them. Even if Baccy has no idea, or only a suspicion as to who they are, it must give her satisfaction to think they're discomforted.'

He leaned back in his chair. 'You haven't met Baccy,' he said at last. 'She's no murderess; you'll just have to take my word for it. She's odd, eccentric, but murder? No, she's too lazy for a start.'

She picked up his bowl and took it to the washing pail. 'You don't want her to be a murderer because you feel sorry for her, because she's been ill-used by a man. Well, John, there's not a woman in this world who hasn't been ill-used by a man at some time.'

He followed her and stood by the fire, warming his back before he had to venture into the cold. 'If Perks was the killer of Louisa, why did he desecrate the bodies with thorns? That's what makes it a crime beyond others, the nastiness, the humiliation.'

'I know you don't believe in witchcraft. Though I'm not so certain as you, I do believe this world is evil enough without summoning imps and demons. But, what if Perks was superstitious? What if, in his jealously, he thought that by binding the man's eyes with thorns he could prevent him, in the next world, from gazing upon the body of his beloved?'

'Lucky man, getting to gaze in any world,' muttered John, looking lustfully at her and wishing she wasn't so encased in linen and wool. He awaited the inevitable explosion but instead she simply frowned at him.

'Are you always thinking about *that*?'

'Yes, because you never let me do *that*. If you only did, I could stop thinking about *that* and start thinking about this!' He jabbed his finger into the papers he held. Now he expected to be subject to an angry tirade. Except she merely rubbed her hand across her lips and was quiet for a while. He wondered if she was stifling a laugh.

'I'm sorry,' she said at last, no mirth in her voice. 'I'm sorry for the way things are. I'm sorry for the way I spoke to you last night. I was happy, and then I was sad when the evening ended, that's all. I know you make all sorts of sacrifices, to … to … well, you know.'

'Thank you.' His voice was soft with gratitude. He stepped closer.

She held up her hands. 'I said I was sorry. I didn't say anything would change.'

It was enough. Once more she'd ensnared him. The night before he'd wondered how he could continue to love her. Now emotion flooded through him and he was as besotted as ever.

'Nothing will change, but I *am* sorry,' she reiterated, but it was too late, he had begun to hope again. That little escapee from Pandora's Box chirruped in his ear, even if only softly. One day he and Zipporah would truly be man and wife.

He put on his hat and coat. 'If you've got time, give our puzzle some more thought. I don't think you've quite solved it yet. For a start, why did Perks ride all the way from Whixall to Wem, just to turn round and go to Hornspike, which is but a few furlongs from his home? And we've no proof that Baccy knew anything of the Moss bodies until she was told about them by the gaoler in Wem. She certainly wouldn't have known details about the position of the thorns.'

She frowned. 'You may have some points there, John. I'll be proved right, though, see if I'm not.'

He smiled all the way to Noble Street, which, though not very far in yards, was long for a smile.

'It's good to see someone looking so cheerful,' said Crowther as he let him into Spibey's study.

'Sorry,' said John. 'Life goes on for some of us.'

'Indeed it does, I'm pleased your mood is so improved. Master Wellings has left for Whixall Grange already; he went at first light. We await the return of Sir Moreton, or at least some instruction from him.'

'I've plenty of notes to transcribe for him,' said John. 'I'll have no trouble keeping busy this morning.'

John rubbed his tired eyes and stacked the papers upon which he'd written his reports. As there was no sign of Spibey, he might as well go to the garrison headquarters and see what could be gleaned from Perks's horse. He told Crowther of his plans, and while being vague as to the exact description of Perks's regular mount, Spibey's servant was sure it was a serviceable cob, of gingerish colour and named after liquor, possibly Brandy or Whisky.

The main camp was on the opposite side of town, and even though Wem was of no great size, John's leg was aching after his walk. The sentry at the gate let him pass. Immediately he was confronted by the familiar sights, sounds and smells of a military encampment. Pots bubbled over fires and tents rippled in the breeze, their material making a distinctive flapping sound as it did so. Men and horses were coming and going. There was the ringing of hammers on metal. He heard the crack of a musket being discharged, followed by a sharp cry, but he recognised it as one of disappointment at missing a target and thought no more of it.

'Whoah! Captain!' called a voice, and he looked across to see Benbow running towards him.

'Cornet, I've come to see this horse you mentioned,' he said when the younger man joined him.

Benbow was at his side now and took his arm. 'So you shall.' He leaned closer to him and spoke quietly. 'I've heard the vile lies people here are telling about Mistress Carne. I'm putting them right about her, don't you worry. It's a disgrace, how can such an evil rumour have started?'

John was spared from replying as a tall angular man, clutching several rolls of paper, emerged from the largest tent in the compound.

'Captain John Carne, pleased to see you, sir,' he bellowed, holding a hand in front of him and pulling John into an embrace, before slapping his shoulder.

'Colonel,' said John, bowing to him. 'It's plain Master Carne now, or John. And I'm pleased to see you, too, though it grieves me this conflict continues.'

'There's nothing civil about a civil war and, sad to say, all the evidence points to a long haul ahead of us. But keep that to yourself, my man. Come, sit down, take a drink with me.' He waved his hand. 'Back to your duties, eh, Cornet.'

Benbow took his leave.

'Impetuous young man, but I like him,' said Colonel Mytton, jerking his thumb towards Benbow and then indicating a seat for John once they were inside the tent. Drinks were poured and the Colonel started an account of everything that had happened since Edgehill.

'And still this wretched war continues,' Mytton concluded. He leaned forward. 'Thanks to young Jack Benbow, I've heard of your circumstances. You'll have no one billeted with you, but if you need a strong lad about the place to help out, just say the word.'

John was touched. 'I thank you for that, Colonel, but we manage well enough.'

Mytton's sergeant arrived and asked if the captain would be dining with him. 'I hope you shall, John, though we can only offer army rations. I hear, from the garrulous Benbow, that your wife is a magician who can transform a humble pigeon into a banquet. And, I rather fancy, enchant a young soldier at the same time.' He chuckled. 'Set another place, Sergeant.' John joined the colonel and his officers there for a most congenial meal.

'I thank you for that, sir,' said John to Mytton as the other officers drifted away. 'I'd be obliged if you'd let me see the horse captured by Benbow and his troop, together with anything found with it.'

The horse flicked its ears forward to the name Brandy. There was a bag containing a spare shirt, a pair of gloves and a notebook full of figures, with PROPERTY OF THOM. PERKS. WHIXALL GRANGE written inside the front cover.

'This is the man's horse,' said John. 'May I keep the bag and contents?'

'Yes,' said Mytton. 'We've only requisitioned the animal and its harness. It's something of a bad do, isn't it? Three murders and mutilations I believe. Presumably they're all connected.'

'There are similarities.'

Mytton smiled. 'Sir Moreton suspects witchcraft. Take my advice, John, don't forget the natural can be equally as destructive as the supernatural.'

'I don't forget, Colonel. It's puzzling to me, though, that this horse seems to have disappeared for the best part of a week.'

'It's a big county.'

'I must be getting back. Thank you very much for the food, and especially the company, I've enjoyed myself.'

John saw a few people gathered outside Spibey's house. The man himself must have only just returned from Whixall, for he was still on his horse.

'Make way,' he was saying, waving his riding crop. 'Make way.'

'You freed the witch,' shouted a woman. 'We're none of us safe now.'

'She should have hung!' The tall man again. John was becoming thoroughly annoyed by him.

'Ah, John, John,' said Spibey with relief. 'Get these people away from my gate.'

John raised his hands. 'Everyone, please, let Sir Moreton into his home.'

'What if she eats my children?' wailed the woman. 'What if she drags them to hell with her?'

'She was released because there was no evidence. You should congratulate Sir Moreton for being such a diligent magistrate. One who upholds the principles of the law.'

'Damn principles!' said the tall man

A breathless Crowther appeared, accompanied by the sergeant from the gaol.

The sergeant held up his pistol. 'This gathering is unlawful. Away now, all of you, away.'

At the sight of the firearm the group began to disperse.

'Witches should be hung,' shouted the tall man, in a last passing shot. 'You've cursed the town with your foolishness.'

Once inside Spibey strode distractedly about his study. 'What am I to do?' he wailed. 'I'm here, there, all over the place. Oh, and that riot just now, I was set upon, John. They were about to tear me apart with their bare hands.' He bit his nails viciously, his dark little eyes darting about in their most abstracted fashion. 'I mean, I don't know what's going on anymore. How can such things be allowed to happen? My dear daughter is here. I need to be with her, yet I'm needed at Whixall. Oh, John, if only my dear wife were alive...'

John remained silent. In a moment Spibey would recover himself.

Crowther put his head round the door and announced the arrival of Reverend Parsons.

'Dear Andrew,' said Spiby to his guest. 'Will you come and see Margaret? And then we can plan Thomas's funeral.' He looked at John. 'Master Carne, on my table there are Master Perks's books of accounts that I brought from Whixall. They're all up to date, but I feel they could be simplified. Have a look at them for me.'

'Gladly, Sir Moreton. I have yet another book found among Master Perks's possessions on his horse. It'll be interesting to see how they all tally together.'

John enjoyed the afternoon. As Spibey said, Perks kept his accounts in good order, but in many separate books, almost as if he was keeping secrets from himself. John devised a way in which all the financial transactions could be recorded in two books. His wife would be proud of him for creating such order and organisation. He sighed. Zipporah, He was sure, in her own strange way, she had sent him an olive branch that morning. Then Baccy came into his mind. He remembered something she said. That she'd been prepared to accept her husband's male lovers, if that was the price of keeping him. Now he realised he'd never really tried to understand Zipporah. He'd tolerated her behaviour but never attempted to see things from her point of view. His main concern was that her madness should never be revealed to the world. If he wanted her to change, perhaps he must make himself change, too.

Spibey was a lot calmer after his time with the rector, and at least the funeral arrangements were now in place. He was also impressed with John's ordering of the accounts of Whixall Grange and the estate.

'You've a clear mind, Master Carne,' he said. 'I like that.'

John wished that was true. He wished his mind was a lot clearer concerning the death of Perks and the strange bodies from the Moss. Some clarity regarding his relationship with Zipporah would be welcome, too.

Chapter Fourteen

Zipporah was upstairs when he returned home.

'I'll be down in a moment,' she called.

'It's all right, I'll come up.'

He stepped into the nursery. The little clothes she so lovingly made and kept so fastidiously clean were either hanging from a line stretched across the pitched roof, or stacked neatly on the chest. The cradle, with the names GEORGE AND ARABELLA painted on the side, was in the middle of the room, a chair next to it. She had one of the children on her lap, gently changing him into a long nightshirt, humming and smiling as she did so. She briefly looked up. 'I'll be with you in a moment. George has made a bit of a mess. He's a greedy boy, and then … well, you like to make a lot of washing for your mama, don't you? Go downstairs, John and pour yourself some ale.'

'No, it's all right.' He swallowed hard and stepped towards the cradle, where he knew the other child must be. She was there. Out of swaddling now and dressed in a dark blue gown, a miniature version of her mother's best dress. She was a pretty child. Her rounded cheeks were pink and her lips perfect rosebuds. Her blue eyes gazed sightlessly upwards from her beautifully carved and painted, but expressionless wooden face.

He swallowed again. 'They're coming on well, a real credit to you.'

She stood up, gently cradling George in her arms, as if he was real. John knew that under the children's clothes were bodies made from linen filled with straw and wool. He felt sick, his heart beating fast. No matter how much he loved her, there was no mistaking the cruel hard fact: his wife was a lunatic.

'It's your step-papa,' she was saying to the doll. 'He's come to see you; that doesn't happen very often does it?' She stood close to him, the George doll stared blankly up at the rafters. John leaned down and with the greatest effort took Arabella from the cot.

Zipporah frowned. 'Careful.'

'We're all right,' he said softly, cradling the doll in his arms and stroking her woollen hair.

'Why are you doing this?' she asked. She remained close to him.

'I've been unfair. You're my wife, these are your children. I have responsibility for them, and I should ... um, care for them. As I care for you.'

Her lips trembled. 'I can't believe this. You won't regret it, though, John. Not for one minute. They're such fascinating little creatures. Already they have their own personalities. Arabella is the braver of the two. She'll walk before she's a year old, for sure. Now, George, he watches; he considers. His eyes follow me everywhere, though he's really fascinated by you as well. If he were your son, I'd say he'd inherited your cleverness. He isn't yours, but if you're there to guide him, I think he may have a great future.'

John couldn't answer. He wanted to shout at her, shake her even, and make her realise they were merely timber and fabric. How could the bright, rational Zipporah truly believe these damned dolls were real? He forced a smile.

'They're such a credit to you, yes, clever, pretty, bright babies.'

'They need a father. A good stepfather is better than an unknown sire.'

Unknown? Why did she say that? What *had* happened to her? He wished she would confide in him, tell him how she'd got with child, perhaps then he'd understand her better.

She laid George gently back in the cradle, then looked up at John. 'Come downstairs, you must be hungry and thirsty. Later, may the children come down and sit with us?'

'Just for a while, I don't want them to get overtired.'

She shot him the widest beaming smile and skipped downstairs. He heard her, busy with her pots and pans, singing carelessly. He threw Arabella into the cot with disgust. Evil toys. The sort of dolls that could convict a woman of witchcraft. By indulging her fantasy was he helping or hindering her recovery? If recover she ever could.

He remembered the day he'd discovered her. She was filthy and had been begging, wandering aimlessly about the lanes and sleeping under hedges. He recalled her huge, frightened hazel eyes, gleaming brightly against the grime of her face. He'd held out his hand and she'd grasped it, and let him pull her up.

'How did this happen?' he asked.

She didn't answer him then, nor had she since.

'I'll care for you, Zipporah. You're safe now.'

She'd simply nodded, all spirit gone from her.

He blinked and wiped his hand across his face, as if to clear away the memory. Then he crouched by the cot and arranged her 'children' neatly, side by side and pulled the blanket up to their wooden chins. 'You bastards,' he whispered. 'How were you got? In love, or by force? Tell your mother to tell me. I'm the one who loves her more than anyone else in this world. I'll understand, no matter what happened. Tell her to tell me.' He stopped short. Now he was the one talking to the malevolent little effigies. Was her madness contagious?

She might be mad, but at least she was alive. The dolls had saved her. She'd lost her mind during the days she spent in labour, when she screamed until it seemed she could scream no more, then seconds later started all over again. She screamed so loudly, with such terror, that no matter where he went he could hear their echoes. Then there was silence. He waited a while, but could bear it no longer. Despite Molly Kade's cries of disapproval, he went into the bedroom. He glimpsed two small shapes on the table; she was covering them with a cloth. She shook her head firmly, telling him in one gesture that the babies were dead, and he shouldn't look at them. He stared wide eyed at Zipporah, lying pale and motionless, she and the bed so splattered with blood she might as well have been blown up at Edgehill. He leaned over her, and her eyelids flickered. 'Two,' she croaked through cracked lips. 'Twins.'

'That's right,' he whispered, his voice watery with the tears that threatened to burst forth. 'You've been brave. Braver than many a soldier I've seen.'

Her eyelids opened and he briefly recoiled. There were no whites in her eyes,, they were blood red. Then he composed himself and took her hand. 'You need to rest, sleep, recover.'

'The babies, I haven't heard them crying yet.'

'Leave them to Molly, you sleep.'

She seemed to drift off. He turned to Molly who stood by him now. 'What happened? Her eyes, they're like a demon's.'

'It took a great effort. There were two, lying awkwardly. I didn't think she'd manage to deliver them, but she's strong. She managed, but the cost to her is great. If they'd had normal heads though, I think they'd have killed her. They still might.'

'What do you mean? Let me see them.'

'No, they're strange ill-formed creatures, their limbs twisted, their faces half what they should be, with tiny flattened skulls. One drew breath, if only briefly, which was amazing, for they were surely never meant for this world.'

'How am I going to tell her? She thought she was having one

child. She wanted that baby. She'd made all the clothes. We bought the cradle.' Now tears slid from his eyes and he didn't care. 'How can I tell her that after everything she's been through, there's nothing?'

Molly shrugged. 'She's not the first and won't be the last to lose a child. If she can conceive again, she'll probably lose another. As it is you may as well dispose of the cradle. Even if she lives, she's been ripped to pieces. I doubt she'll carry again.'

John slumped onto the end of the bed, put his head in his hands and sobbed. Even though he'd determined he would look after Zipporah's child as if it was his own, he'd also looked forward to the time when they'd have children together. He felt hopelessness seep through him. When he looked up he saw that Molly was bundling the babies into a basket.

'They can't be buried in hallowed ground, but I'll see to them. It'll be respectful. I always show respect.'

After that Zipporah teetered on the edge of life and death for a week. Fever raged through her. They cut off her long chestnut hair, soaked her with cold water, and eventually she showed signs of recovery. Molly's work was done and John was left alone with a woman who was little more than a shadow. Most of the time she lay still, gazing sightlessly at the ceiling. She took the food he offered, and allowed him to pull her from her bed and walk her around the room. Sometimes she called for her child, forgetting that she had two and that they were both dead. Eventually, she got up and dressed herself and started to make him food and keep the house, though she barely spoke and her expression never changed. It was like having a sleepwalker in the house, but one who never awoke.

Then there was the dreadful day when he found her hanging from the rafters, unable to continue to live with the pain. He'd reached her just in time, and once again she recovered.

'I might as well go to my damnation now as later,' she said to him, expressionless.

'You're not damned, my love.'

'I am. That's what my brother says. The children I conceived out of wedlock are a sign of my damnation. Then they died. Surely that's another sign.'

'What happened, Zipporah? Tell me, I'll understand.'

She shuddered. 'It's never to be spoken of.'

He pleaded with her and eventually got a solemn promise that she'd never attempt to take her own life again.

She spent hours in the room that would have been the nursery. He couldn't understand why she'd taken the spherical newel caps from the top of the staircase, or why she needed clean straw. He hoped that taking her box of paints into the room meant she was at least returning to one of her previous hobbies, as she'd been a decent artist.

Then one day, she burst out of the nursery, her face bright, her eyes shining, her cheeks pink. 'Come, husband, I've made my children live again.'

Then he saw what she'd done. The newel caps had been refashioned into painted faces, the straw stuffed the bodies. He hated them from the moment he saw them. He tried to snatch them from her, fully intending to burn them, but she'd protected them with the ferocity of a mother. And so they began their uneasy alliance. John realised that they gave her a will to live. Her physical recovery was rapid after she created them. She cooked beautifully and kept the home better than most. And John made the decision to protect her, to keep her within the house and its small grounds. If anyone ever found out she had two wooden children, it wouldn't be good for her, especially with men like Moreton Spibey about, determined to find witches and devilry where none existed.

John sighed hard and looked into the cradle again. He straightened the blanket over the dolls. If only Zipporah would let him love her. Even if there was only the tiniest chance she could bear another child, he must try, as he was sure that would cure her of this madness. He prayed to God that she'd let him take her as a man takes his wife, and not just to satisfy his own desires, which were so intense as to be physically painful at times. They had to move away from this make-believe world, and become real, even if that meant accepting grief and disappointment. And yet, here he was, letting himself be drawn into her fantasy.

'Leave them alone, you'll tire them out,' she called up the stairs, her voice light with happiness. 'Come and eat.'

He ran his finger down Arabella's deftly carved cheek. If there was any magic to bring these puppets to life, he'd use it. But there was none, so he must feign affection for them, in the hope it would eventually lead to his wife's salvation.

———

As he promised, after they'd eaten and when the shutters were pulled tightly closed and the doors barred, he let her bring the children downstairs, something which, until then, he'd strictly forbidden her from doing.

'Just occasionally and when I say so,' he said. 'You understand why I want to keep them safe and private don't you?'

'Yes, because of the war.'

So he sat with his pipe and a mug of ale at his side, George upon his knee.

Zipporah's face was radiant as she turned to him, Arabella in the crook of her arm. 'This is how it should be, husband, you, me and our children.'

'Yes, it is.' He didn't know if he should laugh or cry.

After their pleasant evening John's desires were overwhelming. They were in their nightclothes and preparing to retire when he kissed her, and for a short moment he was sure she responded. The sensation of the kiss was so intense and the closeness of her body so arousing that he lost his seed. He stopped, ashamed, and she saw the stain on his nightshirt and gasped in horror. She spent the rest of the night curled away from him, sobbing into the bolster, he huddled to his own side of the bed.

Zipporah's face was pinched and her eyes red rimmed the next morning. John hardly looked any better.

'I'm truly sorry about last night,' he said, his voice hoarse. 'It's just that when a man loves a woman as much as I love you … it can be difficult. Please forgive me'

She poked the fire into life and added some more logs but said nothing.

'Why are you so frightened, my love? Maybe I was wrong to kiss you last night, but I'd never hurt you. I hugged you too close, that's all, but I didn't force myself upon you, and I never shall.'

'I don't want you to love me,' she said. 'I don't understand why you do. You could easily repudiate me; it's not as if our marriage has been consummated. You're still young; you're handsome; you'd soon find another. Someone who'll love you as you deserve to be loved.'

'It's only you I want, Zipporah. It's only ever been you.'

She turned away. 'Will you break your fast?'

'No, I'll be off.'

'Oh, dear, life goes on, Master Carne,' smiled Crowther, knowingly.

'Some days good, some not so.'

Even Spibey noticed something was amiss. 'My, you look ill, but then, what a business this is. It's enough to make any man peaky. And I forget that you're in pain most of the time. Some good news, though.' He tapped a piece of paper on his table. 'It's a short note from your brother to say his wife is safely delivered, and Mistress Kade will soon be on her way. I just hope my Margaret can hold out for her.'

'I'm sure she has some time to go.'

'She does, of course she does, but all this shock, who knows what trouble it could cause?'

'It's good news for my brother and his family.'

'Yes indeed.' Spibey motioned for him to sit down. 'I hoped you'd go to Whixall Grange and work with Master Wellings today. Your efforts with Tom's accounts yesterday have set me thinking, and Wellings will know what's what and where's where. I've made out a whole list of queries, yet you look so sick I hardly dare ask you.'

'I assure you I'm well enough to go.'

Spibey looked doubtful. 'I don't want to be responsible for any greater malaise taking a grip of you.'

'No, not at all. In fact, Sir Moreton, I think all the activity you're putting me to is beneficial to my health. My leg is definitely growing stronger. I believe that soon my stick will be little more than an affectation.'

'Oh, I don't think so,' said Spibey. 'You put a brave face on things, but I can see you're more than a little queasy today.'

'Just a flux, a bit of a flux.'

'Where?'

'In my heart, I suppose,' said John without thinking, tiredness making him stupid.

'Your heart. This is serious!' Spibey looked alarmed.

'No, no, sir,' said John, tapping his chest. 'Heartburn, you know, that's all.'

'Oh, I'm a martyr to that myself. Have a glass of my best brandy before you go. By the way, I never had a chance to thank you for bringing Tom's possessions back from the garrison.'

Spibey's face was grave as he poured John a drink. 'Now, take that down in one. If nothing else it'll keep the cold out. And here.' He pushed a folded and sealed piece of paper into his hand. 'A communication from your brother, no doubt he wants to tell you more of the new child.'

Recently every day had started misty but that day there was a deep frost and it was even more bone-achingly cold than usual. With his coat fully buttoned, the collar of his cloak fastened tightly and his hat pulled well down, John still felt ice seeping into his body, even with Spibey's brandy inside him, which had actually made him feel sick, as he'd had no breakfast. As his sturdy pony walked quietly, he thought he'd better open Dick's letter before his hands became completely numb. It was written in his brother's familiar untidy hand.

Dearest John,

Thanks bee to God my wife is safely delivered of our Child, our new son Edward John. No trouble this time, Molly Kade was hardly needed, but it was good to have her here. She will soon be with your Employer in Wem.

What is this concerning old Thom Perks? His manner of Demise is most Peculiar (tho' til I hear it from yourself, I'll belive none of it). Mistress Perks is left in an Interesting Predicimant. Once deliver'd of her child I'll Venture she'll have many a Suitor for her hand. Tis a pity you were Bewiched by that Hoare. Tho' Mrs Perks Father's godliness wont go down well with our father, but then nothing you do pleases him now, so you could do worse than form an alliance with the Young Widow.

John looked up, the watery sun was burning off the mist. His eyes followed a swooping flock of starlings, flying so close together they made shapes in the sky. He crunched the paper in his hand, anger warmed his body as clothes and brandy could not. Still he had to read on, even though he hated the way Dick referred to Zipporah.

Dearest Bro', I know you Hate what I write (I'll wager my Paper is crumpled by now!)

John had to smile.

and you know I have tried to help you with the House & all, but I feel so keenly for the Unhappy Situation you are in. If what you have told me of your Situation with Z is still true, then you are no more tyed to her than a Vague Aquentance. I hope you get My meaning. There is little that is done that cannot be Undone. You are miss'd my Dearest Bro'

Your Most Loving Bro'
Richard Carne.

He pushed the paper into his pocket. He knew Dick loved him, but if he really did, why couldn't he, if not like or love, at the very least accept Zipporah, too?

Chapter Fifteen

John stopped briefly at the main entrance to Whixall Grange. He looked up the short track that led from the road to the house and its outlying buildings. To the right was the old timber framed hall, now converted to a stable. Attached to it was the new brick-built house. It was smartly constructed, three storeys high and with lighter bricks marking out a lozenge pattern between the glazed windows of the ground and first floor. The imposing main door was set in a carved stone surround. The roof was tiled with slates as grey as the sky which glowered above. John shivered in his coat. He ached as well. Freddy had been positively mule-like for the last half of the journey. John was looking forward to being off the wretched pony and inside if nothing else.

The house must have cost a fortune. And Perks made this investment when there was no sign of an heir. He lived in hope, it seemed. John couldn't really understand his character though; from what he'd heard of him he seemed a miser, yet enjoyed luxury. He supposed he never would fully comprehend the squire now, and even if he did, how would it help in discovering his murderer?

Isaac Wellings was at the side door. 'Come inside, sir, you look poorly.'

'I assure you I'm well, but most hungry. I'll bother you for some food and a mug of warm ale and then we'll be about our work,' said John.

After finishing the last of some delicious thick cut ham and freshly baked bread, John felt invigorated. 'So, Master Wellings, we have a busy day ahead of us; Sir Moreton has provided me with a great list of questions he needs answers to.'

'Then we'd best begin.'

They were briefly interrupted by a maid who came to collect the plates. 'I've a message for Master Carne.'

'Yes,' said John.

'Nanna Grey, the old lady in the laundry, she asked if you'd go to her. It's about something she's seen. No, I'm sorry, it's about something she hasn't seen.' The girl giggled a little. 'No, I must have got that wrong. It must be about something she's seen, because if she hadn't seen it, she couldn't tell you, could she?'

'She's a very old lady,' whispered Wellings.

John nodded. 'I've met her. Tell her I'll certainly pay my respects to her before I leave.'

The maid took the plates. 'Oh, there's another thing. Nanna will only tell you what she saw, or didn't, whatever it is, if you're a married man and know the ways of women.'

John heard Wellings snort and tried to keep his own face straight. 'You can assure Nanna that I'm a married man, though wise as she is, I'm sure she realises I still know little of the ways of women.'

The maid left. Wellings was frowning. 'As I said, she's very old. You don't need to see her, and she'll have forgotten what nonsense she had to tell you by now, anyway.'

'I'm respectful enough to spare a few minutes with her.' John returned his attention to the papers they were studying. 'So, Isaac, the most recent estate map we have was drawn in the days of the queen. What's changed since then?'

Wellings talked about the estate and its running, while John making made copious notes. After a couple of hours he leaned back and yawned.

'I'm sorry this isn't interesting,' said Wellings.

'It is. There's just so much to take in.' John rubbed his eyes.

'How is Mistress Carne? Does she know about the strange discoveries on the Moss and about Master Perks?'

'She does,' said John. He liked the fact that Wellings had only ever shown respect for Zipporah.

'Is she worried? I mean, worried because such crimes have been committed so nearby and you're away from home so much.'

John couldn't prevent a little shiver. 'No, she's not worried, though maybe *I* should be. Still, let's finish off here, and then I'll see what Nanna Grey has to say and get home to Zipporah.'

Wellings smiled slightly. 'I'm sure she's safe enough in your house in Wem. Now, Master Carne, you were asking about the land to the north that Master Perks purchased from a neighbour. I think the documents will be in the master's room. May I go and look for them?'

'By all means,' said John, pleased to have a break. He settled himself by the fire and within seconds his eyes closed.

'Master Carne, Master Carne.' It was Wellings, gently tugging his sleeve.

John jerked awake. 'I must have dropped off. I apologise.'

'I'm sorry it took me longer than I thought it would,' said Wellings. 'You looked so peaceful I wasn't sure if I should wake you.'

'Yes, you should. Now, I see you've retrieved the documents. Let's continue.'

It was mid-afternoon before John felt satisfied that most of Spibey's queries had been dealt with.

'Many thanks, Isaac. You know this estate as well as any, and I'll venture you love it, too.'

'It's been the happy home of my family for generations.'

'There'll be changes, just as there must have been when Thomas took over from his father, but I can assure you, Sir Moreton will be a good and fair master until the squire's son is old enough to take over.'

'I'll admit I worry about Mistress Perks. She's so young to have to withstand such tragedy.'

'She's shocked, of course, but what little I've seen of her leads me to believe she's resilient and will recover.'

'I most fervently hope so.'

'Are you staying here, Master Wellings?'

'As I've no other instruction I may as well ride back to Wem with you later and see what Sir Moreton wants of me.'

'Are you a married man? Accompany me to see Nanna if you are.'

'No, sir, I'm still a bachelor. I'll get the horses sorted for our journey. Nanna will be in the laundry, next to the kitchen. I keep telling her to give up and rest, but she says as long as she can, she'll work.'

'I'd like to get off pretty promptly. If I'm not in the stables in a couple of minutes come and rescue me, eh?'

Wellings smiled, his broad face dimpling pleasantly.

What an unassuming and capable young man he was, thought John, as he made his way downstairs. He also liked the fact that he clearly respected Zipporah, which not many people did. He stopped and nodded to the cook and thanked her for the food she'd provided and then limped down the corridor to the laundry. He could smell boiling water and damp linens as he opened the door. He coughed, the room was so full of steam. He went to the cauldron. It had almost boiled dry, and he swung it away from the fire.

'Nanna Grey,' he called. 'Come on, Nanna, no need to hide.' Where was she? The next batch of washing was laid on the table next to the cauldron.

He grinned, surely she'd not forgotten she'd asked to see him and gone tottering off somewhere? She'd hardly leave her cauldron unattended, though. 'Nanna,' he called again. He sighed. Whatever it was she had to say, it couldn't have been important. It would have to wait for another day. He turned to leave, then something caught his eye and he looked up.

'No!' He gasped and held onto the edge of the table. The body of Nanna Grey hung limply from the ceiling. 'No,' he moaned. He no longer smelled the lavender of the wash water, or felt the warmth of the bubbling cauldron. An icy chill stabbed into him and his heart pounded. 'So wrong,' he muttered. 'So wrong.' As the steam dissipated he could see the old woman's eyes and lips were pierced with thorns. Why was this happening? What could this poor, decent, hardworking woman have done to deserve this? Nothing, he was sure. Was it a manifestation of evil, committed for no reason than pure wickedness itself? Was Spibey right? Not about Baccy, he was still sure about her, but were they trapped in events beyond reason? He mustn't think like that. He must remain rational. He must investigate. He limped to the door and called for help.

—————

'What a dreadful shock for you,' said Wellings, passing John a glass of spiced wine.

'It wasn't what I was expecting,' said John. He sipped a little of the drink and then put it to one side. He looked up again and shook his head, unable for the moment to articulate any thoughts.

'It doesn't seem decent, leaving her up like that,' said Wellings with a sniff.

The head groom entered the laundry carrying a ladder.

'Not just yet,' said John, holding out his hand. Suddenly his head felt clearer. He wanted nothing more than to bring the poor woman down, but he needed to examine her first. I'll find out who did this and bring them to justice for you, Nanna, he said to himself.

'Perhaps *you* should take some wine,' he said to Wellings, passing him the glass. 'I know it doesn't seem decent, but she's been murdered and the killer may have left some evidence, so I don't want anything touched for the moment. Now, Master Groom –' he turned to the man who was reluctantly propping the ladder against the wall by Nanna Grey's body '– send your cleverest boy and your fastest horse to Wem. Tell Sir Moreton what's happened. He needs to be here. And another thing, and this is most important, the boy must get a message to my wife to say I shall either be very late or not back at all. Her name is Zipporah Carne and we live at The Dial, on High Street. It has a grey lozenge-shaped sundial with white Roman numerals above the door.'

'Master Carne,' said Wellings. 'Let me do this, my horse is fast and ready and I know where to go, and I'll most certainly make sure your wife knows what's happening.'

'Then I'll let you go, Isaac, but tell no one except Sir Moreton what's happened here.'

With a nod, Wellings was off.

'Dark and devilish work,' murmured the cook, who'd been the first to answer John's call. She'd immediately and without fuss sought out the head groom, who seemed to be a most responsible person.

'I need to speak to everyone, call them to the kitchen, please.' John looked to the cook and the groom. The two servants looked at each other as if unsure what to do. 'It's what Sir Moreton would ask for,' he said. 'I'm his assistant and I know his ways.' Given that Spibey was prone to panic in such extreme situations he wasn't sure this was what the magistrate would have ordered, but it seemed to work, and he was for the moment left alone with Nanna Grey.

She hung from a rope passed over the furthest beam in the room, then tied to the table leg. He was sure that, like Perks, she must have been attacked on the ground and then hoisted into the air.

He painfully pulled himself up the ladder, until he was close to her face. As he expected, there were no signs that stringing up had killed her. Her tongue did not protrude, nor did her eyes bulge. There was little blood where the thorns pierced. Three closed her mouth, two for each eyelid. Fewer than were used on Perks and much less than on the Moss bodies. He reached out and held her hand. She was still limp; there was even a little warmth to her, though that might be due to the boiling cauldron heating the air.

The groom returned and said all the staff were assembling in the kitchen. John called over his shoulder, 'Be a good man and untie the cord from the table leg, then gently lower her.' John eased himself down the ladder, holding her steady, and he and the groom carried her to the central table and covered her with one of the clean sheets she'd been sorting. They bowed their heads and remained in silence for a while.

'Are you all right, Master Carne?' said the groom. 'We all know you have an injury to your leg. That must have pained you.'

'A little,' said John, with considerable understatement. Though, his physical pain was nowhere near the anguish this barbaric act caused him. The groom left and John put his hand on Nanna's chest. 'Oh, Nanna,' he whispered. 'What did you see? What were you going to say?'

By the time Spibey arrived, red faced and flustered, John had taken statements from the servants. The two of them sat together in Perks's study.

'Today was a day as any other,' said John. 'The cooks cooked; the maids cleaned; the grooms groomed. And the laundress boiled, dried and sorted linens, until she was killed.'

'No callers, no one suspicious sneaking about?'

'Not today, though this might interest you: I've been told that yesterday one Samuel Blanchard called. Husband of Baccy.'

'Blanchard? I thought he lived in London. You told me, John, that he lives in London.'

'I believe he does. I suppose he's visiting his wife.'

Spibey spluttered. 'Evil seeking out its own. What was he doing here? Did he say?'

'He'd heard about Master Perks and came to pay his respects. They were neighbours in the past. He was keen to make your acquaintance, too, and Mistress Perks. Apparently he met your daughter when she was living in London.'

Spibey jerked to his feet and thumped his fists on the table. 'Well, that's a damned lie and a half, Master Carne, you can take my word on it! Margaret was in town but three months, and living with a most respectable relative. Even though it's a godly town, I brought her home swiftly. For all big towns, godly or not, harbour those such as Sam Blanchard.'

'So he didn't find you?'

'Master Carne, you disappoint me. You think I'd allow such a seasoned sinner into my home? A creature who mocks the Scriptures and flaunts himself with another man, no, never, never!'

John looked down and smiled to himself. 'No, Sir Moreton, I don't think you'd entertain such a person for even one minute. Nevertheless it's a fact that he's the only unexpected visitor here for many weeks. I'll have to speak to Baccy again.'

'Why? We agreed, didn't we? She's nothing. There's a great

evil in this place but I doubt that tobacco-stained old whore is the cause of it.'

John frowned. Not only had Spibey apparently changed his opinion of Baccy, but he'd also never heard him speak so intemperately before.

The magistrate sank heavily back into his chair. 'I know what you're thinking. But you're the one who persuaded me that the Blanchard woman had nothing to do with Tom's disappearance.'

'I'm sure she didn't.'

'So, we agree. Tell me about this Nanna woman. The killer must have been in a hurry, for time would have seen her off soon enough.'

'She was very ancient. No one is sure exactly how old, maybe even more than eighty years. She lived and worked on the estate all her life. For the last ten years or so in charge of the laundry. She married, had five children, and she's been a widow many years. Her two surviving granddaughters both work here. I met her myself, on our previous visit. She seemed well for her age. Apparently she had something to tell me, but was killed before I could speak to her.'

'You don't know what she had to say?'

'No, it was something she'd seen or not seen; the message wasn't clear. When we last spoke, I asked Nanna to let me know if she remembered anything. I presume she did. If that's the case, it leads me to an unfortunate conclusion.'

'Which is?'

'That someone in this household murdered Nanna Grey, before she could tell me what she knew.'

'Surely not!'

'I can't think of any other reason. And as I consider what little evidence I have, another darker thought comes into my mind.'

'Which is?'

John paused. He might as well say it, as Spibey had probably come to the same conclusion himself. 'The person who killed Nanna Grey is also the murderer of Thomas Perks.'

They sat in silence. Spibey's jowls sank lower into his collar and vibrated slightly. He rubbed his finger along the grain of the wooden table. 'And do you have any idea who that might be?' he said eventually.

John put his notes and pencil down. 'Not one single suspicion. Every statement I took had the ring of truth about it. All these people are decent. They may not have loved Master Perks, but he was certainly respected. Everyone here is well fed, well dressed and where possible, fairly well educated.'

Spibey nodded. 'The first Mistress Perks saw to it that everyone in the household was taught to read if they had the aptitude. It was for the sake of their souls, so they could study the Bible.'

'Very commendable. Your son-in-law kept his estate well. This was no harsh landlord, but a decent man who took his responsibilities seriously. He may have counted every penny and known its exact whereabouts, but he wasn't mean spirited. He didn't pester the girls or beat the boys. There'd be many a servant in this county who'd be more than happy to live here.'

Spibey pulled himself tiredly from the table and laid his giant puffy hand on John's shoulder. 'See,' he said, leaning over him, 'with every word you answer your own questions. The manner of these deaths is not normal. The hanging, though the body is already dead, and those despicable thorns, don't you see, they all point to witchcraft. We're in a fight against the very devil himself. Are you strong enough for that, John?'

'Are you, Sir Moreton?'

'With God's help, yes.'

'But where do we look for these wraiths, or demons, or whatever they may be?'

Spibey went to a cupboard and took a bottle and two glasses from inside. He pulled the cork.

'I'm normally modest in my consumption, as you know. But have some of this. It soothes the stomach, for mine churns about at the moment.' He poured a dark ruby liquid into glasses so fine John hardly dared grasp his for fear it would shatter. Spibey sipped. 'Tom liked the finer things in life. Like this.'

'It's the smoothest wine I have ever tasted,' said John. 'What do we do next? I'll admit I can't think of anything.'

'Your theory may not be completely incorrect. Perhaps it is a member of the household, possessed by a demon, yet unaware of it. We must tread carefully. Do you think I should take everyone, duck them in the river and see who floats?'

'I think not, sir!' exclaimed John. 'For the righteous would drown, and there'd be no one left to keep your grandchild's estates running.' John had thought Spibey a clever man, but sometimes that intelligence was hard to discern. 'For the moment, if you think it prudent, I believe we should keep any suspicions to ourselves. At the very least it will lull the perpetrators into a false sense of security.' He had no more idea than Spibey how to proceed, but felt he had to say something.

'Yes, indeed,' said Spibey. 'Then we pounce.'

Spibey decided to stay at Whixall Grange. He had no objection to John going back to Wem, even though he couldn't understand why he wanted to, as it was fully dark.

'I need to,' said John, hoping Spibey was too tired to ask for any further explanation as to why. From John's point of view it was simple. He didn't like to leave Zipporah alone any longer than he had to. He pulled on his coat. He heard Dick's letter rustle in the pocket. It was best to dispose of that before he got home. He screwed it into a ball and threw it into the fireplace.

By the look of the moon and stars it must have been nearly midnight when he finally got back to The Dial. He expected

Zipporah would be in bed, but she was still up, writing in her journal. She immediately closed it, and tied the leather straps tight around it. She'd removed her cap, and John saw the kinks were returning to her hair as it grew. It made him smile as it reminded him of the long gloriously wavy chestnut locks she once had.

'I didn't expect you back,' she said.

'Then why are you still up?'

'I couldn't sleep. You look dreadful by the way.'

'I thank you for that, dear wife. I've not had a good day of it. I started with brandy on an empty stomach. Once in Whixall I ate a crust or two, but I've not had a hot meal all day. Then I drank a strange thick wine with Sir Moreton. Now everything gripes.'

'Take your clothes off; they need a good brushing. I've a comforting stew here that will put things right, and have some claret; your leg must be paining you.'

'Everything is paining me.' He moved his chair closer to the fire and gratefully sank onto it. 'There's been another murder.'

Zipporah looked up from the cauldron, her hand fluttering across her lips. 'Dear Lord, no? What's happening, John? Who's been killed now?'

'Nanna Grey. An ancient laundrywoman. Her eyelids and lips pierced with thorns.' He couldn't stop a little sob escaping. He must be exhausted to allow himself to feel such sorrow for someone he hardly knew.

Zipporah knelt next to him. 'Why?' was all she said.

He shrugged. 'I cannot fathom that. All I know is there was something she wanted to tell me, then she was dead.'

'And you think they're connected?'

He paused and swallowed hard. 'That is a possibility I must consider. As I must also suspect that someone in the household at Whixall is the killer. Which, since every last one of them seems as decent a person as you could hope to meet, is something I can hardly countenance.'

She ran her hand over his hair. 'My poor John,' she whispered.

Then she pulled herself upright. 'For the moment, we must forget the old woman. You need to eat something. Leave this vile crime for another day.'

He hungrily ate the stew. As it was made by Zipporah, it tasted far better than its humble ingredients of pork, carrots and cabbage would if stirred by another hand. The claret as usual did the work of numbing the pain in his leg.

'Claret again?' he said, feeling both his body and spirits reviving. 'Are we living on the stuff now? We can't afford it.'

'A present from Jack,' she said over her shoulder as she brushed his jacket. 'As in Cornet Benbow, I mean. He called today hoping to see you. He'd heard from his family in Shrewsbury, that your brother's wife has given birth to a son.'

'I had a letter from Dick, delivered to Sir Moreton,' said John, between mouthfuls, grateful he'd destroyed the missive as she was emptying his pockets.

'Then you know more than me,' she said.

'I'm not sure I approve of young Benbow visiting you whenever he pleases.'

'He visits you, not me. Jealous husband doesn't suit you, John. I'm no good wife to you, but I'll never make you a cuckold.'

He smiled into his bowl. She was right, on that score he trusted her implicitly. He beckoned her over.

She sat opposite him and her lips twitched mischievously. 'Not that Jack was my only gentleman caller today.'

He raised an eyebrow.

'First there was Master Crowther. He most politely told me that you were delayed at Whixall.'

'Crowther, are you sure, not Master Wellings? I asked Master Wellings to tell you. In fact he eagerly volunteered to take a message to you.' John felt unaccountably annoyed that Wellings hadn't kept his word.

'No, he introduced himself as Crowther. A Welsh gentleman, with a bright smile and amazing eyebrows, like two furry caterpillars. I've seen him in church. Master Wellings I know is a much younger man.' She grinned. 'Master Crowther did say he'd been sent by Master Wellings. I got the impression that he wasn't too happy about being given orders by him. He said Master Wellings considers himself a favourite of both Sir Moreton and Mistress Perks and forgets he's merely the steward at Whixall Grange.'

John raised his eyebrows. 'That sounds like a bit of jealousy from Crowther. Master Wellings is simply a helpful young man.'

'Anyway, that's all by the by. Before Crowther, a stranger came to our gate. Never fear, I didn't let him through it. He said he was Samuel Blanchard, husband of the witch Baccy, though he called her Becky and didn't refer to her as a witch.'

He looked up. 'Him again.'

Her lips curled down. 'I was hoping to surprise you but you've met him already.'

'No, not met him,' he said between chews. 'But I heard he called at Whixall Grange yesterday, to express his regrets concerning the death of Perks. What was he doing here?'

'He'd come to see you. You're a popular man all of a sudden. Perks will be buried tomorrow by the way, so Master Crowther informed me.'

John nodded. Spibey had already told him that. 'Did Blanchard say why he wanted to see me?'

'Yes, to thank you for everything you did for Baccy. He was polite enough to say how much she'd enjoyed my meals, despite the circumstances in which she had to eat them. I must say his manners were impeccable.'

John sighed as he handed his empty bowl to her. 'For an estranged couple they seem very chatty.' He couldn't help a small burp escaping from his lips. 'Just showing my appreciation,' he said, as he saw her frown. 'Presumably the exquisitely mannered Master Blanchard would do no such thing. I believe he wanted to see Sir Moreton as well.'

'I got the impression he intended to have some strong words with Sir Moreton. He very much emphasised he had no complaints about *your* behaviour.' She took the bowl and placed it in a bucket. 'I know I said leave things for another day, but an old woman ... a laundress,' she mused softly. 'Spending every day going through dirty washing, what might she have seen? John, John, your eyes are closing. To bed with you.'

Chapter Sixteen

When John returned to Whixall the next morning. Spibey was striding up and down the kitchen, his arms flailing wildly. He was bawling at Tom Perks's staff. Some of the younger maids had been reduced to tears.

'One of you knows something. Tell me now and it'll be easier for you in the end. Tell me this very moment, before I have to start beating it out of you one by one.'

One of the weeping maids' legs gave way and she had to be pulled back to her feet by her companions.

'Why do you fall?' demanded Spibey.

She shook her head, her red-rimmed eyes terrified.

'Is it because you know you're possessed by a devil?'

She fainted clean away at that.

'A-ha!' exclaimed Spibey, only just noticing John was there. 'You arrive just in time, Master Carne. See how this woman collapses under the weight of her sins.'

John twisted his lips. He'd never seen Spibey so out of his wits with anger. He had to stop him but had no idea how to.

'Leave her,' Spibey ordered another maid who'd dropped to

her knees by the side of the fainted girl. 'Let's see if her demon raises her. Watch carefully.'

The head groom edged closer to John. 'She's a silly girl, as likely to faint at her own shadow as anything else,' he whispered.

'What's that? What's that?' snapped Spibey.

John beckoned him over to the doorway. 'The man simply said she's one of those silly sort of girls who wilts for no reason.'

'Just the weak-willed type the devil preys upon,' spat Spibey under his breath. 'Why will none of them speak?'

'Maybe they have nothing to say.'

'That's something coming from you. You're the one who supposed the murderer came from within the Grange. I never thought that likely, until *you* persuaded me.' Spibey was in one of his more malevolent moods.

'I'm merely your assistant, and an inexperienced one at that. I could be wrong.'

'You more than likely are.'

'Sir Moreton, don't you think it's time to make your way back to Wem.'

'Huh! Can't you see I'm busy here?'

'I was only thinking of Master Perks's funeral,' whispered John.

'I *hadn't* forgotten that, not for one second. How could I, when my poor girl mourns her unburied husband.'

John realised Spibey had forgotten.

'Did you see Margaret?' demanded Spibey.

'Very briefly this morning. She was at breakfast and I think she was taking more food than previously.' She'd looked quite bonny actually, slicing her way through a plate of cold meats, and talking to her maid about the new gowns she'd need after the child was born and she was out of mourning. She showed every sign of recovering rapidly, though John doubted if she was so hearty when her father was around. 'Sir Moreton, you're needed elsewhere. Leave me here, I'll do more probing.'

Spibey strode back to the assembled staff. 'As you know, Master Perks, my old friend Tom...'He paused and sniffed. 'My dear son-in-law is to be buried at Wem today. Master Carne will be asking more questions, and don't forget, he has my authority. Talk to him as you'd talk to me. Lie to him and you are lying to me.' He turned back to John. 'I'm beginning to wonder if every one of them hasn't sold their souls.'

'I think that unlikely,' said John.

Spibey was chewing his thumb. 'Could it be the witch, that Blanchard woman? You made me release her. She could have flown here and killed the woman—'

'You really should be on your way, Sir Moreton. You cannot be late,' said John with some urgency. He didn't like the direction Spibey's thoughts were taking.

Nanna Grey's room was built high in the attic of the Grange. The final staircase to reach it was narrow and twisted. Megan, Nanna's granddaughter, led the way.

'Your grandmother was nimbler than me,' said John, somewhat breathlessly.

'She was wiry, sir. Her joints never seemed to stiffen. She used to laugh that she was living on borrowed time, having had more than her three score years and ten. We were grateful we had her as long as we did.' She stopped briefly. 'We knew she'd be gone soon, but the manner of her going... Can you manage, sir? I hear your leg was shot to pieces in battle.'

John had no idea how the people at Whixall had gleaned that information. 'Thank you for your kindness. I'm slow, but I get there. I too deeply regret the manner of Nanna's passing. It's a shameful thing that was done to her, and I'll do everything in my power to find the perpetrator. Did your grandmother always live here?'

'Not in this house, it wasn't built when she was young. She lived in one of the estate cottages, and then when our mother died, my sister and I wanted to look after her, so we brought Nanna here. We all shared this room.'

John glanced around the chamber they'd just entered. A dormer window looked out over pleasant grounds. There was a bed, some shelves and a small table, upon which lay a little book. A wooden chest in the corner presumably held their clothes.

'So there were three of you in this room?'

'That's right. We used to lie there in that bed, sir, and Nanna would tell us her stories and we would laugh and laugh—' she stopped short. 'Am I wrong to say that?'

'Not at all. You loved your grandmother and you remember her with fondness and joy. In what way can that be wrong?' He picked up the book. 'The psalms. Did your grandmother read this?'

Megan smiled. 'She couldn't, sir, not well and certainly not small printing. Despite the lessons, she never learned to read or write properly. But my sister and I read to her every day.'

'The psalms are beautiful.' He flicked through the pages of the book. '"Deliver me, O Lord from the evil man: and preserve me from the wicked man." Amen to that, Megan. It was a wicked man indeed who killed her.'

She frowned slightly. 'May I speak?'

'Yes, I'd like you to. Remember you're speaking to me, alone. I may have Sir Moreton's authority, but I also use discretion. No one else will hear your words, unless you wish them to.'

She went over to the window and stood in the eaves of the dormer. He followed her.

'Sir Moreton is wrong,' she said softly. 'No one here would kill Nanna. I'm not saying she was perfect – she had her share of arguments and falling-outs over the years – but no one would harm her. What with her being by far the oldest person here it would be sort of bad luck if you did. Believe me, no one from Whixall did this.'

He nodded. 'I'm inclined to believe you, except for one problem. No one else was around.'

She looked out of the window. 'Nanna was godly, truly she was, she listened to the Bible readings. She loved Christ as her Saviour.' The girl paused.

'Go on,' said John, trying to sound as kindly and encouraging as he could.

'There were other things. She could recognise signs. She knew if a woman with child would have a girl or a boy. She often knew when a woman was with child even before the woman herself. It was a sense within her. She saw shapes in the clouds which would foretell the future.' She stopped again and looked at him. 'These gifts were all God-given, I'm sure.'

'Doubtless they were, Megan. Nanna wanted to speak to me herself. Do you know what that was about?'

'It was my sister who passed the message to you, but we don't know what she had to say. It made us think we could trust you, though.'

'You can. Tell me what you cannot tell Sir Moreton.'

The girl's eyes darted from side to side. 'I don't think I should.'

'I think you must. It might help to catch Nanna's murderer.'

She stared out of the window and shook her head. 'I don't think it will, but I'll tell you anyway. My grandmother didn't like the latest Mistress Perks, and she'd seen enough of them. She said there was something wrong about her.' Megan stopped again.

John assumed his most encouraging expression.

Her voice became even lower. 'My sister and I have told no one else this.'

'Go on, we cannot be overheard.'

'You know the whole household is now in uproar that the mistress is with child and yet none of us knew.'

'I did wonder how such an event could be kept secret.'

'Oh, it was easy enough. The mistress rarely left her room and when she did she wore her big cloak. But Nanna knew. One night, as we lay in our bed, my sister and I wondered who would take over the manor when the squire was no more.' She looked swiftly at John. 'Master Carne, we wished the squire no harm, quite the opposite, but he was an old man.'

'I understand that.'

'Anyway, then Nanna said that the mistress had a boy child in her belly, and it was no good; the child wasn't right.'

'Did she mean he would suffer from some impairment, some deformity?'

'Maybe. She didn't say any more, just that the child "wasn't right".'

'Did that frighten her?'

'No, nothing frightened Nanna. It was just as if she felt something bad might happen. And, alas, it has, hasn't it?'

'Are you sure she didn't say anything of this to anyone else?'

Megan shook her head vigorously. 'Just my sister and myself. As she got older, Nanna kept herself to herself. She didn't gossip, and we never dared tell a soul.'

John hid a small smile. He imagined Whixall Grange thrived on gossip, though he was inclined to believe that Megan and her sister kept Nanna's ramblings to themselves. 'Thank you, Megan. I think maybe Nanna wanted to tell me about the child.'

Megan bit her lip. 'We're all so worried. Sir Moreton seems such a harsh man. Squire Perks was strict, but we knew him. He never accused us of witchcraft, or being in thrall to the evil one.'

'You haven't seen Sir Moreton at his best today, but I believe him, at heart, to be fair. When everything has calmed down, you'll all get along well enough.' Well, that was what he hoped. He put his hands on her shoulders. 'Thank you for talking so openly to me. Whether it will help or not, I don't know, but I'm grateful for your trust.'

He carefully negotiated his way downstairs. When he reached

the ground floor he was told that a visitor approached the Grange. Fully expecting the return of Samuel Blanchard, he went to the front of the house, only to be surprised to see a most familiar figure ascending the short set of steps which led to the door. It was Zipporah's brother.

Randall Goodman stopped in his tracks, then bounded up. 'John, I never thought to see you here.'

'I could say the same of you,' said John, grasping his brother-in-law's hand and inviting him inside.

Randall explained himself. 'I'm on my way to Wem; the great preacher Richard Baxter is to join the garrison there, if he hasn't already done so. I couldn't miss a chance to hear his sermons. When I reached Wem, I intended to call on you, and the woman of course,' he added quickly.

'Of course,' said John. 'Your sister progresses well. She's fully recovered from the physical damage caused by her illness.'

'Hmm, hmm,' muttered Randall, looking away. 'Last night I heard of the awful events that have occurred here, so I took a detour to Whixall in order to offer my condolences to the family.'

'And that explains my presence here, too. I'm employed by Sir Moreton Spibey. He's the magistrate investigating these terrible deaths.'

Unexpectedly Randall pulled him into a tight embrace. 'Oh, John,' he cried. 'What splendid, splendid news. You're working with a godly and righteous man. A man who's sworn to do everything in his power to rid this county, nay, this country if he has to, of witchcraft, devil worship and any other vile wickedness and corruption.' He grasped John by his upper arms and shook him gently, his usually sombre features transformed by the widest and happiest grin. 'How long have I looked for signs that you're saved, John, yet seen none. But now I see the greatest indication of your salvation. That you've allied yourself to such a man and dedicated yourself to his mission, which is God's mission.' He let go of John and looked up, his light blue eyes squinting, his hands held out, palms upwards. '"I lift up mine eyes to the Lord—"'

'I'll get you some refreshment,' said John. 'I've a few more interviews to conduct here, then we'll travel to Wem together.'

On arriving at Wem, it was soon clear that the taverns were full, with both soldiers and followers of the Reverend Baxter. Much put out, Randall said he'd have to stay with John, and hoped a room would be made ready for him, though he cared not whether he saw his sister or not. John was dismayed but thought he couldn't refuse. He dreaded what Zipporah would make of the situation.

Randall was determined to meet Spibey, so John took him straight to the magistrate's house. Spibey was in his study with Rector Andrew Parsons.

'My brother-in-law—' began John.

Without waiting to be introduced Randall dashed forward and took both men's hands in his own.

'I see you're a fellow clergyman,' said Parsons to Randall.

'I am. I took over my father's parish, though I leave my curate to the day-to-day running of the place. I'm here to listen to Reverend Baxter.'

'His sermons will be so uplifting,' said Spibey.

John stood up, poured himself a mug of ale and walked to the window. Dusk was falling. The day had been so grey it was as if dawn had never fully broken. He turned round, leaned against the wall, and observed the three pious, self-righteous men. They could quote the Scriptures, that was for sure, but he saw little he liked, even less, admired.

Randall swivelled round, narrowing his cold calculating eyes. 'You do know, don't you, John, that the devil finds many disguises.' He turned back to Spibey and Parsons. 'My brother-in-law considers himself a rational man, but I keep reminding him, never underestimate the Evil One. He'll be found where you least expect.'

John looked back out of the window.

Spibey addressed Randall. 'Reverend, I've already asked Andrew here to dine with me tonight. Simple fare, as always. We've buried a loved one today, and we wish to remember him, and I've no hesitation in asking you to join us.'

Parsons was nodding effusively. 'I can think of no better dining companions.'

Spibey was wriggling. 'And you, Master Carne?'

Poor man, thought John, forced out of politeness to invite him. He shook his head. 'My leg is paining me, I must leave you soon, if I may.'

Spibey waved his hands. 'Yes, of course, you're not a well man.' With relief he returned his attention to Randall. 'But I forget my manners. We've not been properly introduced. I don't know your name, though you must be married to one of Master Carne's sisters,' he said.

John sucked in his cheeks. He couldn't wait to see Spibey's reaction when he discovered the true relationship between him and Randall.

'Sadly, no,' said Randall. 'Poor John is most unfortunately married to *my* sister. I'm Randall Goodman of Nantwich, son of the late Parson Goodman, who educated your daughter I believe.'

Spibey and Parsons gasped aloud. The magistrate's face tensed and his eye twitched, as, John guessed, he was frantically thinking of a way to politely withdraw his invitation to dine.

Randall held up his hands. 'Gentlemen, I must explain that as far as I'm concerned, I have no sister. I thoroughly assure you of that. I was the first to publicly denounce her as a whore, and would never see nor speak to her again if she weren't married to my old friend. My sister, my *former* sister's behaviour was sent to test me, but even seeing my own erstwhile flesh and blood pulled down and embracing depravity, never once did I wobble.' He sighed, shakily. 'My poor father, weakened by an illness that sapped his soul, was tempted to take her back. "Never, sir" I warned him. "Her soul is lost, father, always has been. I have no sister, and you have no daughter—"'

'Excuse me,' said John, 'I'm truly pained now. I'll take my leave.'

Chapter Seventeen

Zipporah was silent as she cleared out the nursery. The cradle and the dolls had been put into the small storeroom which led from the bedroom she shared with John.

'They'll be nice and cosy in there,' said John, trying to sound encouraging. 'Right next to the chimney. They certainly won't catch cold.'

'I must leave the door ajar, in case they cry.'

'You do what you have to do,' he said kindly, thinking how much he preferred the flawed, sinning Zipporah, to any number of the self-styled godly, such as her brother.

'Do you need some salve on your leg?' she asked, when they went downstairs.

'No, my leg never pained me that badly. It was the delight Randall took in boasting his own righteousness that caused me greater agony.' And the way he'd gloated at his sister's downfall, though he didn't say that to her. 'Why has your brother become like that? That summer when I met you, we were all happy together, weren't we? I know Randall always loved his Bible, but he was training to be a clergyman after all. We had fine times together at university. I remember him saying: "When we get to work, John, you'll look after their property and business deals, and I'll take care of their souls. Between us we'll never be out of employment." He laughed when he said it. Did he ever tell you what changed him?'

'Not really. God claimed him, it's as simple as that. Randall saw the truth and knew he was saved. He'd always had his doubts about me, and then, with what happened, he knew as surely as he knew his own salvation that I was damned.'

'I don't like him anymore.'

'He wouldn't care if he heard you say that. He's beyond human affection now. You should envy him; he feels no pain.' She went to the pot over the fire and stirred it. 'I'll finish making supper. Then we'll eat, though it will be poor fare compared to that served at Sir Moreton's.'

'It'll be far better. Both in taste and company. That's one thing *I'm* completely convinced of.'

As she bustled in the kitchen area he pulled a chair closer to the hearth and opened his Bible, but the words remained unread, the pages unturned. He looked at the fire, the yellow and red flames dancing a merry jig, their flickering limbs momentarily linking then snapping apart. Occasionally one of the logs hissed and spat, then the gentle crackling accompaniment to the fiery dance continued. His eyelids felt heavy. The pleasant smell of wood smoke and cooking tickled his nose. With a great effort he forced his eyes open and, seeing that a goblet had appeared by his side, drank a large mouthful of wine. The book couldn't claim his attention, though, and he returned his gaze to the fire.

His thoughts drifted back to a tavern in Shrewsbury…

'You're a mess, John. How did you not die?' his brother had said in his candid fashion. 'I've spoken to father, but he won't take you back. You know what he says. Once you joined up for Parliament against the rightful king, you were no longer a part of his family.' Dick passed him a money pouch. 'That'll buy you a room for a few nights. I've no more. Father keeps the purse strings as tight as ever.'

'Thank you. What about our mother?'

'She weeps because she misses you, but she dare not disobey Father.'

John had sighed. His mother was a soft, kindly woman, but obedient to the point of servility.

'Oh, and Father says you're not to try and get anything out of our sisters or their husbands, either. If he hears even a rumour you've been to see them, he'll ruin them.'

'I'll press on to Cheshire, then. I don't think my friends the Goodmans will turn me away.'

———————

'John, is it really you?' exclaimed Randall, who had taken him in a tight embrace and steered him into the parsonage at Nantwich. 'Sit, sit. My, you're trembling all over.'

He'd gratefully sunk into a chair. 'It's a while since I ate.'

'Say nothing,' said Randall, calling for a servant and ordering food and ale.

Strengthened by the victuals John had told Randall about the injuries he'd sustained at Edgehill and that his family had disowned him. 'I hate to impose, but my father won't take me back. I'm no good to the army anymore. I've no money, nowhere to sleep, nothing.'

'You'll never be turned away from this house.'

John could only smile weakly.

'My father's here,' continued Randall. 'But I warn you, he's suffered a dreadful seizure and is no longer the man he was. When you have the strength, I'm sure he'll be pleased to see you.'

'I'm strong enough to see my old friend now,' said John.

Reverend Goodman was propped up in bed. 'I was very angry with you, young man,' he slurred through a desperately lop-sided mouth that dribbled somewhat. 'Taking up with Parliament like that. I thought you'd more sense. But you are John, our dear friend John, and what's a war between friends?'

John had barely controlled himself. He sniffed loudly, struggling to hold back his tears. He'd been close to death, and travelled painfully half the length of the country, only to be rejected by his own family. The kindness of the parson was too much for him. He grasped the old man's hand. 'How can I ever thank you?'

'Don't cry, although why shouldn't you? The pain of this life brings tears to my eyes.'

'You've suffered greatly.' Then he had to ask the question he dreaded. For some reason he hadn't felt he could ask Randall about Zipporah. It was clear though that she wasn't living in the parsonage anymore. 'Where's Zipporah? Is she married?'

Now it was Goodman who sobbed.

'No, no. Please don't tell me she's dead.' John swallowed hard. Thoughts of Zipporah had kept him alive and given him the strength to recover from his injuries. Though he was now a poor cripple, he'd been determined to see her. While he may never be in a position to ask for her hand again, he hoped they could at least renew their friendship.

'Worse than dead,' slobbered the parson.

'How?'

The old man reached out and he gripped both John's hands again. 'She's with child and unwed. What I'd taken for spirit and intelligence, was wilfulness and vice. Despite that I'd let her live here, but Randall won't countenance it. She's ungodly, he says. I had to throw her out. I didn't want to, but he made me. I don't know where she is.'

They held each other close for a while.

Eventually, John said, 'Zipporah would never disgrace herself like that.'

'I don't care what she's done. Where's she gone, John? I do

miss her so. I don't care what she's done; I want her back. You're a strong young man, please find her for me.' He couldn't see that he'd passed this task to a cripple. 'I want her back, but Randall won't let me, and he's the parson here now. I am but his guest. Bring her back to me, John. Together we can stand against my son.'

John had waited a while and calmed the old man, then he heard Randall's voice call him. So great was his rage, he ignored the pain in his leg as he sped down the stairs.

'If it wouldn't cause me to fall, I'd strike you,' snarled John, watching the smile fade from his friend's face. 'How could you do it? What happened? How long ago did you cast her out? Will she have had the child by now?'

Randall looked away. 'I presume you are referring to the whore. She's dead to me. Dead and damned.'

John had found enough strength to jump forward and grip him by the throat. 'You inhuman monster! You take in a friend, yet cast out your own sister. What part of your faith demands you treat a woman so?'

Randall pushed back, but John somehow kept his balance.

'Never question my faith, John. The woman is a whore. She disgraced herself and her family. I didn't throw out my sister, for I have none, I banished a depraved creature from this house, that's all.'

Despite the pain ripping through him, John surged forward and pushed Randall's head hard against the wall. 'Never did a man's name so little suit him, for you're no good man at all. I can't stay here. I'll limp along any street I can, until I either find your sister, or at least know what happened to her.'

Randall at last had pushed him away. 'Forget her, John, forget the whore, be sensible, stay here.'

'John, John, where are you? Certainly not in the Gospel of Saint Luke.' He heard Zipporah speaking.

The fireplace at The Dial refocused before his eyes and the Bible slithered onto the stone flagged floor.

'Were you asleep, or thinking about those murders?'

'No, not even that. I was dreaming, a sort of recollection really.' He picked up the book.

She didn't say anything, but simply twitched her lips and eyebrows in a quizzical and rather beguiling way.

He sighed. 'You won't like this, but I was dreaming about the day I went back to see your father, after Edgehill, only to find him a dying man.'

'You're right, I don't like it.' She studied the tips of her long, strong fingers and entwined them one through the other. 'Not good memories. My poor father, I'll always blame myself for his illness.'

'You shouldn't. You're a good person, Zipporah, I know you.'

She shrugged.

'At the time I wanted to beat Randall to a pulp,' said John. 'If I'd been strong enough I would have done. Now he invites himself into our house.'

'When we married he brought my clothes and possessions here. I'm grateful to him for that.'

John snorted. 'And it was just after then the rumours began that you were a whore. No doubt started by your loving brother.'

'He thinks it his Christian duty to denounce sinners.'

'But I don't consider you a sinner. I wish you'd say what happened. You know I'll not judge you.'

She turned away. 'On and on you go. How many times do I have to tell you? It will never be spoken of. You should be thinking of more pressing matters. I have.'

He looked at her. She seemed calm. She'd neither run upstairs nor shouted angrily at him. Dare he hope she was improving? 'Will you share your thoughts with me?'

'When I've finished my sauce, we'll eat and I'll tell you my ideas, then you may tear them to shreds.'

'Or be inspired by them.'

Zipporah had a way of cooking simple bacon, beans and leeks in a creamy sauce that raised those humble ingredients into a delicious feast. He was happy to let her talk as he savoured every mouthful.

'So this old woman, Nanna, works in the laundry and pays special attention to her mistress's linens. Now, Master Perks and Margaret had been married less than a year. You may wish to find out exactly how long, but I doubt Sir Moreton will be forthcoming.'

John frowned.

'Molly Kade is on her way, so Mistress Perks's child must be due soon. What if Nanna noticed there were never any stained linens amongst Mistress Perks's washing? It isn't second sight. It's observation, plain and simple.'

John frowned again and raised an eyebrow.

'Women have courses, John.'

'Oh, yes, I see. But even if there was no evidence of them, it isn't significant. Margaret may well have conceived on her wedding night, or close to it. In fact, given that she's near to her time, we know that's probably what happened.'

'My children were born less than a month after our wedding. Not all brides are pure, not all wives give birth to their husband's children. I wouldn't be surprised if Nanna Grey knew that Margaret wasn't a virgin on her wedding night, or that Perks hadn't managed his duties.'

John tutted under his breath. 'How could the old lady have guessed anything like that?'

'Dirty linen, John, that's all Nanna knew, but it would have told her a lot.'

'When I first met her she did say if anyone pissed their pants at The Grange she knew about it.'

'There you are.'

'I doubt Sir Moreton allowed his daughter enough freedom to disgrace herself.' The minute he spoke he threw his spoon down and buried his face in his hands. 'Forgive me, Zipporah. I didn't mean it like that.' When he dared to raise his head, she was looking fondly at him.

'Spibey couldn't be with his daughter all the time. In fact, we know he wasn't, since she was in London prior to her marriage,' she said.

'Staying with a fanatically pious family.'

She shrugged. 'Who knows what happened there? Eat up, don't let your food go cold.'

John leaned forward. Despite the subject matter he was enjoying their conversation. Relishing the way they were sharing ideas. 'So, you're suggesting that Nanna Grey knew not only that Perks and Margaret had never lain together as man and wife, and there's a lot of gossip says he wasn't capable, but she also knew that the new Mistress Perks already had a child on her. The pregnancy was kept secret from everyone at the Grange. Sir Moreton says that was because, given her own mother's sad history, Margaret was frightened to make the fact public. I must say his explanation has a ring of truth about it.'

'I'm simply thinking aloud.'

John shifted in his seat. 'I can never share these ideas with Sir Moreton, of course.'

'No, you cannot, and even if true, would it have any bearing on the murders?' Zipporah tucked into her food and they ate in silence for a while.

John spoke first. 'But if somebody knew Nanna Grey wanted to talk to me, and guessed what it was about, then perhaps they killed her.'

'And the only person who would benefit is Margaret Perks, and she's safe in Wem, awaiting her confinement. And even if the old lady had told you and then you'd confronted Sir Moreton, who would he believe? His daughter of course. You see my thoughts have got you nowhere.'

He pushed away his plate, satisfied.

She took it from him. 'The blackberries are plentiful this year. Enough for me to have a wine brewing in my still room, and to make a pie for you.'

He rubbed his stomach. 'In a minute, let me rest awhile. Are you trying to fatten me?'

'No, I try to make you happy.' She immediately looked flustered and swiftly removed their bowls and made a great fuss of pouring him another drink.

'Make me happy?' he mused.

'No, not that, no, I didn't mean *that*. I try to be a good wife, I mean a good housekeeper for you, that's all. I wonder when my brother will arrive.' She was trying to change the subject.

'Now there's a problem,' said John. 'It's a godly thing to be early to your bed, yet Randall, Sir Moreton and the rector must each burnish their righteous credentials. They have the whole of Scripture to quote to each other. It could be a late night.'

'You have a flippant attitude to religion.'

'I have a sense of humour.'

As it happened John was reading aloud to Zipporah when Randall let himself in.

'"Thy lips, O, my spouse, drip as the honeycomb, honey and milk are under thy tongue, and the smell of thy garments is like the smell of Lebanon"'

'Hah,' said Randall, sniffily. 'So, you do read your Scriptures.'

John said nothing.

'Solomon's Song,' said Randall. 'You read of the love the Lord has for his Church.'

'Is that so? I merely opened the book and read the pages as they fell. Did you dine well with Sir Moreton?'

'We ate sufficient for our needs.'

'Did Mistress Perks join you?' asked Zipporah.

Randall looked away from her.

John snapped the Bible shut. 'You're a guest in my house and will treat my wife with respect, even if you can't manage any affection.'

'I share no blood with this woman. Though, as the wife of a good friend, I'm obliged to be polite, I suppose,' said Randall grudgingly.

'I'm honoured, I'm sure,' said Zipporah.

Now Randall did look at her. 'To answer your question, Mistress Carne, I did meet Mistress Perks, if only very briefly, simply to say good day and express my sympathies at her loss. We do, after all, have a prior, if small acquaintance. I dined with Sir Moreton and the rector only.' He took a seat at the table. 'I've heard more details of the dreadful events which have happened around these parts. A couple caught in sinful congress nailed to the ground, the godly Squire Perks not only hanged but mutilated, and now, likewise the old woman.' He squinted his hard flinty eyes towards her. 'How easily a place becomes tainted by sin.'

Zipporah's face likewise hardened. John knew both she and her brother could have an icy quality about them, though Zipporah still managed, despite all her troubles, to leaven hers with some good humour and kindness. 'Do you accuse me, brother?'

'Should I?'

'Don't you dare,' said John.

'All I'll say is that evil slips amongst us, often unnoticed, until it's too late. Still, Sir Moreton is a fine man and given that you need to work, John, you must be grateful to be employed by such as him.' He sniffed. 'You know Sir Moreton considers the use of tobacco unsound, as do I. I trust I don't smell its vile odour in this house.'

'I'm sure it's just the stench of my sins, stinking out the place,' said Zipporah.

John stood. 'I'm tired. Randall, help yourself to anything you need. Wife, to bed.'

Zipporah nodded to her brother and went up the stairs.

Randall grabbed John's sleeve. 'Be careful, friend, the whore's soul is lost and, despite your employment with Sir Moreton, I still see precious little sign of godliness about you at the moment. I pray that I'm wrong.'

'You are a very bad man,' said Zipporah to John. She was sitting on the floor of the makeshift nursery in the storeroom, Arabella on her knee. 'What a naughty papa,' she whispered to the doll.

John pushed open the shutter and leaned out.

She chuckled. 'Did you choose to read that passage on purpose, knowing that of all the Scriptures it would be the one Randall liked the least?'

John's position looked precarious as he lit his pipe. 'It comes to something when a man can't smoke in his own home.' He twisted himself into a slightly more comfortable posture. 'I was determined that Randall would find us in some godly pursuit when he returned, so the minute I heard the gate squeak I let the Bible fall open where it would. Whether it fell on that page by chance, or whether the spine is broken there through over reading I don't know. That passage does refer to love between a man and a woman, though.'

She gently laid Arabella in the cot and lifted out George. 'You must be very quiet tonight,' she told the doll, then turned back to John. 'Do you think Randall believes I'm the murderer? Oh, do be careful, John, you'll fall out.'

'It's no good,' he said, tapping out his pipe and slipping back into the room. 'A smoke should be enjoyable and not involve all these strange contortions. As to Randall, I don't think he was actually accusing you. He simply likes to take every opportunity to remind you of your alleged sins. He should take the great beam of pride out of his own eye first.' He paused and smiled. The candle flame flickered as he closed the shutter. 'You look so beautiful. If you loved me only half as much as you love those –' he paused '– as you love your children, it would be enough for me. I'd be content. I'd be happy.' Did he detect a look of wistfulness on her face?

Her words suggested he did not. 'But I don't love you at all.'

Chapter Eighteen

The church bell rang earlier than usual the next morning, and John had little time to savour lacing Zipporah's dress as Randall was chiding them, calling from downstairs that they'd be late. The reason for the early service, and a blessedly short sermon, was that nearly everyone was going to the garrison headquarters to listen to the great preacher, Richard Baxter. John pleaded extreme pain to excuse himself, and of course, nobody wanted or expected Zipporah to attend, though when they left church John noted with approval that both Crowther and Wellings nodded and smiled to her in a friendly and respectful way.

When they got home John was overcome with tiredness.

'Take the Lord's advice, have a day of rest,' said Zipporah, passing him a hot spiced ale. 'Don't think about anything, especially not Whixall, Hornspike or that benighted Moss.'

John agreed that was a good idea. He cleaned his musket and pistol, something he always found relaxing, and read through a couple of newsbooks that Randall had brought with him, while his wife busied about, singing and humming to herself. He felt a closeness between them that hadn't been there before. Though experience taught him not to imagine that this was finally the start of her recovery.

A knock on the door startled him. Then Benbow's impish face was at the window.

'Come in,' called Zipporah.

'How are you, Captain?' he asked, frowning slightly.

'Very well,' said John.

Benbow's face split into its usual wide grin. 'That's what I hoped. May I dare to suggest you're escaping from this dreadful outbreak of righteousness, as am I?'

John laughed. 'I'm admitting nothing, though I wonder what I'm missing, since the whole town seems keen to hear Baxter's words.'

Zipporah handed Benbow a drink.

'Now, that's what I call righteous,' he said. 'And the whole town is *not* hanging on to his every word, since every tavern I passed seemed filled to cramming point.'

'You'll eat with us I hope,' said Zipporah.

'Another prayer answered.'

After eating, John sought out his chess board and he and Benbow enjoyed the most pleasant afternoon. They played and talked, with Zipporah never far away, whispering advice into both men's ears.

It was nearly dark when Randall poked his head round the door, simply to say he would be dining with Spibey again. He sniffed slightly at Benbow's presence, especially when the soldier enthused about the nectar and ambrosia he'd enjoyed at John's table, but Randall said no more except to bid them all goodbye.

'That's handy,' said Zipporah to Benbow. 'Now you can have his portion of supper.'

The next morning Randall was off bright and early to the garrison, as Baxter was to preach yet again. John was glad to see the back of him. The godly fellow had finished off the last of their claret the night before and eaten all the bacon that Zipporah had cooked for everyone's breakfast.

'I like porridge anyway,' said John, trying to calm his wife.

'I'm declaring a fast for the rest of his stay,' she snapped, tapping her ladle bad-temperedly on the side of the cauldron. 'Bread and water it is. I don't care if I faint. I don't see why he should gobble all the food I make for you. You work hard and always try to do what's right. So who cares that he knows his Bible backwards, frontwards and sideways, what good does that do anyone? He's a parish to run, souls to care for, how does he have the time to prance about, drinking your wine and eating your meat?'

'Apparently he has an able curate who does all the boring bits for him.'

'Boring! How ashamed my father would be of him. He never found it boring to visit the sick or comfort the dying.'

She was so angry he managed to drop a kiss on her forehead before she noticed. She wiped it away. 'Be gone, you're as bad as he is.'

As John walked to Spibey's house he thought about his wife's theories concerning Margaret Perks. He knew he should speak to the young widow, but that was not going to be possible. Given her status and condition it would be most improper for him to question her. Nor did he think for a moment that she was in any way involved. The little he had seen of her, together with Zipporah's comments upon her as a girl, pointed to her being empty-headed and frivolous, albeit with a somewhat nasty streak. There was some rational motive for the murders though – there must be – but there was no way she could be involved, even if, in the wider sense of the word, she may not be innocent.

When he arrived at Noble Street, Spibey was agitated. It

seemed to be his normal condition these days. Though that morning there was some justification for it.

'Margaret has pained all night. I had to call a local woman. The child's not yet coming, for which I thank the Lord's goodness, but I'll not rest easy until this Molly Kade is here. What's the use of a man in a situation like this? If only my dear wife was alive. I don't remember this stress when our own children were delivered, though her confinements ended so sadly. We saw it as our testing time. Oh, I know I've told you all this before. But my worry for Margaret, is so... John, I've never lacked faith, or complete confidence in the Lord, so why do I harbour this fear for my daughter?'

John took Spibey's arm. 'Sir, calm yourself. You've answered your own question. What man wouldn't worry about his daughter, especially as she's his only child?'

Spibey gripped John's other arm tight. 'But should I not be beyond such human affection?'

'No, sir. When Our Lord heard of the death of His friend, Lazarus, did He not cry? Even as He hung on the cross, did He not ask Saint John to care for His mother?'

'Yes, of course He did. I know I sin, Master Carne, but it's because I love.'

A couple of evenings with Randall Goodman and even Spibey doubted his own godly credentials. What was it about the man that he inspired nothing but guilt and doubt in everyone he met? 'Let's say our prayers and then turn our minds to the events in Whixall. I confess I've no ideas, Sir Moreton. There must be some deep animosity somewhere to cause these murders.'

Spibey's face brightened. His spirits were lifting as swiftly as such moods always did. 'Your most excellent brother-in-law warned me that you are prone to an excess of rationality. Do you still refuse to believe the evil behind these crimes?'

'I believe them to be truly evil, but as I've no idea how to find a witch, I'm looking for other motives.'

Spibey narrowed his eyes. 'We could examine everyone at Whixall. I mean thoroughly examine, as in look closely for the marks of Satan, such as an extra nipple, where a demon is suckled.'

John looked away.

'You've still not the stomach for it, Master Carne?'

'I'm your assistant, and happy to be so. I'll write reports and take your instructions, but as for identifying the marks of the devil, that's beyond my knowledge.'

'We have to find a culprit for these murders.'

Was Spibey suggesting that anyone would do? John wished they could be rid of the whole thing. Although he'd dismissed Zipporah's theories concerning young Mistress Perks, they continued to intrigue and confuse him. And he was completely puzzled as to how anything related to the bodies from the Moss, which, now they were buried, everyone seemed to have forgotten.

'Dear, dear, what am I thinking?' said Spibey, looking distractedly about. 'I'm to hear Master Baxter preach again this morning. You can't begin to believe how inspiring he is. Are you sure you won't accompany me?'

John shook his head.

'I'll leave you to your own prayers, then,' said Spibey. 'My rough reports are over there if you wish to look at them, though in my opinion you'd do as well to come and listen to the preacher.'

'I'll stay here, I'm sure to hear it all word for word from my brother-in-law.'

John was so absorbed in his work that he didn't hear anyone come into the study, until a small cough alerted him to another presence in the room. He immediately jumped to his feet.

'Mistress Perks!' He bowed his head. 'Your father's not here. He's gone to the camp to hear the preacher.'

'Oh.'

'If you wanted him I could go and get him, or better still I could send Crowther; he'd be faster.'

'Oh.' She looked around the room, rubbing her swollen belly, eventually she turned towards him and her lips briefly curled into a weak smile.

'I'm sorry to hear you've been so indisposed,' he said eventually.

She looked down at the bump, which she still caressed. 'I didn't think it would be like this.'

He didn't know what to say. 'I'm sorry you have such pain,' he said lamely.

'How fares Mistress Zipporah?'

Her comment surprised him. 'She's well, yes, very well, thank you. Would you like to take a seat?'

'No, I'm better when I move around. I was rude about your wife when we met in the cellar with those horrid bodies.' She shivered slightly. 'I don't know why I said those things, except it's what everyone says about her.'

John did not reply.

'Mistress Zipporah really tried with me, you know, when I went to her father's school.'

He nodded.

'She was a good teacher; it wasn't her fault I refused to learn. I could never find enthusiasm for reading or history or sitting still.'

John grinned. Her honestly was disarming.

'Actually, I did like Mistress Zipporah, even though she was so very bossy.'

John's smile broadened.

'A-ha, I see she's bossy with you, Master Carne.'

'She speaks her mind. That's one of the reasons I love her so.'

She turned away and wandered to the other side of the room, the fingers of her small pink hands tapping at the sides of her dress. She turned again and walked back to him, fondling the bump once again. 'And you do love her, don't you? I mean really, really love her, so that you ache inside?'

Could she read his mind? That was exactly how he felt most of the time. He wished she'd go, or at least change the subject of the conversation. 'I'm sorry for all your troubles, madam. To lose your husband, and in such a manner, is truly dreadful.'

She shrugged, almost as if she'd forgotten about him. 'Her babies died, didn't they?'

'It was very difficult. They were too close together. It will be better with you, mistress, for sure.'

'He's a lively fellow; he gives me no peace. If fellow he is.'

'That can only be a good sign, and –' he licked his lips '– I believe that Nanna Grey, who apparently knew about such things, was convinced that you carry a boy child.'

'Did you find out what Nanna wanted to say to you?'

'No, and I'll never know now.'

'Is there anything that could happen that would stop you loving your wife? She's disgraced and yet you stay with her, obviously enamoured.'

Now he looked away. Though at times he wondered how he could continue living with Zipporah, experience taught him that, in the end, nothing could dampen his feelings. He turned back. 'No, I cannot think of any circumstance.'

Her mouth twisted. 'You said, the other day, that if she died, you'd find another.'

He didn't think he'd said exactly that. 'I believe I said I hoped, Mistress Perks, that in time, *you* will find another. You are young. You will love again.' His advice sounded so hollow. Who was he to counsel her?

Yet her expression brightened. 'You're a kind man, Master Carne.'

He jerked backwards as she suddenly lunged towards him and gripped his arms, her little hands vice like even through the thick fabric of his jacket.

'Tell me, Master Carne, for no one else will, shall I scream? Will I wish myself dead? Did Mistress Zipporah scream? If she did, then surely I will. Will I die? I'm so frightened. My mother died. Help me, I cannot do this—'

He tried desperately to push her away. 'Mistress, Mistress, these are questions for women, not for me.'

Her grip tightened. Her face, flushed and red, her eyes bulging, was close to his now. 'Did she scream, Master Carne? You must tell me.'

He wondered how she could have lived even to her own tender years and never been aware that childbirth wasn't painless. She was Spibey's cosseted daughter, though; he must have protected her from the world. 'Yes, she screamed. She screamed a lot. Now please, let me go.'

She relaxed a little but still held on to him. 'Were you there?'

'No, of course not. Listen, Mistress Perks, I know something of pain, I was injured in battle. I know agony and I know that it passes. I pray you'll feel nothing more than discomfort, but whatever happens remember, pain is temporary. Now I must beg you to release me, for you are causing me an agony of embarrassment.'

She laughed and stepped away. 'You speak well, Master Carne. I have much to overcome, but as I cannot escape any of it, then I'm forced to endure, though it goes against my nature.' At last she left the room. The conversation disturbed him and he wondered how she knew that Nanna Grey had had something to tell him? It seemed unlikely that Spibey would have told her that. He doubted she'd been in contact with the maids at Whixall Grange, so the only other person who could have informed her was Wellings. Since he was a servant, whose duties meant he had no need to speak directly to her, it seemed equally implausible she'd gained that knowledge from him. And, even if they did talk, why would they speak of such things?

Spibey and Randall were bursting with enthusiasm when they returned.

'Truly, we should never doubt the goodness of the Lord,' said Spibey excitedly.

'His judgment is final and firm. Sin will be excised, expunged, excavated from every last pore and cavity of our bodies,' trilled Randall.

John winced.

'Sir Moreton had the opportunity to mention our troubles to Master Baxter,' Randall continued breathlessly. 'He was most encouraging. Demons cannot stand the word of the Lord. Of course they cannot, for the Scriptures are truth and the devil speaks only in lies.'

Spibey's eyes sparkled. 'Rector Parsons is keen. He'll happily go to Whixall, and together with the parson and any curates available, read the Scripture to the household of poor old Tom.'

'I myself have volunteered to help,' added Randall. 'Master Baxter thought a three-to-four-hour reading would be enough to cast out any demons.'

'This will be shown by way of great jerkings and shudderings of the possessed person,' said Spibey, himself jerking about somewhat. 'The other possibility is that the sinful creature will become insane. One way or another we'll know if the murderer is from Tom's people.'

John thought insanity could certainly be one of the consequences of such an event. He'd had a strange morning and his head began to ache.

Spibey sidled up to him. 'How's your leg today, John?'

'Much recovered, thank you. I still feel pain, but every day I think I gain strength.'

'He's a good keen fellow,' said Spibey to Randall, as if praising a half-decent hound. He turned back to John. 'So, I've no hesitation in setting you the task of organising this reading. He's a good little organiser,' he said to Randall. 'Right, then, I'll leave you to it. That game little pony you use is available for you any time, as you'll be up and down to Whixall quite a bit I should imagine.'

'Very well,' said John, not at all relishing the thought of riding up and down to Whixall "quite a bit" on that stubborn pony, Freddy, who was anything but game.

Spibey turned back to Randall. 'Now, dear friend, when are you due back in Nantwich?'

Randall gave a slight cough. 'I'm my own master, nay, I am servant to the Lord, but where I come and go, that is my business.' He coughed again and lowered his voice. 'I can stay for as long as I like, but my former sister's house... Well, I don't have to explain, it's a small mean place, and her company is not conducive to prayer and contemplation of godliness.'

Once again John was forced to deal with his anger in impotent silence. Both men needed a thorough beating. 'I'll be off about my organising, then,' he managed to utter, through clenched teeth.

'And I'll relieve you of your guest,' said Spibey. 'If you concur, come and stay here, Randall. You'll be most welcome.'

'Why, that would be more than acceptable.'

'Indeed it would,' said John, not caring how relieved he sounded. 'I'm more than grateful to you, Sir Moreton.' He couldn't wait to get home and tell Zipporah, both the good news about Randall and the strange conversation he'd had with Margaret Perks.

Chapter Nineteen

U pon hearing the news of her brother's departure, Zipporah swiftly restored the nursery to its rightful place. She cuddled Arabella, and seeing her eyes dart to the cradle John obediently picked up George and sat next to her.

'It's such a relief to be rid of Randall,' she said.

'I can take no credit. Sir Moreton and your brother decided upon it themselves. Truly, two men were never so suited to be friends.'

She tweaked the tiny ruffles on Arabella's bonnet into place. 'I thought Sir Moreton had better taste. Well, whoever is responsible, I'm grateful. I couldn't relax with him around.'

'Nor could I,' said John. 'A man needs to enjoy his tobacco sitting comfortably, not hanging out of a window.' He pulled his pipe from his pocket and lit it from the candle. 'There, what could be better, one happy family sitting quietly together. Though I can only spare a moment, since I must be off to Whixall and arrange this dismal Bible reading.'

Zipporah looked wistful. 'And I must savour this moment, for Randall continually assures me I have an eternity of torment ahead. The only hope I have left is that you are saved.'

John put George back into the cradle and snorted. 'Your brother's so proud he considers he has the ear of God. And not any sort of god I'd want to meet.'

She took a sharp gasp of air. 'No, John, don't say that, never say that. Randall's right, I've polluted you, I've dragged you down—'

'Listen to me.' He dared to squeeze her arm. 'Randall has a spiteful streak. He's not a decent man and you shouldn't give his words any weight. Now, let me tell you of an encounter I had with Mistress Perks.'

Zipporah twisted her mouth when he'd finished. 'Poor child, I don't envy her what's to come.' She kissed Arabella's forehead. 'Though it'll be worth it to have a babe.'

With a regretful sigh, John stood. 'I must be away, but hopefully not for too long.'

She narrowed her eyes. 'Interesting that she knew Nanna Grey asked to speak to you. And if she did hear that from Wellings I'm intrigued as to the nature of their relationship.'

'Since we know for sure that Margaret was nowhere near Nanna when she was killed, I don't think it's significant,' said John.

John was satisfied with his work. Especially as he'd arranged the Bible reading for a time and day when neither Spibey nor Randall could have any excuse to avoid it, though as godly people they would no doubt be keen to attend anyway.

Being back at Whixall Grange also meant he was able to continue questioning the staff. They all seemed equally shocked, with many being tearful. They'd known Nanna all their lives and no one had a bad word to say about her. He learned nothing more, but noticed how many of them seemed keen to blame Baccy, whom they referred to as the 'witch of Hornspike'. He felt sure somebody was putting this idea into their minds, as no one had mentioned her previously. He hoped their suspicions didn't reach Spibey, who'd be keen enough to re-arrest the poor woman.

His enquiries leading nowhere and certain as he was that the Bible reading would prove useless, John was at a loss as to where to turn. He managed to establish one fact, though: the marriage had taken place in April. So if the child had been conceived within wedlock, Mistress Perks should still have at least a couple of months to go.

He was in the nursery, telling Zipporah of his day at Whixall, when they heard the front door bang below. John had only got halfway down the stairs when he heard his brother's voice.

'Can't stop, John,' he called breathlessly. 'I'm called to Lord Capel's troop. Wem will be back in the King's hands before the end of the week. Keep your head down and you'll be all right. I'll leave Molly with you—'

Dick hadn't finished his sentence before Zipporah pushed John out of the way, and on reaching the room launched herself upon the small figure who stood next to Dick.

'Murderess!' she screamed, pushing Molly backwards against the tabletop. The midwife's bag fell to the floor, as did both women, grappling with each other, their caps flying off. Molly managed to pull herself to her feet, but Zipporah threw a punch which clipped the side of Molly's face. 'You killed my babies. You sucked the life out of them! If it wasn't for you—'

Molly leapt forward and scratched at Zipporah's eyes, but Zipporah was taller and stronger. She grasped the midwife by her throat and shook her. It was only when Molly began to go pale and her lips started to turn blue that the men eventually intervened and separated the warring women.

Zipporah struggled against John's grip, while Molly wept into the front of Dick's jacket.

'Stop it now,' ordered John, pulling his wife's arms behind her back, the only way he could think of restraining her. 'Molly didn't kill your babies.' He tried to reason with her.

'She did, I saw her. Why doesn't anyone believe me? I heard them cry, then they were silent—' Now Zipporah choked on her own deep sobs.

John held her tightly, and rocked her. 'You dreamt it. You were only half alive; you dreamt it. The babies never cried. Molly saved your life.'

She still struggled. 'Why do you believe *her* over *me*?'

Molly was calmer now. 'Mistress Carne,' she said breathlessly, 'your children were too small and not properly formed; they could never have lived.'

Zipporah began to scream, struggling against John's grasp again as she did so. It was as much as he could do to hold her. 'Who are you to say who lives and dies? You think yourself God Almighty, Molly Kade, but I know you! You killed my babies. I saw you do it. Will nobody listen to me?'

'This is too much,' snapped Dick. 'I'll leave you to your foul-mouthed whore of a wife and take Molly straight to Sir Moreton's. Come, woman.' He tugged at the midwife's arm.

Zipporah finally broke free and rushed towards Dick, pulled him round and spat a long strand of spittle into his face.

For a moment he simply stood there, before wiping his cheek. Then he raised his hand.

John pushed her away just in time and gripped his brother's fist. 'Don't you dare touch her.'

'She needs it, John,' he said, through clenched teeth.

Zipporah ran off to the corner of the room, where she now stood, looking over her shoulder, her lips stretched across her teeth. She appeared to be hissing.

'Go, just go!' said John, pushing his brother out of the door before turning to his wife. He'd never felt so angry towards her before. She cowered slightly as he approached and she pressed her back against the wall, her hands each side, their palms hard against the plaster. She was still hissing. He gently held her shoulders. She became limp and made no attempt to struggle. 'Zipporah, Zipporah! Talk to me.' He began to worry. He shook her slightly. 'Why did you do that? Why did you spit at my brother?'

At last her eyes seemed to focus, and he felt her shoulders pushing against his hands. 'Why, Zipporah?'

'His fault.'

'His fault for what? Giving us a roof over our heads?'

'Bringing her and calling me a whore.'

'He shouldn't have said that, but he had to bring Molly to Wem.'

'The murderess. She killed my babies, and then made me live when I had nothing to live for.'

'I begged her to do everything she could to save you, and she never left you, day or night. Is that the action of a murderess? I think not. Though why either of us bothered I don't know, since your life has been nothing but misery ever since—' He stopped short, instantly regretting his words, spoken so stupidly in anger.

Her face hardened and a strange, triumphant smile twisted across her lips. 'At last, John, at last, even you despise me.'

He tried to pull her close but she resisted. 'I didn't mean it like that,' he said.

She freed herself from his grip and looked back at him. 'Now you see me for the evil woman I am.'

Feeling cold air on the back of his neck, he turned round to see Dick standing in the doorway. 'I'm wasting time, where does this Spibey fellow live?'

John snapped out some directions and heard the door close behind him as he stared hard at his wife. He wondered if it was possible that she would eventually push him so far away that his love would die. Was the agony he felt now nothing more than the death throes of that emotion dying of starvation? For it had had nothing to feed it but hope, and now that was disappearing fast. He limped to the table, and sat, staring ahead, unable to think, feel or speak any longer.

'You've never really understood, have you?' she said, her voice betraying no softness. 'You simply made it worse, trying to make me happy, trying to give me hope, when neither is possible.' Her footsteps were heavy as she ascended the staircase.

Her words wounded him far more than any battlefield injury. Without hope they were both damned.

'I'm not happy,' said Spibey, to John the next morning. 'Molly Kade is here, with a shiner of a black eye, making vague hints that it was caused by your ... by that woman in your house. That's not natural behaviour, even for a—' Spibey stopped, clearly unwilling to say more.

John said nothing. The last thing he wanted was for Spibey to show an interest in his wife. Though she was even less of a wife now that she ever had been. For the first night since she'd recovered from childbirth, Zipporah hadn't shared his bed, nor had she spoken to him, remaining in the nursery, staring at nothing, even her babies no longer giving her any solace. He wished he could curl up somewhere quiet and sleep. But his bedroom had been quiet enough, and sleep had eluded him there.

'Master Carne, John!' Spibey snapped his fingers. 'Answer me.'

John suddenly focused on the magistrate. 'I'm sorry, Sir Moreton. My wife is unwell, but if she's caused any problem to you, then release me and you'll be free to employ another assistant.'

Spibey shook his head. 'No, no, my dear John, that's not what I meant at all, don't talk like that. The fact that you try to be a decent husband to such a woman is a testament to your good character. In fact, if you'll let me talk frankly, as a friend to a friend, which is what I like to think we are, I understand from Randall, that your marriage may not have been ... may not have any validity.'

'You've seen the register in the church. I am married.'

'Oh, well, that's it, then,' said Spibey, sounding slightly embarrassed. Then he narrowed his eyes. 'I'm not sure you should have released the witch, Baccy.'

Damn, thought John. 'As I said at the time, I don't think she's the murderer.'

'Everyone I meet is asking why she was released. Apparently her crimes are worse than we knew. She was caught sucking the blood from a sheep. Did you know that Master Carne?'

'Baccy's story grows more outrageous by the day. It's idle tittle-tattle. We shouldn't pay heed to such gossip.'

Spibey leaned closer. 'But is it just tittle-tattle? I have it on good authority from one of the most respected men in our town, that she gave birth to one of her cats after consorting –' Spibey coughed slightly '– after consorting in a most unseemly manner with a goat.'

John closed his eyes. He could almost hear the wagging tongues of Wem vying to outdo each other with their knowledge of Baccy's depravity. 'I can assure you, Sir Moreton, that if we investigated these stories they'd have no foundation. I guarantee not one of the gossipmongers had heard of Baccy before you brought her here.'

Spibey puffed out his cheeks. 'You're too naïve, Master Carne. I've said this before. I don't hold it against you but it does mean you dismiss the obvious too readily.'

John had no desire to continue this conversation. 'Sir Moreton, may I speak to Molly? I believe I owe her an apology.'

That seemed to knock Spibey off course. 'Yes, yes, I suppose that would be the right thing to do. Wait here, I'll have her sent to you.' He turned to leave. 'But after that, we continue with our investigations and we discount *nobody*.'

Although she was considered a most experienced midwife Molly Kade could only be in her early twenties. Her complexion was soft and fresh; she wasn't tall and though by no means plump her body had a pleasant roundness to it. Her full lips spread into a friendly smile and her dark eyes, one ringed with purple, crinkled at the corners.

'I can only apologise for your injury,' said John. 'Zipporah isn't usually like that. She's not well.'

'I think we all got a little overexcited yesterday,' she said. 'How is Mistress Carne today?'

'I think she may have a scratch or two about her face. She's keeping to her room; as I said, she's not well.'

'Shall we sit down?' She pointed to two chairs by the fire. Once settled there she continued. 'Let me try and explain. Sometimes a mother will have a child easily: it's pink, happy; it gurgles and feeds, yet the woman mourns, and for a time nothing is as it should be. There's no reason for her sadness, for she has everything she could hope for, but after a child, some women are taken like that. Most, eventually, will recover. For your wife, that was not the case. Her labour was long and hard, and there were no pink, gurgling, happy children at the end.'

'Will she always be like this? Is there any chance she can recover?'

'I don't know. She's strong, that I know for a fact.' She touched the skin beneath her eye and winced slightly. 'How she survived that birth I'll never understand.'

John took a deep breath. 'Did you kill the twins, Molly?'

She licked her lips and stood up, walking slowly away from him.

He followed her. 'Molly?'

'I was trained by my mother and grandmother, as they were trained by theirs. Sometimes a midwife knows that it is best if a child is –' she twitched her lips '– rested. Newborns are tiny. Your fingers softly pinch the nose; the rest of the hand covers the mouth. Because these children are not meant to be, it never takes long. They don't struggle or twitch. Their eyelids flutter briefly, then they're rested.'

'You haven't answered my question.'

'As I told you at the time, the twins hadn't properly formed. They were like mirror images, each with a wizened side, the limbs but little buttons. Their faces were not like those of a normal child: they simply had holes for a nose, just the one unopened eye each. It was even impossible to know if they were male or female. The firstborn was already dead. It had begun to fester in the womb. The second had breath. To this day I cannot see how that could be. I held my hand over it. I didn't even need to touch it; what little life it had was gone. If there's any way I can save a baby, I will, Master Carne. I'll blow into its tiny mouth, and I have revived a couple that way, but there was nothing I could do for Mistress Carne's children.'

He believed her. 'Thank you for being honest.'

She stood close to him, smiling. 'I'm sorry that a man like yourself is so unhappy.' She ran her hand down the front of his jacket. 'I hear that Mistress Carne is no real wife to you.'

John frowned and took a step back. Suddenly his private business had become common knowledge in Spibey's household. 'She should let you love her,' continued Molly, coming closer so that she could touch him again. 'It would do her good. It would do you both good. I know all about babies, how they are made, and I know how a man and woman can enjoy each other with no resulting child.' She gripped the front of his jacket now. 'Look at me, Master Carne, John. You're a lustful man, I can tell, and so you should be. It would be good for your health; a man cannot stand rejection after rejection. Don't you want to kiss me?'

'No,' said John, but he didn't move away. Molly's open face did appeal to him. There were no complications here. She was offering him simple pleasure and, as he wasn't truly married to Zipporah, it wouldn't even be adultery.

Her hands slipped inside his jacket and around his waist. 'How strong you are. How I long to caress you. You need love, John, not discord.' Her hands moved up and reached around his neck, drawing his face close to hers.

At last he tried to pull away. 'We're in Sir Moreton's home,' he stammered.

'And he's given me my own little room. We'll not be disturbed. We can lie together, John, our bodies entwined, my legs tight about you, you feeling nothing but pleasure after pleasure. When was the last time you felt that? We'll please each other, John, because you're not only lustful, you're kind. I longed for this when I nursed your wife, but I didn't know how things were between you then.' Her lips grazed his.

For a moment he thought he'd respond, but Zipporah's beautiful, hard, hurt face loomed before his eyes and at last he had the strength to push her away. 'No, stop now, Mistress Kade. I'm a married man. No matter what the gossip around this place is, I swear to you I'm truly wed to Zipporah, and I'll not betray her.' He felt sick. Molly was right; he needed a woman.

She pushed him hard in the chest. 'Zipporah, Zipporah, Zipporah! What's she got that the rest of us haven't? She can't breed; her temper is foul and, no matter what you say, your bed is cold with her in it. You're a fool, John. See things as they really are.'

He shook his head. 'I don't like you. I don't like what you're saying.' He was frightened of her because she stirred him.

Her previously pleasant features soured. 'I'll tell you one more thing. We have a name for children like hers. We call them Satan's

Babes, for they're not got by any man. We throw them back into the Moss, because that's where the demons live and that's where they belong.'

He was shaking now. He thought his head would explode and his heart burst through his ribs.

She shrugged. 'Never mind. I won't be here long. I'm sure Sir Moreton will be generous with my payment. I've not had a wasted journey.' She raised an eyebrow. 'Let me know if you change your mind.'

He turned away from her, strode out of Spibey's study, down the stairs and narrowly avoided colliding with a most surprised Colonel Mytton. An equally bemused Crowther stood next to him.

'John, you don't look at all well,' said Mytton. 'Crowther, my good man, help me rest him on this bench. Dear me, you should be improving, not deteriorating.'

Crowther had somehow come by a glass of wine and was pressing it to John's lips.

John held up his hands 'Really, I thank you, sirs, I was suddenly a little dizzy, but it's passing.'

'Take it steady, now,' said Mytton. 'We all forget how seriously you were injured. Even after all this time a setback may happen.'

'No, it's not that. I've a bit of a flux in my belly, a chill on it I think. The wine is warming. I'll be better presently.'

'I hope so,' said Mytton, 'for we've business at the camp for you and the magistrate.'

'Oh,' said John, 'in what way?'

'In the way that a civilian by the name of Samuel Blanchard has been half cudgelled to death. Our surgeon binds his wounds as I speak.'

'Sam Blanchard?' said John, grateful that talk of cudgelling and violent attack took his mind off his own problems. 'Is he conscious?'

'Surprisingly enough, he is now. You can thank your friend Benbow for that. He and his troops were out on patrol and found him knocked senseless by the track. It was their swift action which saved his life. Now, finish your wine, and if you feel strong enough, will you and Sir Moreton, if he's available, come with me?'

———————

Spibey, Randall and Parsons were deep into a study of St Paul's epistle to the Romans, and though shocked by John's news concerning the attack on Blanchard, the magistrate was happy to let him investigate on his own.

'The man has reaped what he's sown,' said Spibey. 'You can't flaunt your sin and expect the lord's protection. And John, believe nothing he says. Given what we know about his abominations, we can hardly expect him to be honest, can we?'

'I'll bear that in mind,' said John, blandly, keen to be gone.

'Oh, by the way,' said Spibey over his shoulder, as John took his leave, 'is the Kade woman mollified?' Then suddenly his shoulders shook. Parsons's and Randall's tight mouths twisted into pursed smiles and all three men began to giggle.

John felt sick again. He thoroughly despised them. 'Mollified, yes, that's very amusing, Sir Moreton.'

Chapter Twenty

S am Blanchard was propped up on a camp bed in the surgeon's tent. A bandage was wrapped around his head, leaving wisps of long, light brown hair, matted with blood, sticking out at the bottom.

'Master John Carne, we meet at last. Forgive me for not rising but I see stars every time I move.' His neatly trimmed beard twitched as his full lips curved in an attempt at a smile which became more of a pained grimace.

John nodded and wished him a speedy recovery.

'Well, for once Becky didn't exaggerate,' continued Blanchard, sipping from a tankard that smelled strongly of alcohol. 'You are very easy on the eye. Take a seat, and perhaps the good doctor will pour you some of this wine. It's marvellous stuff.'

'I'd better not,' said the doctor to John. 'It's laced with a tincture of poppy seeds. If you want to find out what happened to Master Blanchard you'd better be quick for he's a few hours of oblivion ahead of him.'

John wished he could have some blessed oblivion, too. He turned to Blanchard. 'Have you any idea what happened?'

Blanchard slurped some more wine. 'None at all, there's the

devil of it. I was on my way back to Hornspike. I'd been to Prees, as I've got some property and business there. I'll admit, it took me longer than I expected, so it was dark when I left and perhaps it was a little foolish travelling so late at night in these dangerous times.'

'You were going to Baccy were you? Sorry, I mean Mistress Blanchard. Forgive me. I thought you were estranged.'

'Not a bit of it. We live separate lives most of the time, I suppose. But I make sure I see her at least twice a year and stay with her for a few days. We're man and wife, you know.'

John twisted his mouth. He hoped Baccy was suitably grateful for her husband's occasional attention. 'Were you followed? Have you any recollection of anyone you met on your journey?'

'There were quite a few folk just outside Prees, people coming back from the fields and such like, I suppose. I certainly had no idea I was being followed, and once well away from the town I saw no one.'

'So, you felt a blow?'

'No, I felt nothing. I was riding along and the next thing I was lying in the mud with a troop of soldiers trying to revive me.'

'The head injury is serious,' said the doctor. 'But I'm pleased to say that Master Blanchard has a strong constitution. His skull is depressed, but not broken. I'm sure he'll recover. It was a heavy blow, though. It would have seen off a woman or an older or weaker person.'

'Was anything stolen?' asked John.

Blanchard attempted to shake his head, then stopped. 'Uh, that does hurt. No, I have everything.'

'Your horse?'

'He was standing next to me, the faithful fellow.' Blanchard rubbed his lips; John noticed he did that quite frequently. Then he yawned. 'Your potion is finally working, doctor.'

'I told you he was strong,' said the surgeon. 'Usually half that amount sends the patient into a deep sleep.'

'If it wasn't for this prickling.' He rubbed his lips again.

'Something troubles you?' said John.

'Something here, ouch, stuck in my beard.'

'I'll have a look,' said the surgeon, holding his magnifying glass over Blanchard's face. He turned and took a pair of tweezers from his box. 'There we are,' he said. 'Nothing to it, just a splinter.'

'May I see,' said John. The doctor passed it to him. 'It's not a splinter, it's a thorn.'

'Whatever, that's better,' said Blanchard, his eyelids drooping. 'I'll sleep now. I meant to thank you for keeping an eye on Becky, Master Carne. In a strange sort of way I think she enjoyed her experiences, especially meeting you. She said you were a comely—'

John abruptly shook his head. 'I don't know,' he said, under his breath and slipped the thorn into his pocket.

Outside the tent John met Benbow, though his friend was hardly any more help. 'We saw no one else, apart from Isaac, Master Wellings.'

'Where was he?'

'With us. We met up just before we found Master Blanchard. He quite sensibly asked if he could ride with us back to Wem. He looked pretty shaken up if you ask me.'

'He'd not been assaulted as well, had he?'

'No, I think he wasn't enjoying being out on his own, what with the countryside being full of cavaliers, murderers and who knows what. I don't know what he was doing out so late. I didn't think to ask.'

'Master Wellings is steward at Whixall. With everything that's going on, he travels between there and Wem a lot. As for cavaliers and murderers, let us hope not more than one of the latter. So how did you find Blanchard?'

'It was Trooper Evans's dog. He ran off on a side track and wouldn't stop barking.'

'So you followed the hound.'

'Evans wanted his dog back. At first we thought Blanchard must be dead. Even by moonlight and lanterns we could see he'd taken a real bashing to his head. Then he started to groan. Isaac had a little flask of brandy. He got some into the poor fellow's mouth and he began to revive.'

'The surgeon says he's a strong man.'

'He must be. I'd say that blow was meant to kill.'

'Yet nothing was taken, so this was no thief.' John carefully took the thorn from his pocket. 'I'm a little worried, Jack. This was found in Blanchard's beard. It was piercing his skin.'

'A thorn?' said Benbow, shrugging.

'One of the bodies on the Moss had his lips and eyes pierced with thorns. Tom Perks and Nanna Grey had their lips sewed with thorns, and I suspect, if something hadn't happened to stop it, the same would have happened to Master Blanchard.'

Benbow narrowed his eyes. 'Thorns piercing the lips, that's weird. Why would you do that?'

'Magic,' said John, without conviction.

'You don't believe that.'

'No, I don't. I'd better have a word with Wellings, in case he saw something.'

Wellings was still in the camp and talking to some of the officers.

'Don't you dare enlist,' said John. 'Sir Moreton would be sure to blame me, and I'd never be forgiven.'

'I won't say I haven't been tempted,' said Wellings. 'But I've plenty to keep me at Whixall, though if it comes to a fight in Wem, and rumour says it will, then I'll do my bit.'

'I cleaned my musket on Sunday and I'm glad I did, as I think it may be needed sooner rather than later,' said John. 'Now, last night, did you notice anything strange before Master Blanchard was found? Cornet Benbow says you looked shaken.'

'I wasn't shaken, not at all, but I did wonder if it was wise to be out alone and in the dark,' said Wellings. 'So I was especially pleased to see the soldiers. It was a crackly sort of night.'

John smiled. 'I think I know what you mean, when trees groan more than usual and there always seems to be something scuttling around in a hedge.'

'Or behind it.' He lowered his voice. 'I'm sure I was being watched. I would be surprised if there weren't royalist spies lurking everywhere.'

'Really! So you did see something? Have you told Colonel Mytton?'

'No, no. There was nothing I could swear to. Perhaps I'm being too suspicious. It was probably just the moonlight, or the wind and shadows playing tricks.'

'Quite likely, though someone armed with a club of some sort must have been abroad, to attack Master Blanchard. Why were you out so late?'

'I didn't consider it that late. It was simply dark. I was finishing all the tasks you'd left me, sir, getting things ready for the Bible reading. Sir Moreton wanted me back in Wem, for I'm to stay at his house tomorrow, to protect Mistress Perks, while everyone else attends the reading.'

'Very well, Isaac. This does make me think that while there is such a threat of battle, it may be better if we stop travelling alone during the hours of darkness.'

'That's probably a good idea, sir.'

'Although I don't think it was renegade soldiers or robbers who attacked Master Blanchard. The surgeon found a thorn in his beard, piercing his lip.'

Wellings stared at the tiny object in John's palm. 'No, sir, you're not suggesting that the fiend who murdered Nanna had a hand in this?'

'I am, and though fiendish, I don't think a fiend was involved.'

'Everyone says it's the witch from Hornspike.' Wellings held up his hand. 'I know you don't believe that to be the case, Master Carne, and I respect you for that. But these monstrous acts do seem to have started occurring since her depravity became common knowledge.'

John let out a long sigh. 'Isaac, I pray you not to succumb to the ridiculous gossip concerning that woman. She's lived in Hornspike for years with nothing untoward happening. Every one of the stories I've heard about her is simply a fouler exaggeration than the last.'

Wellings nodded. 'If you say so, sir. Though I'd hate to think the murderer had been right under our noses all this time.'

'I'm sure that's not the case,' said John.

'I'm relieved to hear you say that,' said Wellings.

'Come,' said John. 'Let's go back and report to the magistrate.'

As they walked, John remembered: Zipporah thought that Crowther had seemed rather put out that he'd been asked to pass on John's message. He asked Wellings why he'd not gone to The Dial, as promised.

'I'm sorry about that. I was looking forward to meeting Mistress Carne. However, Mistress Perks wanted to know what was happening at Whixall, so I had to go to her. I sent Master Crowther with the message. He delivered it, I hope.'

'He did.' So, Wellings had spoken to Margaret. Maybe he had told her about Nanna Grey.

On arriving at Noble Street, Spibey, predictably, became agitated. 'I don't like it. I don't like it at all. The evil is stalking us, getting closer and closer. What do you think, Randall?'

'I'm not sure it's getting closer to us, as such. I'd say the evil is mounting, though to what end, I don't know.'

'So far, the only connection would seem to be Whixall,' said John. 'Squire Perks and Nanna lived there, Master Blanchard not far away.'

'But what of the bodies from the Moss?' asked Wellings.

'The Moss is but a few furlongs from the Grange,' replied John.

'Sir Moreton, did you ever meet Sam Blanchard? I know he was looking for you.'

Spibey's mouth twitched. 'No, never. And see, I happen to be holding my Bible as I say these words, so I cannot be lying.'

'I don't think you lie, Sir Moreton,' said John.

John had not long left Noble Street when he heard a voice calling him. He turned round. 'Mistress Perks!'

'Wait for me,' she called breathlessly. 'I'll come with you and pay my respects to your wife,' she said once she'd caught up with him.

John was alarmed. 'I think not, my lady. You shouldn't be out and about, best you go home.'

'The babe makes me restless. I told you, I cannot sit. I need to be active.' She set off, walking a little ahead of him, forcing him to follow. 'You live at The Dial I believe.'

'Mistress Perks, I implore you, go home. Think of your condition, and I assure you that meeting my wife will not be acceptable to your father.'

She turned and beamed an innocent smile at him. 'Oh, Master Carne, haven't you realised yet that whatever I do, no matter how shocking, my father will forgive? Nay, not forgive, for he believes me incapable of sin in the first place.' She laughed her pretty tinkling laugh. 'I hear Mistress Zipporah blacked the eye of my midwife. Is there something I should know about this Molly woman?'

'She's most experienced, and Zipporah is not herself at the moment. She's not accepting visitors.'

Margaret pointed. 'But there she is, in the garden.' She paused, her lip curled. 'Dear Lord, she's digging. Why is that?'

'So we can plant,' said John, wearily.

Margaret speeded up and crossed the road. 'Mistress Zipporah!' she called and waved.

Zipporah dropped her fork and looked shocked. 'Margaret, Mistress Perks, I should say.' She went to the garden gate.

John caught up. 'There, Mistress Perks, you've seen Zipporah, time to go.'

'You hit the midwife, why?' said Margaret.

Zipporah looked mulish. 'I hit her and I had my reasons.'

'Should I dispense with her and use a local woman?' said Margaret.

Zipporah shrugged. 'Do as you please. I've heard the Kade woman is respected, though I've no liking for her.'

John took Margaret's arm. 'No good is being done here. Let me escort you home.'

Margaret shivered. 'Won't you even invite me in for a warm drink?'

'No,' said John, firmly. 'I told you Zipporah is unwell.'

'I just saw her digging. She's well enough.'

'There's no need for you to enter my home,' said Zipporah. 'I wish you well with your confinement.' She turned and went inside.

'Come, Mistress Perks,' said John.

'You have a mean house and a mean wife,' said Margaret when they got to Spibey's house.

'I'm content with both,' said John, deciding not to react to her insult.

Margaret took his hand. 'It doesn't have to be that way, you know. I hear you and Mistress Zipporah aren't married, not in any real sense.'

'You hear wrong.'

She looked up at him, the corners of her wide blue eyes crinkling with amusement. 'So, there's nothing to stop you having a comfortable home and an affectionate, accommodating wife. Think about it. How nice would it be not to have to till your own patch? How nice to rest on a soft feather bed.' She stood on tiptoe so her face could be nearer to his. 'And how nice to share that bed with a wife willing, eager to embrace you. A wife willing, eager, capable of giving you children.'

'I am as I am,' said John, pulling his hand from hers and stepping away.

'I told you, there's nothing my father won't let me to do, and there's nothing he won't do for me. You don't have to stay as you are.' She rubbed her swollen belly. 'Just as I will soon be returned to my former self. Things can change. Think about it.' She headed to the house. Then she turned and beamed a broad smile at him. 'I always get my way.'

He was relieved when Crowther opened the door and she went inside.

Zipporah was sitting close to the window and darning stockings when John returned to The Dial. She didn't look at him when he came in.

'Trust me I have no idea why Margaret Perks decided to come here.'

Zipporah shrugged and bent over her needlework.

He hoped she wasn't about to disappear into another form of madness. He wondered if he should tell her about the strange conversation he'd had with Margaret. He couldn't really believe she was suggesting that she wanted him, or that her indulgent father would somehow make that happen. And had she meant anything when she said Spibey would do anything for her? He threw the thoughts aside. Maybe she was suffering with some fancifulness caused by her condition. 'Someone has attempted to kill Sam Blanchard,' he said to change the subject.

Zipporah looked up from her sewing. 'More than likely Baccy herself.'

'He was hit so hard a weaker man would have died. Baccy is small; I doubt she would have managed such a blow.'

'Anger gives you great strength. She did it all right.'

'I suppose I'd better speak to her again,' said John, without enthusiasm.

'You might as well arrest her.'

'There's no evidence. Though your thoughts are in tune with the rest of the town who've convinced themselves she's a witch and responsible for all manner of ills and crimes.'

'Your soft spot for her blinds you.' She put aside her sewing.

He picked up the mirror he used for shaving, which was propped up on the sideboard.

'That's vanity, husband.' Her reflection appeared behind his.

'Baccy asked me if I ever looked in the mirror, and Sam Blanchard said I was easy on the eye. What do you think they meant?'

'What do you see?'

'You.'

She moved away. 'Now?'

He shrugged. 'Freckles, blue eyes, sandy brown hair, that's it.'

She laughed. 'Then we can cross vanity off your list of sins.'

He put the mirror down. 'Dare I ask how you're feeling today?'

'I don't know. All these months I've loved wooden dolls.'

'You loved them and they made you happy. They made *us* happy. I was getting used to them.'

'Thank you for saying that.' Her lips twitched. 'I liked my madness; it gave me a purpose, but seeing…' She paused and bit her lip. 'Seeing her, Molly, made me remember. I don't want to but I do.'

'You make very beautiful dolls, though. Perhaps we could go into business.'

Her mouth twisted into sadness. 'Is there any circumstance you think irredeemable?'

'Not you.'

She snorted. 'Do you know what I saw when I looked in the mirror?'

He shook his head.

She took it from the sideboard and held it in front of them. 'I see sad, tired eyes, ringed red, darkly shadowed beneath. I see lines around the mouth that shouldn't be there. I see unhappiness. I see despair and I see two people destroying each other. We can't go on like this. It has to end. I have to find a way to finish it.'

He took the mirror from her. 'I can't tell you how many times I have prayed for you to be well again, not to love the toys—'

'God always answers prayers, but not always in the way you want Him to. Leave it to me. I'll talk to Randall; he'll know the right way to undo a marriage that should never have been. A way that leaves you free. This is me, Zipporah Goodman, talking. The real Zipporah, the same who said years ago she'd never marry you.'

His head buzzed. 'Stop what you're saying. We can work something out.'

She turned her back to him. 'John, go to Baccy, go to her husband, go to anyone who thinks you handsome. Send Randall to me. I need to get everything arranged.'

It was time to stand up to her. 'This is my home – I'll not leave – and I'm hungry. Feed me, then I'll go to Molly Kade, another who thinks me handsome, and who has offered me pleasure with no pain.'

'Go to her, then. Be careful as you sleep, though, for she may lay her hand across your face and still your breath, as she did to my children.'

'She didn't need to; one child was already dead. She would have put the other out of its misery – yes, she admitted that – but it breathed its last before she needed to.'

She stood close to him. 'But I'm right. I saw what I saw, didn't I? Even though I was barely alive when it happened.'

He looked away.

'She might not be an actual murderess, but she thought the thought, and isn't that just as bad? I heard what she said to my babies, too. "Satan's babes". That's what she said. What did she do with them, John?'

He didn't move.

'You know, tell me.'

He turned to her. 'You won't like it.'

'I don't like anything, but I need to know.'

'Why do you need to know something which will cause you great pain?'

'Because they're my children. I have to know what happened to them.'

He let out a juddering sigh. 'Will you never let anyone help you, Zipporah? I'm trying to be kind, to protect you. None of this will change the fact that not only did your babies die, they could never have lived.'

She grabbed hold of his sleeves. 'What did she do with them? Tell me!'

'They're in the Moss.'

She whimpered a sob. 'Then at least I'll be reunited with them in hell.'

Now he took hold of her arms and shook her. 'Stop this, stop it now. You say your madness is in the past, but you're more of a lunatic than ever. If there's any love in the Almighty at all, the souls of your children rest with Him. If you'd just let me love you, Zipporah, we could at the very least have found contentment, but you wouldn't have it. You continue to wallow in your grief, your guilt, and I'm beginning to wonder if perhaps you enjoy it. Maybe the woman I love has always been a creation of my own imagination.' He paused. 'This is the hardest thing I've ever said, but I don't think I can help you.' He meant to push her away from him, but all strength left his body, and his hands dropped limply to his sides. They stood staring at each other for a while. John wondered if, now he'd said those words, now it was all over between them, now there was no reason for living, time had stopped. Had his life actually ended there and then? But it hadn't. He felt a breath escape from his mouth, and his heart still thumping in his chest.

Then she smiled and took his hand. 'Thank you, John. That was kind. At least now I've no guilt concerning you. Do you want me to leave? I'm happy to stay here as your housekeeper until such time as you find a wife, but you may not wish that.'

Her words echoed around his head. He couldn't think. He'd got angry and despaired of her, but had he really intended they'd part? 'Where would you go?' he asked, thinking aloud. 'Of course I don't want you to leave. Please stay, we can be company for each other.'

'Thank you. When Randall has had our marriage annulled, I'll find a position somewhere. There must be a household in need of a woman with a decent education to tutor their daughters.'

This wasn't right. She looked happy, suddenly relaxed as if the greatest of weights had been lifted from her shoulders, but when he spoke so harshly to her it had been because of anger and despair. Had he meant any of it?

'There's no need to rush into anything.' In his head the words 'for better or for worse' rang out. She and Randall might think her marriage to him could be ended simply because they had never known each other carnally, but he'd made that vow before God and didn't see how it could be undone.

A tap at the window stopped any further discussion and John beckoned Isaac Wellings inside.

'Mistress Carne, it's good to meet you properly at last,' he said, nodding to her, most politely.

'You're a busy man, so I hear,' she said, after John introduced them. 'Up and down between Wem and Whixall most days.'

'These are difficult times, and that's why I'm here now. Sir Moreton has become most anxious following the attack on Master

Blanchard. He has the opportunity of travelling to Whixall this afternoon with a scouting party from the garrison, and is keen to take up that offer. I'm sorry this will mean your husband is away overnight, mistress, but I'm at Sir Moreton's house and if there's anything you need, please come to me there.'

John sighed. 'I'd better go,' he said to her. 'Sir Moreton wants us all to be at the Bible reading. If we start early tomorrow I should be back before nightfall.'

'Very well,' she said. 'You're obviously a man above suspicion, Master Wellings, if you're excused this trial.'

Wellings's charming smile spread across his face again. 'I'm simply here to watch over Mistress Perks while her father is away.'

'And as I can vouch for Master Wellings on the day of Nanna Grey's murder, there is little point in him being there,' said John.

'Then you can vouch for each other, and you need not go, either,' she pointed out reasonably.

'Except that I am Sir Moreton's assistant, but if you really wish me to stay, I shall.'

'Go, then. I have Master Wellings's kind offer, though I doubt I'll need it. I'll get a few things together for you.'

'I believe your father spent some time in the Americas,' said John to Wellings as they walked to Noble Street.

The steward looked surprised.

'The cook told me. When I first went to Whixall Grange, I asked about everyone who lived there. She said that your father had been abroad for a while.'

'Not very long at all,' said Wellings.

'I wondered if he ever told you about it. It's just that ... well, I might be moving from here, making a fresh start somewhere, and I wondered about New England.'

'Oh, I see. That's a shame, you'll be missed.'

'I'm thinking aloud, that's all,' said John.

'I'll not say anything to anyone. But of the Americas I know little, though I was actually born there. May I speak frankly, sir?'

'Of course.'

'My father was a strong man, and even he found life over there too hard to endure.'

'I take your point. It would be much harder for a cripple.'

'And it killed my mother, or at least my father blamed the harsh conditions on her death. It was then he decided to return to Shropshire. I was barely two years old at the time. I believe the squire was happy to have him back. In truth they were friends; I think they missed each other.'

'When did your father die?'

'Just before the latest Mistress Perks came to Whixall.' Wellings sighed.

'You sound as if you still mourn him.'

'I do. He was a good man. We worked well together and all I want to do is be a credit to him.'

'That I'm sure you are,' said John, wishing there were more decent souls like Wellings in the world. They reached Noble Street.

'Well, here we are. I see Sir Moreton has the horses already harnessed. I'll wish you a good journey.'

'Thank you, and thank you for the kind offer you made to my wife. It's good to know you're around if she needs anything. It's appreciated.'

'It was honestly meant, sir. Though if you didn't mention it to Sir Moreton, I'd be grateful.'

'I won't, and I'm the one who's grateful.'

The day was bitterly cold, and the little band of pilgrims and soldiers kept the pace brisk. Jack Benbow seemed unusually quiet and any attempts to engage him in conversation were kindly rebuffed.

'They're all around us' was all he said. 'Cavaliers, Captain, can't you smell them? They're here, somewhere, if only we could find them first. They'll be upon us before long, and we'll be at a disadvantage.'

Even though Benbow seemed to be focused on his duties, John sensed there was some other reason for his reticence.

'Cornet Benbow had a letter delivered,' whispered Trooper Evans, whose dog had been instrumental in saving Blanchard. 'He's had a face like thunder since he read it.'

John smiled. 'Now I understand, no doubt a romance has not developed the way he wanted.'

'When do they ever, Captain?' said Evans, with a wisdom greater than his soft unshaven chin would suggest.

Chapter Twenty-One

S heer exhaustion meant that John enjoyed a full night's sleep, which was just as well as it was Reverend Parsons who started the reading the next morning and his dour delivery would have rendered anyone even slightly weary completely unconscious.

The local curate from Whixall gave a more spirited rendition of his passages. He was followed by Randall. Whatever John thought of him personally, he was a good orator and his reading of St Paul's epistles to the Corinthians was moving.

Spibey still seemed shaken by recent events. 'If it wasn't for my daughter, I'd be tempted to stay here, bolt the doors and wait till this trouble is over. All this talk of the royalist attack is more than disturbing.' He rubbed his hands over his face, John noticed they were shaking. 'It's all right for you, Master Carne. You may be a non-combatant now, but you're used to war and I'm not. Do you know what I overheard one of the soldiers say?' He didn't wait for John to answer. 'That the garrison and the defences at Wem are not yet strong enough to withstand an assault. You know those cannons going up on the walls? Some of them aren't real;

they're made of wood. What good is that going to do? We could be slaughtered in our beds. It's a worrying time.'

John gripped Spibey's shoulder and stared hard at him. 'As for the wooden drakes, you keep that information to yourself, please,' he said softly, but firmly. 'Whether they work or not is immaterial. If our enemies think they do, they're almost as good as the real thing and may, hopefully, make them more hesitant to attack. Take heart, Sir Moreton, surely today's readings have inspired you?'

'Of course they have. The Scriptures never fail to hearten. Yet why did no one writhe around in an agony of torment?'

'Because no one present was the murderer.'

Spibey shook his head rapidly. 'Then who is? An invisible wraith, most likely conjured up by that witch. The more I think about everything, the worse it gets.'

John sighed. 'May I suggest we head back to Wem while the light holds? Once you're reunited with your daughter, you'll feel better.'

'You're calm, Master Carne. See how your military background stands you in good stead. I'll order the horses saddled immediately.' He beckoned Randall over to them. 'Are you back to Nantwich or Wem?' he asked.

Randall seemed unperturbed. 'Whichever way I go, I'm likely to find trouble. As Wem is closer and if your kind offer is still open, then I'll return with you.'

For once the sun made an appearance. It glinted low, gilding the countryside as they left the Grange. Spibey was jumping at every crackle and shadow.

'I cannot see for this light,' he said, pulling down the brim of his hat and holding his hand in front of him. 'What's that over there? Did I hear a clash of swords? Did I see the flash of a musket barrel?'

'The path turns south just ahead and the sun won't bother you then,' said John, but the magistrate would not be placated. As they rode alongside the Moss, a group of peat cutters emerged, singing as they left their work. Such was his agitation, he nearly fell from his horse.

John was desperate to stop this unsettling behaviour. Again he noticed starlings flocking together, swooping and swirling, making great shapes in the sky. 'Look, Sir Moreton,' he cried, pointing. 'The birds of the heavens have made the shape of Our Lord's cross. A sign we have God's blessing and protection.' Surely that would calm the man down.

'And yet now it curls into the shape of a sword,' moaned Spibey. 'We're all going to be cut down.'

John made no more attempt to soothe him after that.

They'd just crested Lowe Hill and Wem was in sight, when they saw a small group of riders coming towards them. Spibey was all for turning tail and making a run for it. John had to raise his voice to convince him that he recognised the men as friendly.

The troop pulled up next to them, breathless. 'Make haste,' called one of the soldiers. 'The enemy will be upon us again by nightfall. We've already seen off one attack. Get into the town as quickly as you can. We're closing the gates ... well... propping them up, as most haven't got hinges yet.'

Spibey was already thundering down the hill, Randall close on his heels.

'You too, Captain,' said a trooper.

'Me and old Freddy here haven't got much in the way of pace, but if I'm to die, at least it will be in battle, not tumbling off a bolting horse. Take care yourselves.'

'Are there any others in your party who've fallen behind?'

John assured him there were not, and as the troops cantered away he nudged Freddy into a reluctant trot.

'The enemy's been sighted, over by the Drayton Gate,' said the sentry as he hauled the thick wooden door closed behind them.

'I'll fetch my musket and get over there,' said John.

Zipporah was waiting at the garden fence, despite everything he was still pleased to see her.

She seemed relieved too. 'Praise the Lord, I thought you'd been left behind. I've loaded your musket and pistol and your sword is ready.'

'Good girl,' he said, slapping her shoulder as he would a comrade at arms. He swiftly donned his thick leather jacket, buckled his sword belt and tied his tattered orange sash across his chest. 'Might as well do this properly,' he said, smiling at her. 'It's traditional for a soldier to steal a kiss when he's off to battle.'

'That's a lie,' she retorted, but offered him her cheek. She was certainly friendlier to him as a housekeeper than she ever was as a wife. She was pulling on his old, patched gardening jacket and had a pitchfork propped against the wall.

He frowned.

'You needn't think I'm staying here and letting those foul beast cavaliers come in and ravish the women of Wem.'

'Staying here, in this house, you certainly are.'

'No time to argue.' She pushed past him and was out of the door.

Ignoring the pain in his leg, he managed to catch up with her just outside the Lion.

'Hey, if that whore can fight for her town, then so can we,' said one of the chubby trollops lounging about outside and sure enough, they stood up, keen to follow the ever-increasing numbers heading for the town walls.

He heard Colonel Mytton's voice. 'John, thank the Lord, a sensible man at last.' The tall officer ran over. 'My God, the whole town must be out. Most are by the Drayton Gate but I've no hesitation in putting you in charge of that rabble over there –' he pointed '– where the wall is low and weak. And see to it that the tall fierce woman with the patched jacket and pitchfork, is placed somewhere prominent. We've no time for gentle niceties now, and she's got a murderous look on her face.'

John grinned. 'That's my wife, and you've summed up her character perfectly,' he said, over his shoulder, as he walked away, though not before he heard Mytton rapidly apologise.

'Right, ladies and gentlemen,' he said, reaching his command and stopping just long enough to catch his breath. 'Colonel Mytton has the effrontery to call us a rabble. He's wrong, we'll show him. If the rest of the town falls, this part of the wall will stand firm. Wem will not be lost by this way. Wem will not be lost at all.'

'Fighting talk, Captain,' said Farmer Laycock.

John swayed out of the way as the farmer waved his flintlock dangerously in his direction. 'I don't want fighting talk; I want fighting action, and keep that fancy weapon pointing outwards, please,' he said. 'Ah, welcome ladies.' He turned to the two harlots from the Lion, who'd finally caught up with them, armed with a broomstick and a rusty old sword.

'I don't mind hand to hand combat,' laughed the taller of the two.

'We're used to it,' said the other.

'Let's hope it doesn't come to that,' said John, frowning slightly as the women had sidled up next to Zipporah, though the three of them were soon talking in a friendly manner.

'I'll stand with you, Master Carne,' called a familiar voice, and Crowther was soon by his side.

'Sir Moreton sends his apologies, he'd do his bit, of course, but Mistress Perks has just started with the baby.'

'Oh, dear,' said John, who hadn't expected Spibey to take part anyway. 'Where's Master Wellings? We could do with someone like him.'

'As soon as the master returned he was off to the Drayton Gate—'

Everyone jumped as the mighty boom of cannon fire vibrated through their feet. 'Stand your ground,' ordered John. 'That was one of ours; we must have them in range. Hold fast, hold fast, here they come!'

A group of royalist cavalrymen thundered towards them like stampeding cattle. Laycock's flintlock and John's musket discharged simultaneously.

'We can load,' said two lads, both Laycock's sons.

'Then we'll put you to good use,' said John, passing back his musket and letting off his pistol. Crowther's little pistol cracked into action and the two whores from The Lion bared their immense breasts and shouted the vilest of invectives at the enemy, one in English, the other in Welsh.

Zipporah stood like a malevolent statue, her pitchfork pointing outwards and her face inviting anyone who dared to take her on. John and Laycock were armed again and fired, the ball from the flintlock hit one of the cavaliers who tumbled off his horse.

'Good shooting, sir,' said John, then cursing at his own aim as his shot merely swept the hat from an opponent.

The ground shaking, due to several cannon discharging simultaneously, caused some of them to stagger, and there was a whoosh and crashing explosion behind them as a cannonball landed in the town. Soil and splinters rained down on them.

'Don't look back,' ordered John, wiping grit from his eyes. 'There's no casualties, stand your ground.' He discharged his pistol again. 'Better,' he muttered, seeing another cavalier fall to the ground, though he couldn't be completely sure he'd been responsible.

The Lion trollops had re-tied their bodices and were now jumping up and down, squealing excitedly. 'Let's rush them, Captain,' they screamed. Zipporah barred their way with her pitchfork.

'Stand firm until you're ordered otherwise,' she barked.

'Good work, soldier,' said John with a proud grin, his teeth white against his grubby face. 'How are we doing for powder, lads?'

'Plenty, Captain.'

There was another ear-splitting thunder of heavy artillery, followed by a creaking, cracking noise as a branch of a tree sagged and fell to the ground, unhorsing several enemy cavalrymen.

'God is on our side!' exclaimed Laycock, punching his fist in the air.

'As He is on theirs,' whispered John to himself, taking his reloaded pistol back from Laycock's son.

Hoof beats thundered closer.

'Look out!' screamed Zipporah, as a horse launched itself untidily over the half-built wall. Its hind legs caught on the back of the palisade and it tipped, headfirst, into the ground, throwing the rider off. The Welsh harlot grabbed at the harness, but as the horse tried to stand up, its foreleg crumpled under it, and stumbling to one side, it fell on her.

Zipporah was instantly upon the cavalier, her pitchfork stabbing into his thick jacket. He twisted round and aimed his pistol at her.

'No!' screamed John, discharging his own pistol and speeding towards Zipporah.

The bullet slammed into the soldier's arm, his weapon falling at Zipporah's feet. John couldn't stop and collided with her, knocking them both to the ground.

Somehow the royalist, who'd fallen to his knees, got back to his feet, though he was bellowing with pain. He clumsily dragged his sword from the scabbard using his left hand. He swiped towards Zipporah. There was a hard crack, and the man dropped to the ground.

Crowther stood stock still, except for his hands which, though they still gripped his little pistol, were trembling. Smoke snaked from the barrel. 'I'm sorry, so sorry,' he muttered.

'Good shooting, Master Crowther,' exclaimed Laycock. 'You saved Mistress Carne.'

Gripping each other, John and Zipporah staggered back upright.

'Dear Lord,' she whispered, before going to Crowther and putting her arm around his shoulder. 'How can I ever thank you?'

'I never thought I'd kill,' said Crowther, still shaking.

'You're a good fellow. There's a war on and you did your duty,' said Laycock, slapping him hard on the back. 'Now, let's finish off this ruined horse, and see if we can save poor Gwyneth.'

Miraculously 'poor Gwyneth', though badly winded and bruised, was conscious, and once extracted from under the charger, was within a few moments able to sit up and suck in noisy gulps of air.

'Back to your stations, those who can,' shouted John. 'They're coming upon us again! Boys, are we ready?'

Despite the drama, Laycock's sons continued with their duties, even Crowther's weapon had been prised from his trembling hand and reloaded.

Once again the men fired and Zipporah thrust her fork at any enemy soldier who came within range.

Gwyneth recovered and was soon back by their sides 'It's personal now!' she screamed, as she flailed her sword.

Another cannonball from the town flew outwards and once again soil and turf exploded into the air.

That was enough to see off the remaining cavalrymen, but they were swiftly replaced by a small band of infantry.

'This is it, troops, stand firm,' shouted John above the ever-increasing cacophony. He fired his musket for the last time before passing it to Crowther. 'Use it as a club,' he said, drawing his sword.

For a group of untrained men, women and boys, they were a fearsome opponent to their enemies. Time and time again they repelled a wave of invaders. Zipporah's pitchfork flailed, pushed and jabbed, the end soon tinged with blood. Gwyneth and her sword acquitted themselves admirably, while the whore with the broom literally swept all before her. Laycock was no slouch with his sword either, and Crowther, his shakiness gone, was clubbing steadily.

Smoke and darkness surrounded them thickly now, and they were reacting more to the sound of the attackers rather than their movement. The booms of the cannon subsided, and an eerie calm descended. They suddenly realised the enemy had fallen back. One of Laycock's boys threw a lighted torch into the darkness. It landed on the ground and burned long enough for them to see that any of the enemy left were motionless on the ground.

'Well done,' said John. 'Well done, my fine troops.' Then he leant forward momentarily feeling winded and tired. 'I think we've won.'

They had. A cheer went up around the town, replacing the ugly sounds of war. They lit more torches, illuminating their tired, grimy faces.

John sought out Zipporah. She showed no resistance when he slipped his arm around her waist. Rather she rested her head on his shoulder.

'You worked hard tonight, my love.' He nuzzled against her.

'We all worked hard, but we saved the town, didn't we?'

'Yes.'

The landlord of the Lion was making free with his beer, proudly showing off the bent buckle that had saved him from a musket ball. Sam Blanchard was also there, his hat sitting at a strange angle on his bandaged head.

'Will I ever get back to London?' he said. 'What a time to visit Shropshire. It'll be a long while until I come back here, that's for sure.'

'At least you seem to be somewhat recovered,' said John, gratefully taking the tankard that Zipporah passed him and downing most of it in one go.

Blanchard nodded to Zipporah. 'Mistress Carne, what a dreadful day. How awful that a gentle woman such as yourself is forced to bear arms.'

She laughed. 'Now I understand why men make war. It's frightening but exhilarating. My pitchfork tasted blood today.'

John shook his head. 'Today we won and had few casualties. Don't get captivated by it, war's never pretty. Another day it will be the enemy that tastes the blood.'

She leaned against him for a second time. 'Don't worry, I don't care if I never see action again.'

Crowther was the next to arrive at the tavern and accept the free hospitality. Zipporah hugged him tight, much to the man's embarrassment.

'Hello, Crowther,' said Blanchard. 'Well, you're a popular fellow.'

Crowther smiled shyly, obviously pleased to be free of Zipporah's embrace.

'He only saved my life,' she said.

'Just happened, just happened,' mumbled Crowther.

'Almost wish I'd taken part in the battle; it might have been worth it,' said Blanchard. 'Now, all conquering hero, Crowther, did your master get that letter I passed to you?'

'I'd be grateful if no one mentioned what I did ever again,' he muttered, then looked up at Blanchard. 'Your communication was passed to my master, sir.'

John raised an eyebrow but said nothing. 'Any news of Master Wellings?' he asked.

'Alive and unharmed,' said Crowther. 'He didn't hear that Mistress Perks's baby was on the way until after the fighting had finished. Once he did, he was straight back to Noble Street.'

Another round of drinks arrived and Blanchard threw a purse of money to the landlord and asked him to open his wine casks for any who preferred that to ale. The harlots immediately made their way over to him.

'Hmm, good luck to them,' whispered John to his wife, with a wry smile.

'Am I as filthy as you?' Zipporah asked, her eyes bright against her grimy face.

He gently rubbed his thumb across her cheek. 'You're a little dusty for sure. It suits you, though. Shall we go home in a minute?'

She looked away, but he could see she was smiling.

The door burst open allowing a blast of cold air into the tavern. 'A boy,' exclaimed Isaac Wellings. 'Mistress Perks is safely delivered of a fine, big, lusty baby boy. Pass me a tankard of ale, or five!'

'You'd think the babe was his,' Blanchard muttered to John and Zipporah.

'Maybe it is,' whispered Zipporah into John's ear.

They finished their drinks and said goodbye to Blanchard who seemed to be eyeing the whores speculatively. 'A change is as good as a rest,' he said to John, with a barely perceptible nod.

Outside a freezing wind hit them, and Zipporah took his arm. 'Just to keep warm,' she said.

'Dare I ask if we're friends again?'

'We fight well together.'

Damn this cold, he thought. If they'd stayed in the warmth of the tavern and had another couple of drinks, she might have been his that night. He fervently hoped the fire hadn't gone out at The Dial; he might still have a chance of warming her up. He heard footsteps clattering behind them and turned to see Wellings rushing across the street.

'Master Carne, please forgive me.' He stopped and caught his breath. 'The colonel gave me a most important message to pass to you, but what with Mistress Perks and the baby, I forgot. Dear Lord, I hope I'm not too late. Your brother, sir, has been taken prisoner, badly injured and maybe close to death.'

John's shoulders slumped. 'No,' he moaned.

'I'm so sorry, sir. He's being held at the camp; you'd best go to him, I'll walk Mistress Carne back to your house.'

'I have to go,' John said to her. She burst into tears, and not just weeping but deep sobs as if from the very depths of her soul. 'There, there,' said John, holding her close. 'It may not be as bad as feared.' He turned to Wellings. 'Thank you, Isaac, please see my wife home.'

Chapter Twenty-Two

John hurried across town as fast as his aching leg would allow. The garrison camp was well lit with blazing torches, and soldiers were busying themselves, moving ammunition and powder to replenish the town's stocks in case of another royalist assault. He heard quiet conversations and barked orders, punctuated by the groans of the wounded, as he made his way to the surgeon's tent.

'He was brought in covered with blood and quite insensible,' said the surgeon, who ushered him inside the tent. 'Once he was washed, though, we could see he only had a flesh wound, and he revived quite quickly.' The surgeon paused. 'Then something dreadful happened. Once he heard your brother had been taken prisoner, young Benbow burst into your brother's tent, and beat him soundly before any of us could stop him.'

'What?!'

'You might well exclaim. Such behaviour is quite unacceptable. Prisoners of war are the enemy, but once in captivity, they should be treated with respect.'

'They should. Where's Cornet Benbow now? I'd like a word with him.'

'He's been flogged, but we need all the men we can get at the moment, so he's out on patrol.'

'Understood,' said John.

Dick Carne was a mess. His nose was broken, both eyes black, the skin scuffed and weeping, and he'd lost a front tooth. 'The man was possessed,' he groaned, through swollen lips. 'I was lying here, already injured. I posed no threat to anyone, and then this beast laid into me.'

'It wasn't a beast; it was Jack Benbow, whom we've known since childhood. What can have happened that he should turn against you so?'

'Nothing at all. I haven't seen the man since he joined up for Parliament. I tell you, he was possessed. You've got to do something, John. You've got to get me out of here.'

'I'll see Sir Moreton tomorrow and get you a pass, considering what's happened, that shouldn't be a problem. I'll try and get you home, somehow. If not, you'll have to stay with us until you're better and it's safer to travel.'

Dick tried to raise himself, then fell back. 'I want to be in Shrewsbury. I don't want to be here.'

John rested his hand on his brother's shoulder. 'I'll do my best. The surgeon's a good man, and I'm loath to move you at the moment. Stay here for now, and I'll see you tomorrow.'

'I want Benbow hanged.'

'He's been flogged already. That's the appropriate punishment for his crime.'

'If you were lying here, you wouldn't say that.'

John gently squeezed his brother's shoulder before leaving. He asked the sentry on the gate to send Benbow to him as soon as he returned to the camp.

Wellings was still at The Dial, pacing up and down the room. 'Praise the Lord you're back,' he said when he saw John. 'I didn't know what to do. Mistress Carne went straight upstairs and she won't stop crying. I couldn't leave her like this, yet I didn't know if I should try to comfort her.'

'Thank you for staying,' said John, with feeling. 'I'm sorry we've kept you from the celebrations at the Lion. Off you go now.'

'But why is she so sad? She must love your brother greatly. How is he by the way?'

Whatever was causing Zipporah such grief, John doubted it was Dick's injuries, since she'd been antagonistic to him when they met. 'My brother will mend. As for Mistress Carne, don't worry about her. It will be the shock of the battle that's upset her. Get yourself off, the party looked as if it would continue all night, there might be some ale left.'

John tried to explain to Zipporah, who was hunched on the floor in the nursery, what happened to Dick, but as she was so consumed by sobs he wasn't sure how much she took in.

'How can one person have so many tears?' he asked at last. 'You're certainly not crying for my brother.'

She sniffed and smiled up at him wetly. 'You're right, I don't care about Dick. As for my tears, maybe I've been saving them up,' she said. 'After everything that's happened, am I not allowed to weep?'

'Zipporah, for a short while tonight, we were happy. You would have lain with me, I know. Come to our bed, let me wipe away your tears and love you.'

'No, I can't.'

'Just let me hold you, I won't do anything you don't want me to.'

She shook her head.

'Where are your babies?'

She pushed his hand aside. 'The dolls have gone. I don't need them anymore. I have to go. I can't stay here with you. I've become weak.'

'There's nothing weak about loving someone.'

'I know. Love has to be strong. Please leave me alone. See, you've stopped me crying, but I'll be sniffing horribly all night. I'll stay here.'

Reluctantly he agreed.

———

If it was possible for a town to have a hangover then Wem was that town. The smell of black powder hung heavily in the air and there was litter and debris all over the streets. One by one doors were opening and the sluggish inhabitants looked out at the work of clearing up that lay before them. Some were already making a start; others simply reclosed their doors and went back inside.

John and Zipporah hardly talked that morning, though there was no tension between them. In truth they were both too tired to have any sort of emotions.

———

John thought it would be prudent to give his congratulations to Spibey.

Crowther looked exhausted when he opened the door, but beamed when he saw who it was.

'You should be resting today,' John said to him.

'Too busy,' he said. 'All sorts of people coming and going, with news of the battle and then the baby –' he yawned and ran his hand over his forehead. ' – not to mention your brother-in-law with his constant reciting of the Scriptures and Master Wellings prancing about like some puffed up rooster. He doesn't know his place, that one. He even had his arm around Sir Moreton at one point. I've worked here for years and never so much as shaken the master's hand.' He shook his head. 'Forgive me, Master Carne, I'm talking out of turn. I'm so tired I hardly know what I'm doing.' He sighed jaggedly. 'I never thought I'd hold a pistol and use it.'

John squeezed his shoulder. 'I thank God you did.' Zipporah was right, though: Crowther *was* jealous of Wellings. 'And Whixall will need its steward back before long,' he said as comfortingly as he could.

Crowther didn't reply but John had the distinct impression that day couldn't come soon enough. When they went into the house he merely said that Farmer Laycock was with the magistrate and John should join them in the main hall.

From the sound and the smell of him, Laycock had come straight from the alehouse.

'And here he is, another of our fine heroes,' he said, wrapping his arm around John's shoulder. 'This is a man who knows how to use a musket. Oh, my, what an honour to fight alongside him.'

Spibey shrugged dismissively.

Laycock was not to be put off. 'And as I told you, the womenfolk of Wem played their part. None more so than the radiant Mistress Carne. Oh, Moreton, you should have seen her. She brandished her pitchfork with valour. In her hands it was transformed into a trident from the gods of old. Royalists fell down before her. She was a woman possessed—'

'Master Laycock,' said John, gripping the farmer's arms. 'I think Sir Moreton has heard enough.'

Laycock shrugged. 'Though, you should know, there's a rumour round the town that if you'd hung the witch, none of this would have happened—'

'No,' shouted John. 'Wem lies on the road from Shrewsbury to Chester. We were always going to be attacked. Now, Master

Laycock, I suggest you go to your wife, who must be beside herself with worry.'

'Ah, I suppose you're right, Master Carne.'

'I'll show you to the door.'

'Was it so terrible?' asked Spibey when John returned.

'It was a skirmish, that's all.' John had no desire to unsettle Spibey by dwelling on the battle or anyone's part in it. 'Actually I came to say how pleased I am to hear your daughter is safely delivered.'

Spibey's countenance brightened and his eyes sparkled. 'Mistress Kade said she was hardly needed, so natural a mother is my Margaret. And little Thomas, he's such a bonny lad, and so healthy, he can scream and shout all right. There's not one bit of sickliness about him. His skin is pink; he's a good head of brown hair, the shiniest blue eyes and the sweetest button nose. He's a delight, Master Carne, a sheer delight.'

'That's the most welcome news. We all rejoice for you and your family.'

Spibey looked wistful. 'Oh, yes, family. We're a family again. Margaret has a babe and now she'll settle.' He added the last quietly.

This was as good a time as any, thought John. 'Sir Moreton, I'll admit I have a favour to ask.'

The magistrate attempted a little chuckle, which invariably sounded false and strangulated. 'Clever John, today's certainly the day to ask a favour of me.'

'My brother, Dick, as you know, fights for the royalists. He's been injured and taken prisoner. If you'd grant me a pass, I'd like to get him back to his home in Shrewsbury. He won't fight again, so he won't threaten our cause.'

'Family's so very important. I've no hesitation in giving you authorisation. Write it out in your fair hand and I'll sign it.'

Spibey was just blotting his signature when there was a knock on the door and Molly Kade entered the room. 'The mother and child are awake now if you want to make a short visit, Sir Moreton.'

Spibey beamed. 'Don't go, John, I still have things to say to you.'

Molly stood aside from the door to let Spibey pass. 'I'm not needed here much longer. You won't forget my pay, or the little extra we talked about, will you, Sir Moreton?'

Spibey looked flustered. 'Yes, yes. I won't forget, not at all. I'll send Isaac to settle up with you.' He left the room.

John didn't look at Molly. Wellings had suddenly become Spibey's most trusted servant by the sound of it.

She smiled at him in her seductive way. 'Always a pleasure to see you, Master Carne. Are you well?'

'Well, but tired, as are we all after last night.'

'It sounded ferocious. I had an easy evening in comparison.'

John said nothing.

'Young women like Mistress Perks birth easily.' Molly came closer, her hands picking at her striped skirt. 'I need to be back in Whitchurch. Will this battle affect travel?'

'You may have to wait. I don't think anyone's going anywhere for a while.'

She rubbed her hands together bad-temperedly. 'Two of my older ladies in Whitchurch are nearing their time. They'll need me far more than Mistress Perks. I must get home.'

'I'll ask around and see if anyone's going in that direction. I've got to get my brother back to Shrewsbury as well.' The assault had made an uncertain situation even worse.

'I need to get away from this household,' Molly said with a shiver. 'Sir Moreton sees the devil everywhere. Master Wellings at his beck and call like a puppy eager to please. And creepy Crowther with his tales of putrid Moss bodies oozing evil—'

John was pleased to see Wellings come in. 'Mistress Kade,' he said, 'Sir Moreton has given me the key to his strongbox, and asked me to settle matters.'

Molly's expression brightened. 'Good, the sooner I get paid, the sooner I can go home.'

'Come this way, Mistress Kade.'

John went over to the window which looked out onto the garden. Everywhere was drab. He wondered how Molly had managed to get more money out of Sir Moreton, for what was obviously an easy job. He smiled. Good luck to her. He hadn't realised how trusted Wellings had become, either. Good luck to him, too. He looked up at the sky, leaden as always, a long winter lay ahead.

'Ah, John.'

Spibey's voice brought him out of his reverie. 'Mother and baby well?'

'Both asleep. How I praise the Lord, for I am the most fortunate of men.' Spibey's expression then became grave. 'Take the rest of the day off, John, but let me walk you to the door.'

Spibey stood with his hand on the catch, shifting from foot to foot. 'Despite what the people are saying, I don't blame you for letting the witch Baccy go,' he said quietly, surprising John with the abrupt change of subject and tone. 'You said it would force the greater evil to show itself, and I believe it has.'

John frowned. 'Has something happened I don't know about?'

Spibey took his hand and squeezed it. 'I'm beginning to see things clearly, John. Far more clearly than I have before. Just as the royalists were defeated, I will defeat the evil in this town. For there is evil here. Have a care, John. Have a care.' He opened the door.

A somewhat breathless Wellings joined them and handed Spibey a key. 'Mistress Kade is keen to be off,' he said.

John frowned. 'I told her, she'll find it difficult to get back to Whitchurch.'

'She took her money, no doubt,' said Spibey.

'Of course, sir.' Wellings looked at John. 'She said she was sure to find someone going in that direction.'

John was happy to be away from Spibey. The man's words, never mind the malicious glint in his eyes, disturbed him. The frostiness in the air was nothing compared to the chill he felt in his soul. Maybe he should have stayed and attempted to discover more about Spibey's plans, no doubt ill-conceived, and then tried to talk Spibey out of them. He wondered if Spibey had actually lost his wits. Constantly looking for evil, finding it where it didn't exist would be enough to turn the most rational of minds. Spibey had been increasingly unstable of late. How he wished Laycock had not described Zipporah as possessed. Had Spibey even heard him say that, given his preoccupation with his grandson? He sighed mistily into the cold. He knew by now that the magistrate was prone to grand statements that meant very little, and hoped this latest outburst was one of those occasions.

The army surgeon still wasn't happy for Dick to be moved, and as the invalid was drowsing peacefully, John had no wish to disturb him. He and Zipporah spent the rest of the day helping to tidy the town, and by the time dusk began to fall, apart from a couple of broken walls and a crater here and there, you'd hardly be able to discern the conflict had taken place. When they got back to The Dial, Zipporah mulled some wine for them.

'How do you propose to get your brother back to Shrewsbury?' she asked.

'Sir Moreton's signed a pass. Dick may be able to travel alone; the wound on his shoulder isn't a deep slash, but he'll have no horse. If I can find a carter to take him it would be better, though I doubt there'll be many people travelling for the next few days.' He sipped his drink. 'Hmm, just what I needed. I still can't think why Benbow would do such a thing.'

She shook her head. 'There may be some history between them we know nothing of.'

'I suppose so. Jack was out of sorts the other day. Apparently he'd had a letter which upset him. I presumed it was from a sweetheart who was no longer keen.' He paused. 'Dick always had a roving eye. I had hoped that now he's married to Hattie and they have children, he'd be finished with all that. I pray he's not involved in any way.'

'Let's consider other matters. All day I've been pondering what Sam Blanchard said. He may have solved the murders for us, well, the recent ones at any rate.'

John raised an eyebrow.

'You know, when Wellings came into the tavern full of the news of the baby's birth, Blanchard said the child might as well have been Isaac's.'

'Not very likely.'

'And why not? Just because she's the daughter of a magistrate and he's a servant doesn't mean to say nothing happened between them. You saw his expression when he came in. He was full of pride and joy. Far more than you'd expect from someone who simply happened to work for the mother's husband.'

John frowned. 'We'd just won a battle. We were all full of pride and joy.'

'There was more to it than that. And we know they've spent time together. He brought Margaret from Whixall. He stayed in Wem, to protect her while everyone was at the Bible reading.'

John bit his lip. 'Yes, perhaps they've had more time together than I thought. He sent Crowther to give you the message that I'd be late, so he could talk to her about Whixall.'

'Hmm, I'm sure she'd have found that *fascinating*,' said

Zipporah. 'Whatever they were doing I doubt they were discussing Whixall.'

'And, when Margaret was looking at the Moss bodies in the cellar, it was Wellings who came to find her. He did seem concerned, too, but then he would be. We know how protective Spibey is of his daughter. If anything happened to her, someone would be in trouble. Wellings wouldn't want it to be him. But none of this suggests anything more intimate between them.'

'Really! There's something going on, I'm convinced. And why not? He's a good-looking man, after all, and *seems* to be a very pleasant person, too.'

'Yes, he is pleasant and he's always polite to you.' John sipped some more wine. 'He was somewhat distant with me today, though that was probably because we were in Spibey's house.' He thought again. 'Yet Crowther said he doesn't know his place and is too familiar with Sir Moreton, though I think that's jealousy on Crowther's part. And Spibey did trust Wellings with his strongbox key when I was there, which I suppose did surprise me, as I hadn't realised he was such an important member of the household.'

'I'd wager the one person he's most overfamiliar with is Margaret. And thinking about it, I begin to wonder if he could be the murderer.'

'What!' John laughed. 'Wellings is no murderer.'

'If he and Margaret Perks are lovers, that gives him motive enough.'

He leaned forward. 'I don't think they are, but go on.'

'Perks was killed for obvious reasons, either simply to get him out of the way, or because he found out the baby wasn't his.'

'All right, that's plausible, even though I don't believe it. Continue.'

'And Nanna was murdered because she'd guessed Margaret was with child before anyone at the Grange knew, and she may have thought she knew who the father was.'

'I'm not convinced of that, either. How could she, alone, have any knowledge of the affair between Wellings and Margaret, which I doubt ever existed?'

'As I said before, from the state of the linens.'

'Sorry, Zipporah, I think that's a lot of supposition. And don't forget, Wellings and I were together for that day, working on Perks's ledgers and accounts.'

'*All* day? Did neither of you have to ease yourselves, eat, get something from another room?'

'All right, we weren't in each other's company continually, but we were apart only for the reasons you state.' He paused. 'I suppose I did snooze while he went to retrieve some documents, but it wasn't for any length of time. And I can't think it was long enough to kill someone, tie their lips with thorns, and then string them up. I don't know why you suspect him so strongly. He's a decent hard-working fellow and he's more than respectful to you, which not enough people are. And I don't see he's gained anything from any of the killings, so why commit them?'

'I doubt it takes long to snuff the life out of an old woman. How many thorns pierced Perks's mouth?'

'Eight.'

'Nanna's?'

'Four.'

'See, no time for more.'

'As you seem to have solved everything, why were the thorns used, and why did someone attempt to kill Sam Blanchard, and stitch his mouth?'

'I'm not saying I've thought of everything, but I'd be cautious of what I said to the handsome Master Wellings.'

'That's twice you've mentioned you think him good-looking.'

'Haven't you noticed?'

'No.'

'He's the kindest eyes, and what a smile, those dimples around his mouth—'

'Stop that, you're a married woman.'

'That's a moot point.' She began to look cross.

He felt brave. 'You may think promises made to God can be undone simply because we never lay together, but I'm not so sure.'

'Don't spoil everything. I'm trying to set you free. It won't be easy, and it certainly won't help if you try and make things more difficult. I'm sure Randall will be able to explain to you how it can be done without breaking any vows. I asked Master Wellings to mention to my brother that I'd like him to visit me. I'm sure he'll pass my message on, murderer or not.'

He stood up and walked across the room, an action he hoped would stop him losing his temper. 'I don't like you going behind my back.'

'I'm not. I'm telling you about it now.' She went over to the cooking pot. 'The stew's warmed through; I'll serve.'

John had only tasted a couple of mouthfuls when there was a knock at the door. It opened slightly and Jack Benbow stood in the doorway but didn't enter.

'Well, I'm not coming out to you; it's freezing,' snapped John. 'So you'd better step inside.'

Benbow acquiesced, holding his hat before him and looking down at the floor. 'You may be interested to know the royalist army has been truly routed and is on the run. We should be safe from them for a while.'

'Excellent news,' said Zipporah, offering him a cup of warmed ale. 'There, that should take the chill off you.'

'I don't think I should,' said Benbow, still not looking up from the floor.

'No, you should not,' said John, going over and snatching the cup from his wife's hand. 'Don't give refreshment to the man who thrashed my brother.'

'*I've* no argument with Jack,' she muttered. 'I hear you've been flogged, would you like me to look at your wounds? Or I could give you a salve for them.'

'Thank you, ma'am, but the weal's aren't so bad,' said Benbow.

'Leave him to suffer his pain,' snapped John.

She shrugged and went back to her meal.

'What were you thinking about? Beating a prisoner of war half out of his wits.'

'Beating your brother half out of his wits is what you mean, since I doubt you'd have been bothered if it had been anyone else.'

'Maybe, but Dick was already injured, wasn't that punishment enough?'

'I'm sorry he's your brother, I am truly, truly, so sorry, but it's a personal matter. If you knew what he'd done, you'd beat him yourself, but I've already said too much. Please accept my apologies. This is nothing to do with you, Captain. My affection and respect for you stand as high as they ever have done.' He looked up at last to Zipporah. 'And to you, my lady. Never let me be at the wrong end of your pitchfork.'

'Nor shall you be,' she said with feeling.

'I'd like you to go, please, Cornet Benbow. Perhaps some other time you'll feel able to give me a better explanation and a proper apology. At the moment I can't be bothered with you.'

With another apologetic look, Benbow left.

John returned to his meal, breathing angrily, but saying no more. He had only just finished wiping the last of his sauce from the bowl when Randall came in without knocking.

'Just what I need,' John said to himself, before turning to the latest unwelcome guest. 'Randall, don't let us keep you from your prayers,' he said. 'Or have you come simply to cadge some decent food from us?'

'Your temper seems a little strained. Be calm, think upon the Lord.'

'Thank you for coming,' said Zipporah, handing him a mug of ale.

John snarled. 'Stop it, woman, why are you so intent on succouring all my enemies?'

'I'm merely being polite. Would you like something to eat, brother? Please sit at the table.'

He did so. 'Some of that mess would be welcome on a cold day like today,' he said pointing to the cauldron. 'Now, sister, why did you want to see me?'

'I thought you'd be the best person to ask about the formalities involved in dissolving the so-called marriage between John and myself.'

Randall's spoon hovered above his bowl, but it never dipped it into his food. His smile was wide and genuine. 'Am I hearing you correctly? At last you want to undo the evil you've done to my dear friend, John?'

John stood, his chair falling noisily backwards onto the floor as he did so. 'I've had enough. This is *my* house and I'll run things *my* way. This marriage is not so-called. It's real and will continue. You.' He jabbed his finger at Randall. 'You have no say in this matter. You, Zipporah, will stop this wilfulness and put your considerable energy and intelligence into being a good wife to your husband. Finish your food, Randall, and be gone.'

Randall's spoon still hovered. 'John, be calm, think about it. I'm sure Sir Moreton, for one, would be relieved to hear that you've decided to make things straight, shall we say.'

'The devil take Sir Moreton. I'll live my own life, in my own house, in my own way, with the person I love.'

Randall winced. 'What a thing to say,' he sniffed, wiping his mouth. 'And I'm not convinced it *is* love you feel for my sister. It's simply a stubborn pig-headedness because you refuse to admit you were wrong to marry her in the first place. A marriage, sister, which I consider so irregular there must be several grounds for annulment.'

'Good,' she said. 'Have some more ale, Randall. John, in time, you'll look back at this day and see it as the start of your happiness.'

'I'll look back and see it as a day when a misguided woman and a religious bigot set out to ruin my life. Except I won't look back, because I'm not going to let it happen.'

'A-ha, you accept she's misguided then?' said Randall.

'By you in most part, constantly reminding her of her own damnation. What sort of a brother does that?'

'A loving one, such as myself. Why should I lie to her? But, John, I'm not yet fully convinced you are damned. Dissolving this sham of a marriage would go some way to persuade me that you show the signs of someone who's saved. Cast aside your sin of pride. Let me find a way to undo what should never have been done—'

John clasped the back of Randall's jacket and pulled him upright, his spoon still in his hand. 'You're leaving this house, Reverend Goodman, and you're not welcome to return.'

'Your very soul is at risk, John. I cannot bear the thought of losing you.'

'Then don't think about it. Go, Randall. We're no longer friends. In truth we haven't been for a long time.'

'Sir Moreton won't be pleased about this.'

'Hang Sir Moreton.' He pushed Randall out and slammed the door shut, hurling the spoon he'd retrieved across the table. 'You, woman, should know your place. No one comes into this house unless invited by me.'

She remained infuriatingly calm. 'Please allow Randall to look into things properly. If there's a way out, we must take it.'

He took both of her hands in his and stared at her. 'You and I made every promise we ever needed to. For richer, for poorer, in sickness and in health, for better, for worse, until one of us dies. There's nothing complicated about it. When the cannon shot was flying over Wem last night, by whose side did you want to be?'

She looked away.

'You wanted to be by me, and I by you. It was that simple. Why do you continue to deny our feelings for each other?'

'Why don't you go and see how your brother is?'

He let go of her. 'Very well. But no contact with Randall, or indeed anyone whilst I'm away.'

'Go, go.' She waved him away. 'I have a lot to record in my journal.' She opened the writing box and took out a pen.

Chapter Twenty-Three

'I was about God's business—'

Journal of Zipporah Carne

Trudging across town in the cold, sharp air helped to clear John's mind. He was pleased he'd stood up to Randall. Though this was tempered by the knowledge that his brother-in-law was probably, at that very moment, denouncing him to Spibey. Even worse he could be spitting bile and, God forbid, making dreadful accusations against Zipporah. Despite having just eaten John felt hollow. He rubbed his head. He needed to remain rational. The town was recovering from a battle and the magistrate was still rejoicing in the birth of his grandchild. Hopefully, he'd have no time for Randall's venom. As he walked he felt that was a slight hope but one he had to hold on to. He needed to see his brother first, though.

At the camp, Dick was up and dressed and eager to be away. John assured him he would try and find him a mount or some other form of transport the next day, as, though still badly bruised, it was obvious he was fit enough to travel.

Zipporah was in the nursery when John got back to The Dial, and refused to come out. Normally this would have sent him into a frustrated rage, but it didn't. He felt something had subtly changed between himself and his wife, the fraught tension, always there when the dolls were around, had gone. The woman he spoke to now was at least sane, even if he'd no liking for what she said.

He sat down in front of the fire with a mug of wine. Procuring a horse for his brother was going to be difficult. The garrison would never relinquish one, neither would Sir Moreton, and any for sale would be at such a premium he certainly couldn't afford it. Still, that was a problem for another day. He wondered if Molly had managed to leave Wem. He'd ask around and find out who was travelling about. He yawned and looked around the room. He might as well go to bed. He noticed that Zipporah's journal lay on the table. Normally she kept it with her. He stood up, winced slightly and paused to rub his leg before walking over to pick it up, intending to take it to her, with the possibility of initiating a conversation. She'd left it open. He couldn't help but read it. It started on the day of their marriage. The date written out and underneath:

Today I married John Carne of Shrewsbury.

Oh well, at least she hadn't written anything bad about him. Although he felt guilty, he couldn't help flicking through the pages, as he'd always been intrigued by the contents of her book. He sat down. Mostly it was recipes, the ingredients and method written out, with comments underneath such as…

Too much salt; too bland; more spices needed; John liked this;
    John appreciated this and it cheered his mood.

And such similar comments. He liked the fact she mentioned him.

Occasionally, interspersed with recipes for meals, medicines, or a potion to polish wood stained with ale, he found other observations. Perhaps a remark about some everyday event, and recently rather more notable incidents, like the gruesome discoveries and her disapproval of the arrest of Baccy.

Additionally there were prayers, mostly for strength. One particularly made him stop and blink.

Dear Lord, today I was tempted to be weak, to kiss when I should keep my
mouth tight, to hold close in my arms what I must keep at arm's length,
to praise and shower with words of love, when I must be shrewish and
keep to my purpose. Make me strong, Lord, I beg, keep me strong.

He rubbed his eyes so hard his vision was momentarily blurred. Was it him she wanted to kiss and to hold, or another? As he was her husband, who could legitimately be kissed and held at any time, he began to feel sick with worry that she'd found another. And yet, though she'd never encouraged his affections, he never believed she was untrue. He knew he was wrong to continue reading, but now he couldn't stop.

Interspersed between all these jottings was a recurring phrase that stood out.

I was about God's business.

But nothing followed, except sometimes a fierce scribble which would pierce the paper. He flicked through more pages, a date was circled and under it written –

I have perfected my receipt for ginger cake and John said it was the best he had ever tasted.

What was going on? One moment a heartfelt prayer, the next delight that a cake had been enjoyed. It was delicious, though, he could still remember it.

He turned the pages and began to learn more.

Today I have seen the murderer of my children and spat in the face of the worst of men. Now I can tell my story.

I was about God's business, though that has never guaranteed to protect anyone from evil and none was afforded to me. I was staying with relatives who live just outside Shrewsbury. My aunt asked me to take some food to a poor widow of her acquaintance, an hour's walk from her house. I was happy to volunteer for this duty, for the day was bright, if a little chilly, and I am more than capable of walking for an hour with a laden basket, which neither my aunt nor my cousin were. I spent some time with the honourable widow and her family, and even though they told me there were soldiers abroad who had been acting with great disrespect, in the way of plunder and violence, I thought nothing of it.

So I began my journey back, it was still full daylight. I had no cares, rejoicing in the countryside and in the knowledge that I was soon to return to my father. I knew that by then his anger at John's joining for Parliament would have abated, and if John would have me, (though I had treated him badly, I still hoped he would) we could be married.

John had to stop. He blinked hard again and re-read the passage, hardly believing the words. Then he continued.

From the moment I refused John I wondered if I had done right. Just before I went to Shrewsbury, John came to our house in Nantwich to see Randall. I wondered how I would feel, seeing him again, especially with him now being a soldier for Parliament. We soon fell into our easy way with each other.

John remembered those days well. He'd come to say goodbye to Randall before his regiment was deployed. Zipporah's father had made his disapproval of John's allegiances vocal. Zipporah herself, seemed unconcerned. And yes, she was right: they'd soon assumed their easy ways together and he fell further under her spell than ever before. If it hadn't been for the war and Edgehill, he would have proposed again. It seemed that he would have been accepted.

I was rehearsing in my mind the letter I would write to him, explaining how my feelings for him had frightened me at first. I was perhaps too young, too bookish, too determined to be independent, to fully understand the power of love. Love I realised I had felt since we first met. Now my mind was clear. Without him, my heart, my soul and my body ached. If he could forgive my youthful wilfulness, if he would accept me, I would gladly be his wife. I was composing the final salutation full of love and devotion when I first saw the men approaching.

John stood and went over to the fire, breathing deeply. His wine was by the chair and he downed it in one gulp. His thoughts tumbled and jangled about his head. She loved him –she wanted him – but he knew, with a sickening certainty, what he'd read next. He had another mug of wine. He felt chilled to the core. He brought the book back to his chair by the fire.

There were three of them, they dismounted and began to laugh and joke. Even then I felt no concern, I laughed along with them, told them not to be silly boys and tried to continue on my way. But one grabbed me and tried to kiss me. Perhaps if I had allowed that kiss the rest may not have happened, but I doubt it. The kiss resisted, his pull on me became tighter, his face close. I was not prepared to be taken without a fight, and battle I did, with hands and fists and teeth, but the one had become all three and in the end, one by one, they did to me what a man should never do to a maid, though by the third attack I was all but completely insensible. I was thrown face down in the mud. They would have left me there, but I heard another horse arriving and my attackers hailed him as Captain Carne. My John was there! I tried to pull myself up and cry out his name. He would save me, and see my assailants punished. But all I felt was a kick and laughter. 'She's done for,' I heard one say.

'No, she'll do.' It was an unfamiliar voice; it was not that of my John. Once again I was violated, while the first three continued to laugh and make jokes concerning their brave captain, Dick Carne. At last they left me. The cold and dark awoke me and I staggered back to my aunt. How I found the way I will never know. At first there was sympathy, but when I realised I was with child, that evaporated.

My brother, always the first to condemn my many sins, banished me from my home. My lack of godliness, he told me, was the cause of my disgrace. I could not be with decent people, for I would taint them with my depravity and cause them to fall from grace. My father, conflicted as he was between his children, was taken with a terrible seizure, from which he never recovered. The only person who remained constant was John. The man who must never know how much I love him, lest I drag him into the pit of hell with me.

There, it is written, the sad tale of Zipporah Goodman, from virgin to whore in one afternoon.

John placed the book carefully back on the table. He pulled on his jacket and buckled his sword belt. As he left The Dial the only thing icier than the night was his rage.

The camp was still well lit. More men were there now and there was some singing going on in a corner. No doubt the victory was being celebrated.

'This is a late hour to be calling,' said the surgeon, as John walked towards Dick's tent. 'Is anything wrong?'

'No, not at all,' John managed to say, through teeth clenched tight, both with cold and anger. 'I've come for my brother.'

'Now?'

'It'll be one less mouth for you to feed.'

'True enough.'

'Is Benbow here?'

The surgeon nodded.

'I'll just take a minute with him, if you don't mind.'

'Yes, by all means.' The surgeon left him to it.

As John marched towards him, Benbow looked somewhat alarmed and then surprised as John took his hand and held him close. 'Thank you, my friend,' said John. 'For starting what I've come to finish.'

'You're not going to kill him?' said Benbow, not requiring any explanation.

'Sadly my religion doesn't permit it, but I'll put a few more marks upon his body before I cast him into the night. How did you find out?'

'I wrote to my sister saying that I'd found you again, and that you were married to a fine woman called Zipporah. My sister wondered if it was the same Zipporah who'd been so badly assaulted by royalists. It would be strange indeed, she said, since one of the attackers was strongly suspected to be Captain Richard Carne. Then, when your brother was captured, I felt such rage I couldn't help but beat him insensible.'

'I've only just found out myself. Do you have any idea as to the identity of the other attackers?'

'None at present, though my sister is making discreet enquiries.'

'Thank you again, Jack. You're a true friend.'

'I am, and for that reason I say, don't ruin yourself or your reputation just for him. Think of Zipporah.'

'I do, Jack, I do.'

Dick was muzzy with sleep. 'Why wake me now?'

'We're going.'

'To The Dial? Oh, well, at least I'll have a comfortable bed. But it's uncommonly late to be out and about.'

'Get dressed.'

Once out of the camp John asked his brother if he'd recognised anyone when he last visited The Dial.

'No, only yourself.'

'Not the woman you ruined.'

'Eh, what are you talking about? I thought your injuries were only of the body, now you're talking like a mad man.'

'That's because I am, brother. Mad at you, that is, livid to the point of murder.'

Dick stopped in his tracks. 'I'm going back to the camp. You're possessed.'

'You're leaving Wem.'

'You're making no sense.'

John drew his sword. 'I'd love to run you through, don't give me a reason. Now, walk.'

The sentry guarding the town's south gate couldn't understand why anyone would want to leave at such a late hour, when there was a chance that some royalist troops might still be about, but as Captain John Carne was so respected he didn't quibble about prising the door open a few inches to allow the men out.

'I won't be long,' said John.

Dick stumbled as John forced him through the gap, then he stopped and turned. 'All right, I've had enough, what's this all about?'

'It's about an afternoon last year. You were out and about in the countryside around Shrewsbury. You came across three of your noble companions who'd already violated a young woman and thrown her face down in the mud. And you, for whatever reason, when you were offered, took this woman by violence.'

Dick, silhouetted against the moon, leaned back, his arms spread wide. 'John, it happens, don't tell me that you and your godly companions have never taken advantage of some peasant.'

'I haven't, no.'

Dick laughed. 'Why do you care, anyway? What's got into you, John? What madness afflicts you?'

'The madness that you, the brother I've always loved and respected, saw a woman much maligned and only added to her troubles.'

'It was too late for her, anyway. What's it to you?'

'You raped Zipporah. You and your comrades made a whore of a maid. Good work for an afternoon, don't you think?'

Dick stepped back, his teeth glinting in the moonlight. 'Stop it, John, how do you know it was her?'

'I do.' That was enough talk. John's fist shot out and made a satisfying thud into his brother's already broken nose. Blood spurted out, John could feel the warmth of it, rather than see it. Dick fought back and struck his brother hard in the face. John now felt the heat of his own blood pouring from his mouth. He let rage overcome him and rained more blows at Dick's body before kicking him firmly between the thighs.

Dick sank to the ground, gasping. 'Brother, have mercy, how am I to get home?'

'Don't care,' said John through short rasping breaths. 'You showed no mercy to Zipporah, why should I to you?'

'I'll take the house off you, repossess The Dial.'

John spat blood and spittle down onto his brother. 'You're already suspected by some in Shrewsbury as a rapist. Let's hope your wife never hears of it. Now go home and do your best by that poor woman you married.'

John slipped back through the tiny gap opened by the gatekeeper.

'All right, Captain Carne?'
'Never better, thank you.'

John let himself into the nursery. Zipporah was fast asleep in the small bed. He pulled off his outer clothes and slipped in next to her, she shifted slightly but didn't awake. He draped his arm over her. Sleep claimed him immediately.

Zipporah was looking over him. Her nightgown was smeared with blood.

'What happened? You look as if you've been in a fight, you've a split lip and your fists are a mess. You've bled all over me.'

He looked at his swollen hands, the skin over his knuckles, soft through lack of hard work, but cracked by the cold, was broken where he'd punched his brother. 'Yes, I was fighting,' he said and rolled over, pulling the bedcovers up to his ears.

'You, fighting hand to hand, when the enemy is long gone? It makes no sense.'

'There are enemies and enemies, Zipporah. Leave me a while, my head throbs.'

'And you drank most of the wine. I'm worried, John. You're usually so safe and reliable but now you seem to have become a drunken brawler.'

He turned back over and held out his hand. Surprisingly, she took it. 'My lovely, clever wife,' he smiled up at her, 'I can't believe that you don't have a salve that can help heal these fighting fists.'

She pulled away. 'Only if you tell me what happened.'

'I met someone bad; I gave them a well-deserved beating; they're gone.'

'Oh, good, that explains it all. Let me get dressed, then I'll see to you.'

She returned a few moments later, dressed, but pale and her lips trembled. 'John.'

The quiver in her voice was enough to make him sit upright.

'John, there's something, no, someone, hanging from our apple tree.'

———————

Outside the air was icy, the ground crisp with frost. John looked at the tree and instantly recognised the striped skirt of Molly Kade's dress.

Zipporah gripped his hand tightly as they went closer. 'Dear God,' she whispered.

John reached out and swung the body to face them.

Zipporah's grip, already vice like, tightened even more. 'Thorns through the lips.' Her voice was barely audible.

John's breath snaked from his mouth in a white plume. 'Why her? Why here?'

'We have to get rid of her,' said Zipporah, her voice tense. 'Now. Get her away from my garden!'

'I have to report this to Spibey.'

She shook her head violently and began to pace. 'No, not Spibey. Someone hung Molly from a tree in our garden? Why? Don't you see how dangerous this is for me?'

'You had an argument and struck her. You think someone might believe you killed her because of that?' he said.

'That's exactly what I think! That's exactly what a lot of people might think. Don't be so slow, husband. People, by which I mean Spibey, will want someone to blame for this. I hit her. I hated her. I wanted her dead. I didn't kill her, you and I know that. But why is she here?' She stared hard at him. 'To make it look as if I did. Quickly, John, before there are too many people around, we must take her down. Throw her in the river, anything, but she mustn't be found here.'

He held her hands, trying to calm the panic he felt rising in her. 'Steady, steady. If either of us killed Molly we'd be unlikely to leave the evidence in our own garden, for all to see, would we?'

She pulled away from him and began pacing again, the frost crunching beneath her feet. 'No, we wouldn't because we're clever, but this town is full of idiots. Idiots who believe Baccy Blanchard is a witch, who believe I'm a whore. Idiots who know I hit Molly and will assume I did this to her.' She stabbed her finger towards the tree. 'Idiots who believe Sir Moreton Holier-than-thou knows what he's doing. No, John, we cannot leave her here.'

'Whoever did hang her would know we'd moved her.'

Her eyes widened. 'Indeed they would! And they may well give themselves away by suggesting she'd been here. That's how we'll catch them. Quickly, we must pull her down and drag her off somewhere.'

'No, Zipporah! What if we're seen, that would make it look even worse. I must inform Sir Moreton. Yes, we both know what he's like but he *is* the magistrate. He has to know and we have to examine the body for evidence.' She didn't move away when he rested his hands softly on her shoulders. 'Think about it. We've no enemies here, have we? I know the townsfolk haven't treated you well in the past, but after your bravery in the battle, you're well respected. Only yesterday Laycock was singing your praises. Why would anyone try to implicate you, or me, in anything? Molly was hung here for a reason, you're right. And it's a reason I can't yet fathom, but it has nothing to do with us.'

'But, John, why else is she here? Is it a warning from the murderer that we're too close?'

'That's for me and Sir Moreton to determine. And since we've kept our suspicions to ourselves, how could the murderer know if we're close to discovering him or not? Anyway, nobody could accuse you of killing Thomas Perks or Nanna, so why would they think you killed Molly, since the perpetrator is clearly the same person.'

She looked sulkily away. 'Better if Spibey never knew she was here in the first place.'

John took her hand. 'A crime has been committed and I have to follow the correct procedure. Do you really think I'd risk you if I thought you were in danger?'

She shook her head. 'No, you'd never do that.'

Crowther shook his head gloomily when John arrived at Noble Street. 'Everything's going from bad to worse,' he said. 'Nothing's been right since those bodies were brought out of the Moss. Master Perks killed, that poor old woman in Whixall. And Sir Moreton's not a well man, Master Carne. He's out of his wits with worry most of the time. Cursed those bodies were, cursed. I'm surprised they've not hauled themselves out of the ground and come back to haunt us. They should never have been brought here, never.'

John held up his hand. 'And I have more bad news for the magistrate.'

Crowther paled as he told him. 'Cursed, cursed,' he muttered as he let John in.

'What's happened? Who's attacked you?' demanded Spibey as John entered his study. The magistrate was instantly alarmed by the state of his assistant's face.

John explained he'd fought with his brother, but simply said it was the result of a longstanding family argument and made no further elaboration.

'This is all wrong! My good solid assistant getting into a fight.'

'Sir Moreton, I have much worse news to impart.'

Crowther was right, Sir Moreton was not a well man. He

staggered about when he heard about Molly. John guided him to a chair.

'My daughter's midwife strung up and the body mutilated. No, no, that cannot be! No, no...'

'Do you want to come and see—'

Spibey waved his arms around. 'No, no! Have her brought here. We'll bury her decently. Oh what evil is among us. What evil. And you've not heard yesterday's developments. The rector tells me Tom Perks's grave has been desecrated. Oh, John, how I long to be off this coil of torment and to be in the bosom of the Almighty. But we're all to be tested.' He gripped John's hand. 'We are to be tested, you and I. Will we be strong enough?'

'The way Molly's been killed must be connected with the deaths of Tom Perks and Nanna Grey. My preliminary investigations suggest she *was* strangled, though it wasn't the hanging that killed her.'

'What have you seen?'

'There were bruises on her neck, but no rope marks. But the thorns in the lips are a message to us. It must be the same person who killed the others.'

Spibey suddenly seemed calmer and nodded slowly. 'Oh, indeed it is. I see it all now. But yes, now I see everything.'

'You speak with certainty, Sir Moreton.'

'I do.'

'You know who did this?' asked John.

'I do.'

'Will you not tell me?'

'Not just yet.'

Zipporah's theory concerning Wellings kept coming into his mind. He could well have been the last person in Spibey's household to see Molly. What happened to her after she was paid? Was there any significance in the extra money she spoke of? But why would Wellings kill the midwife? Unless she'd also realised Margaret's child was illegitimate. But, with Perks dead, could it ever be proved he wasn't the father. John doubted the inheritance would be affected.

'We need to speak to Master Wellings. Molly said she was leaving Wem. Did she give him any idea who she was travelling with? Surely she wouldn't have attempted the journey alone?'

Spibey waved that suggestion aside. 'I don't need to question Isaac, or anyone else.'

'Sir Moreton, are you saying that, not only you know who the killer is but it's someone close to home?'

'Very close. Say nothing.' The magistrate pulled him into a tight embrace, then released him, embarrassed. 'It's a testing, my dear John, but you'll be brave. As will I. We'll look back and see this as the time when right began to exert itself over wrong.'

'Quite so,' said John, wishing everyone would stop saying he'd look back, when in reality he rarely did. He returned to The Dial as quickly as he could, desperately needing to be with Zipporah.

Chapter Twenty-Four

Zipporah and John stood by the gate while Molly's body was carried away.

'You didn't see or hear anything?' John asked her again.

'No. After you left to visit your brother I went to my bed and slept. You were the one out and about, brawling.'

They walked back inside and he told her the truth about his fight with Dick. He thought she'd be angry, but she wasn't. She was simply resigned.

'I was determined not to tell you. I vowed to myself I never would. Your love and respect for your brother was too great a bond for me to break. I didn't realise I'd left my book out. Perhaps in some way I wanted you to read it.' She tightened the leather strap around her journal and knotted it. 'It's strange. When I saw him again I was, at last, able to write it all down. That meant I could see things more clearly, and yet I'm still so confused. I've thought it over, time and time again. I must have done something to cause those men to treat me so. Randall said I'd most assuredly brought the misfortune on myself. Such are my sins, I pollute whoever I'm with.'

'Randall!' he spat the name venomously. He held her hand.

'Your brother is wrong, so very wrong. You did nothing. You're simply a victim of this war and men's vileness.'

Her head drooped.

'And who was vile enough to kill Molly? Was it Wellings? Could it really be him? Spibey gave Wellings the key to his strongbox. Once Molly had been paid she'd be gone. At least that's what Wellings said.'

She looked up, interested again. 'Wellings, Wellings, Wellings. The man's everywhere. And trusted with Spibey's keys now.'

'Molly reminded Spibey that she was to have an additional payment, and yet by her own account the birth was easy. Did anyone see her once she left Noble Street? I must find out.'

Zipporah pursed her lips. 'Perhaps it was a payment to keep her quiet.' She leaned forward. 'Don't you see, as an experienced midwife, she would have known Margaret's child was born full term. She'd have realised Spibey needed to keep that quiet, not only for his reputation, but as you say, it's important that the child is seen to be Perks's heir.'

'Yes. Knowing what I know – knew – of Molly, she'd be happy enough to take advantage of any situation. But why kill her?'

'Maybe she demanded more than Spibey was willing to pay?'

John's eyes opened wide. 'You're saying Spibey killed her? No, he was shocked when I told him. The greatest of players couldn't have feigned such a performance.' He frowned. 'Though, when I wanted to ask Wellings how Molly intended to leave Wem, he dissuaded me.' He shook his head. 'None of this makes any sense.'

He didn't have time to continue as Spibey, together with the sergeant from the gaol barged through the door.

'John, stand aside,' said the magistrate.

'What?' said John.

'Please, sir, stand aside,' said the sergeant.

'Stand aside from what?'

Spibey pulled his normally hunched shoulders upright.

'Mistress Zipporah Carne, you are accused of many acts of witchcraft, the most recent of which is the murder of Molly Kade. You sucked her soul from her body and then sealed her lips with enchanted thorns. The other accusations will be made at your trial, a fair trial, where witnesses will be called and evidence taken before your punishment is decided. Sergeant, take her, use force if necessary.'

Zipporah approached them, her head high. 'You lie, Sir Moreton, and you know you lie. I never murdered anyone. If you know who did this, why blame me?'

John went to her and wrapped his arms around her. 'If you take her, then take me. We're married, we're one flesh. Our sins are like those of any other. We know nothing of witchcraft, nothing of murder.'

She pulled herself away from him. 'Take me then, Spibey. Try me, and see what you can prove. I've prayed for strength over and over again, now let me see if that strength has been granted.' She looked back at John as the sergeant took her by the wrist. 'I have to go, John,'

'Never,' he cried, but Randall entered the house and held John from behind, gently but firmly.

'Let her go, my friend, it's the right thing to do. You know I've always had your best interests at heart.'

John struggled as he watched Zipporah walk out proudly, but Randall was strong and he couldn't break free from his grip as he held his arms fast behind him.

Zipporah turned one last time to Spibey. 'Be careful, sir. Try me, find me guilty, hang me for a witch, but you'll still be nursing the real killer in your bosom.'

John at last found reserves of strength, struggled away from Randall and ran towards Zipporah, but the sergeant pulled his pistol and pointed it at him.

'I'll stop this madness. I'll save you, Zipporah, you'll see,' he called, as Spibey and the sergeant led her away.

Randall was by his side again, holding his arm. 'This isn't madness, my friend. This is the beginning of sanity.'

John was wild eyed. 'How long have you been planning this?'

'I've planned nothing. Moreton has had his suspicions for some time. I may have helped him decide to act, given what I know of the woman's character. Throughout his investigations Moreton was most concerned that you must be kept safe. With the murder of the midwife we couldn't leave you with her any longer.'

John pushed Randall away. 'Zipporah is a thoroughly good woman. She's no whore. She was set upon and attacked by a group of soldiers. That's how she came to be with child. She's certainly no witch. I hope your god is proud of you, for the true, holy God of love must be looking down upon you in despair.'

'See how the witch has perverted your faith. This is what God demands. This must happen. This is right.'

'Then I spit upon you and your god, Randall.' John went to the back of the house and came back with Zipporah's cloak. 'It's a cold day. Spibey must at least allow her some warmth.'

Zipporah was locked in the same cell as Baccy had been. John passed the cloak through the bars and she eagerly pulled it over her shaking shoulders. Her eyes darted to and fro; she was frightened. 'He can't convict me, can he?'

'I don't see how,' said John. 'We've done nothing wrong since we've been here. The whole thing is insane.'

'We did nothing wrong, yet everyone presumes I'm a whore. This is Wem. A few words, probably dropped by my own brother, convinced the people of that. Now Spibey, the magistrate, no less, says I'm a witch. They'll believe that, too.'

'I'll persuade Spibey he's wrong. We have our suspicions concerning Master Wellings, don't we? I'm beginning to think you may be right. If I could prove who the murderer is, surely you must be released.'

'There'll still be the accusation of witchcraft.'

He stopped and listened for a moment. 'What's all the commotion outside?'

'Sir Moreton has already called a special session of the assizes. I'm to be tried today. Word must have got around already.' Her smile was lopsided. 'There are no secrets in Wem.'

He snorted. 'Wem has too many secrets.' He tried to reach through the bars. 'I'll stop this, Zipporah, I will.'

She shivered. 'I'm frightened, I'll admit it, but if this is what God wills, then I must, I shall—'

'This is the work of the devil, Zipporah. Or more to the point, Sir Moreton Spibey, though it's hard to tell the two apart at the moment. Our Lord isn't involved.' He reached through the bars, but she stood away from him. 'Spibey's right about one thing, though.'

She tutted. 'I can't think what.'

'I'm naive. I said I didn't think you were in any danger. I thought by working for Spibey I was protecting you. How wrong I was. I'm sorry.'

Her smile was weak. 'None of this is your fault, John.'

A small crowd had gathered outside the courthouse.

'If the Hornspike witch had been hung, then the town wouldn't have been punished.' The tall man was bellowing. 'This one had better swing or who knows how we'll pay.'

There was a murmur of approval.

'She should have been stopped sooner,' added a woman, her lips pursed piously. 'I remember my grandmother telling me years ago a witch lived at The Dial, yet nothing's been done about it until now.'

'Those bodies from the Moss brought evil to this town,' shouted another.

The tall man was clearly enjoying having his say. 'The Hornspike witch is nothing compared to this one. We all know Mistress Carne's a whore all right, but she spread her legs for the devil. The children she spawned would turn you to stone if you looked at them. She ripped them apart with her bare hands and tore the flesh from them with her teeth, rubbing the blood over her breasts while she and Satan humped—'

Breathless, John pushed himself into the throng and struck the man's chest with his stick. 'Stop, all of you! You're a disgrace, you are, to this town, this country and yourselves.' He paused to pull air angrily into his lungs. 'You were happy enough for Zipporah to risk her life defending the town.' He turned to the woman who'd spoken. 'And you know full well we've not lived at The Dial twelve months, so your grandmother couldn't have known us.'

The woman snorted. 'Witches can change their form, everyone knows that.'

'And', shouted a man from the back of the group, 'Farmer Laycock himself says she fought like a woman possessed, and we know now by whom.'

John raised his hands. 'Listen to yourselves. You know none of this is true.' He turned to the tall man and lashed his stick out again. 'And you, sir, should keep your sick fantasies to yourself.'

'See, she's bewitched her husband, poor man.' He heard someone say.

'Or he's in league with her,' added another.

'Idiots,' John muttered. He looked at them, their dark cloaks flapping. He thought of the crows circling over Tom Perks's body, caw-cawing in anticipation of the feast awaiting them. 'Fools and idiots,' he spat. 'Be careful what you wish for. Today it's my wife who stands wrongly accused. Tomorrow? Who knows where the witchfinder will point his finger? I hope to God you're all as pure as you think you are.'

Then someone accused the tall man of not taking part in the battle against the royalists, and a scuffle broke out. John had no desire to be involved; his argument was with someone else. Ignoring the sergeant on the door, he burst into the courtroom, which was hastily being set up, Spibey directing operations.

John shouted across to him. 'Sir Moreton, think what you're doing. At the worst there'll be a gross miscarriage of justice, as the due process of law is not being followed. This isn't even a true session of the assizes. At best you'll make a laughing stock of yourself, trying to convict a woman without a shred of evidence.'

Spibey's eyes glowed malevolently. 'You're wrong. I've more than enough evidence, and as a Justice of the Peace, I must see justice done. You've been bewitched, but by the end of the trial the scales will have fallen from your eyes. You'll see that the woman you thought you married was no more than the devil in human disguise.'

'Even from you this is beyond ludicrous. Sir Moreton, please listen.' He pulled the magistrate to one side and lowered his voice. 'You know this court has no validity. Zipporah hasn't been subjected to any of the normal tests and nor should she be, since you've not a shred of evidence against her.'

'I've more than enough evidence, John. Trust me.'

The muscles in John's face twitched as he fought to keep himself from striking Spibey, which other than putting him in the cell next to Zipporah, would serve no good purpose. 'Sir Moreton,' he said softly, 'I think I know who the murderer is.' He still wasn't completely certain, but he needed to deflect Spibey from Zipporah, give him cause to doubt and at least postpone the trial. 'I've not mentioned it before because I wasn't sure, but now, I'm convinced. Master Wellings had every opportunity, and may have a motive for all the killing. Stop this trial now, and allow me to prove it to you.'

Spibey grabbed him by the collar of his shirt and pulled him close, face to face. His breath smelled sour. 'Say one word of that out loud, one word, and I'll go to the gaol and wring the life out of your so-called wife with my own bare hands. Do you hear me?'

'I hear you and every word is as unpleasant – and unlawful – as the last. Give me time to amass evidence. Let me defend Zipporah. I'll overturn every argument you make against her.'

'Let the witch defend herself. By the way, Master Carne, I realise the distress you're in, so I'll ignore for now the insults you've just thrown in my face. Once you've seen the truth and you've been released from your demonic possession, you may feel you want to apologise to me. An apology which will be accepted. That's how I show to you my magnanimity.' He looked towards one of the court attendants. 'Let the people in, we're ready enough.' He turned back to John. 'Best find yourself a seat, it's going to get crowded in here.'

There were gasps when Zipporah was brought into the courtroom, her hands tied before her. In her plain dress and cap she was unremarkable enough, except for her radiant beauty, which did not go without comment.

'She's a fine-looking woman.' John heard one man whisper.

'Mamma, she looks like a nice lady, not nasty,' said a child.

'I wonder how much she charged for a go?' was another, less charitable, aside.

Randall now took a seat next to John and gripped his arm.

Spibey thumped the bench with his fist and demanded silence. 'I ask the accused her name.'

'Zipporah Carne,' she replied clearly.

'Zipporah Carne, have you ever been known by any other name?' continued Spibey.

'Before my marriage I was Zipporah Goodman.'

'Zipporah Carne, formerly Zipporah Goodman, you are charged with the murders of Thomas Perks, Nanna Grey and Molly Kade. You are also accused of being a witch and communing with devils. Do you understand the charges levelled against you?'

'I understand what they mean. What I don't understand is why you make them against me.'

'So you admit you understand witchcraft.'

There was a murmuring from the gallery.

'I know no more of witchcraft than the next person and considerably less than you. If you insist on misinterpreting everything I say, I may as well remain silent.'

'So, now you accuse *me* of witchcraft?' shouted Spibey.

John sighed. The more she talked and revealed her intellect the more she was likely to alienate Spibey. He tried to think. There must be some way out of this. He couldn't let a superstitious bigot win the day and kill his wife.

Zipporah took her own counsel and said no more, though her face conveyed nothing but contempt for the magistrate and his hastily assembled court.

Spibey looked confident. 'A-ha, she's no answer, for she knows I'm no witch. The evidence I have against this woman is great. It goes back many years. I have some spoken testimony and some written. Also proof that the woman used imps and familiars in her diabolical practice of the dark arts.' He looked smugly around the courtroom. 'The first evidence I shall read is from my own daughter, Mistress Margaret Perks, recently safely delivered of a fine son and unable to be here in person. Let me explain to you that some years ago I was persuaded to send my daughter to an academy run by a certain Parson Goodman. One of the tutors was Mistress Zipporah Goodman, the accused. Let me read my daughter's statement.

'"*During my time at the Academy in Nantwich, Mistress Goodman said that she could teach her poultry to read and write better than me.*

299

Although at the time I was too young to realise what she meant, now I understand that the hens were her familiars and she talked to them and they talked back to her."'

John couldn't stop himself jumping to his feet. 'That's not what was meant at all, and you know it, Sir Moreton.' Randall tried to pull him back down.

'You're not allowed to speak, unless called, Master Carne. But what other interpretation could be inferred?'

John knew full well that Zipporah had been exasperated by Margaret Spibey's disinclination to learn, though he couldn't say so to the magistrate, so he sat down and sent an apologetic look towards his wife. Her mouth curled slightly; she understood.

'There's one thing that should be explained at this point,' said Spibey. 'Only one person is on trial here, Mistress Carne. Master John Carne, though allegedly her husband, has been bewitched and anything he says in her defence will be discounted. After this trial it is hoped that the demons who possess him will release him from his bewitchment.'

'So, you've made your mind up already,' said John, loudly enough for everyone to hear, even though his wife was gently shaking her head at him. 'But this trial has no validity. Sir Moreton is abusing his position. This isn't a proper session of the assizes; there's no Clerk of the Peace present; no charges have been formally made; no real examination of the evidence has taken place—'

'I think I've proved my point concerning the bewitchment of Master Carne.' Spibey was nodding and wagging his finger vigorously. He seemed to be relishing the proceedings. He was clearly proud of himself. 'The second witness I shall call is Sergeant David Lloyd, from the godly troops garrisoned here. Come forward, sir.'

John recognised Colonel Mytton's sergeant, who stepped forward hesitantly.

Spibey gave his most encouraging smile. It made John feel sick.

'Come now, Sergeant, give us your testimony.'

Lloyd coughed. 'I'd rather not, sir. It's a trifle and I think nothing was meant by it. We all love Captain Carne and have the greatest respect for Mistress Carne, especially after the way she fought for this town.' There were a few murmurs of approval from the crowd when he said that.

Spibey leaned forward across the bench. 'Sergeant Lloyd, you must leave your personal feelings behind. The forces of evil manipulate our emotions so that we see good where there is evil, and evil where there is good. Repeat what you overheard.'

'It was nothing, just a turn of phrase.'

'Tell the court, or you'll be in contempt, and suspected of being in league with the devil yourself.'

Lloyd sighed. 'It was simply that I overheard Colonel Mytton say to Captain Carne that Cornet Benbow had told him that Mistress Carne turned a simple pigeon into a banquet. Then Colonel Mytton said he thought she had enchanted Cornet Benbow, too. But it was said in jest, the Colonel didn't think Mistress Carne a witch, any more than any of us think she is.'

'I'll be the judge of who thinks what,' snapped Spibey. 'The enchanted Cornet Benbow, where is he, can he be brought to give evidence?'

'He's on patrol, a long patrol,' said Lloyd.

'Pity,' said Spibey. 'You may stand down, Lloyd. Now I call our own sergeant from Wem gaol.'

The prison sergeant took Lloyd's place. He was eager to testify and started talking without any prompting. 'We had for a time a certain Baccy Blanchard in detention, on suspicion of witchcraft—'

Spibey held up his hands. 'Stop there, Sergeant, say no more for the moment. I have to confess that I too have been tempted by evil, hard to imagine, I know. Now, I believe the accused, Zipporah Carne, made me believe that a harmless woman from Hornspike, a respectable, good wife, Rebecca Blanchard, was a witch. I state now, here in open court, that no such suspicion

301

should ever have fallen upon the delightful woman, Mistress Blanchard.'

John saw that Sam Blanchard was in court and was nodding towards Spibey. John squinted his eyes. Something had been arranged between Blanchard and the magistrate, what else could explain Spibey's sudden change of heart concerning Baccy?

'So, Sergeant, tell us what you overheard, but ignore anything to do with Mistress Blanchard as that is irrelevant.'

'Very well, Sir Moreton. I overheard Master Carne say to the person you have just told me not to mention that he'd seen his wife kiss the devil's arse.'

A murmur of disapproval rippled around the courtroom.

Zipporah shot John a glance, he could only put his head in his hands. He remembered, when beside himself with frustration and rage, making some fatuous comment which he now utterly regretted.

'Did you make such a statement, Master Carne?' asked Spibey.

John shook his head. 'It wasn't meant that way.'

Spibey turned to Zipporah. 'How often have you kissed Satan's arse, madam?'

'Never.'

'See how lies spill so easily from the witch's tongue.'

'I've seen her kiss the devil's arse!' A man at the back of the room leapt to his feet. John thought he'd seen him working in Spibey's stable.

The magistrate looked triumphant. 'Have you indeed?'

'Yes, sir. When you had the monstrous bodies from the Moss in your cellar, she went to look at them. They were devils, sir, everyone knew that. I saw her bend down and look at the devil's … er, well, his member. She held a lantern, sir, so she could see it and then she kissed it.'

The whole courtroom gasped as if as one.

Damn, damn, damn, thought John. They'd heard a noise that evening, they should have realised they'd been observed.

Spibey looked ever more gleeful. 'Even I wasn't aware of that,' he exclaimed. 'Though it doesn't surprise me.' He stared at Zipporah. 'The creature is even more depraved than I thought.' He paused, as if to compose himself. 'The next testimony is from a most respected member of our community, Farmer Laycock. He told me himself that Mistress Carne was a woman possessed and that she transformed her pitchfork into a magical trident. Men fell at her feet due to spells she wove.'

Laycock jumped to his feet. 'That's not what I said. That's not what I meant.'

Spibey held up his Bible. 'Oh, that is indeed what you said to me, Master Laycock. And I have testimony of my own. While Master Carne and his so-called wife were guarding two cats, suspected of being witches' familiars, I asked Master Carne if they'd changed appearance overnight. He answered, "They have not, but I think my wife wishes they had." You see, even to me he admitted his wife was a witch, though I didn't realise it at the time. Perhaps if I had, people who are now dead would still be alive.'

'And what single reason, or evidence have you got that Zipporah killed, or even knew Master Perks or Nanna Grey?' shouted John.

'You omit to say that your wife knew Molly Kade, the midwife, and had, before witnesses, attacked and threatened to kill her. The poor girl was found hanging from the apple tree in your own garden. Now, Mistress Kade told me herself, that only a few months ago she had delivered Mistress Carne of two monstrous babes, mercifully dead. Satan's babes, she called them, as they could only be got by carnal relations with the devil.'

John finally pulled free of Randall's grip and rushed to the bench. 'You're manipulating the truth, Sir Moreton. My wife was raped; the children were the spawn of royalist degenerates who've no idea how to treat a good and godly woman.'

'John, please, don't broadcast my shame,' cried Zipporah.

'At least the witch knows shame,' said Spibey. 'Sit down, Master Carne, can you not yet see the lies the witch has woven about you?'

'I only hear the lies you spout.'

'One more outburst and you'll be removed from this courtroom.'

John went back to his seat, but walked close to Zipporah as he did so. 'I will save you,' he whispered.

'I'm lost, and you know it.'

'I have two further statements which will convince you all of the defendant's guilt. The first is a letter I found at the back of a fireplace at Whixall Grange, home of the late, murdered Thomas Perks. It must have been thrown there by Master Carne, hoping to burn it, but the good Lord preserved it from the flames so it could be used as evidence.'

Damn my bad aim, thought John.

Spibey continued. 'The letter is from Richard Carne, brother to John Carne. In this letter he pleads with his brother to leave his wife. He states it is no true marriage and at one point he says "Tis a pity you were bewitched by that whore". Again, evidence that Master Carne has been held in thrall by a witch. The last written statement is also from Richard Carne. I know he fights with the enemy but I believe his concern for his brother overrides his unfortunate choice of faction to follow. I shall read the statement in its entirety.

'"*Sir Moreton, I write this by candlelight, courtesy of some good cottagers on the road to Shrewsbury. I shall endeavour to pass this to a member of the garrison for delivery to you.*"'

Spibey looked up. 'Which is exactly what happened, I received the letter early this morning, I will continue.

'"*Tonight my beloved brother, John, took me from the safety of Wem, beat me and left me alone on the road, outside the gates of the town. This is quite unlike the normal behaviour of John, who has ever been honest and honourable. He made some mad accusations towards me, and I believe he is a man possessed. I advised him not to marry the woman, Zipporah Goodman, already known to be a whore at the time of the marriage. Now I believe her to be a witch. Indeed I heard her call herself an evil woman with my own ears. John has kept her close inside The Dial, hoping to keep her from view, but I know the truth. Mistress Carne has two wooden dolls, she speaks to these dolls, she dresses them and calls them George and Arabella. They are her imps. You will find them in a cot at The Dial."'*

There was a hubbub about the courtroom. John stood up again, but Zipporah motioned him to sit down, though his blood boiled so high he thought he would be sure to explode.

'We searched The Dial but the only incriminating evidence we found was Mistress Carne's stained nightgown, no doubt bloodied during the killing of Molly Kade. The puppets mentioned by Richard Carne were not discovered there, though.' Spibey's head nodded knowledgably as he paused for effect. 'Yesterday Reverend Parsons thought he saw some disturbance to the grave of Thomas Perks. As he felt in the soil he found these.' Spibey reached under his bench and brought out a mud-covered George and Arabella. John sat transfixed. How had they got into Perks's grave?

'Are these your imps, Mistress Carne?'

Zipporah shook her head, as tears coursed down her face.

'Are they yours?'

She shook her head again.

'Were they yours?'

She nodded.

'Did you bury them in Master Perks's grave?'

She nodded, her shoulders shaking with her sobs. She tried to rub her eyes, but it was difficult and clumsy with her hands bound before her.

'For pity's sake untie her,' called John.

Spibey ignored him. 'Why did you bury them?'

'I just wanted my children to go to heaven.' She choked, then swallowed hard and sniffed loudly. 'I wanted them to lie in hallowed ground.' She could say no more.

John lurched to the front of the court, Randall stumbling behind him, hanging onto his coat. 'Sir Moreton, I beg you, listen to me. My wife was ill after her babies died; she nearly died of sorrow. She's better now, but don't judge her because she was overcome by grief. Everything we've heard is hearsay, and the testimony from my brother must be discounted because he bears me a personal grudge and desires my destruction.' He turned to the court. 'Please, good people of Wem, use your common sense. This is no witch before you but a decent woman brought low because of the desperate state of affairs this country has fallen into. Zipporah Carne stands accused, but it could be your wife, your daughter, your mother, your sister likewise under suspicion. My wife has done nothing wrong. This is not justice; this is vile prejudice, based on nothing but superstition.'

What started as a gentle murmur became louder as the people in the courtroom took sides and began to shout at each other.

Spibey had to bang his fists on his bench several times before order was brought to the assembly.

'Silence, silence. I order it! Very well, despite all the evidence put before you it seems that some of you remain to be convinced. There is something that will prove this woman a witch once and for all. This court will convene at the bridge by the millpond at daybreak tomorrow. We'll swim her there. The verdict tomorrow will be incontestable, as it will come from God.' He stood up, bowed, and left the courtroom.

Chapter Twenty-Five

J ohn felt someone tugging at the sleeve of his jacket as they
left the courthouse.

It was Sam Blanchard. 'Stupid, provincial, superstitious
nonsense,' he said. 'Let me get you a drink.'

'Thank you, but no,' said John, 'I need to speak to my wife.'
Then he paused. 'I wouldn't mind knowing how you got Spibey
to stop persecuting Baccy, though.'

'It seems that he found an easier target for his accusations. As
in a fine-looking woman, like your Zipporah, if you catch my
meaning. I'm surprised he hasn't thoroughly searched her for
marks of the devil, just to get a good look at her comely body.
Perhaps he has.'

Since John had followed Blanchard to the door of the Lion, he
thought he might as well go in.

'I'm sure he hasn't, for which small mercy I'm grateful. He's
been so keen to get Zipporah tried, he hasn't followed the correct
legal requirements. And despite what he says, he's squeamish and
I doubt salaciousness is one of his vices.'

'Add that to my tally,' said Blanchard to the landlord, who'd
filled two tankards without being asked. 'I'm staying here now,'

he explained. 'Until such time as I can join up with some troops travelling to London. I wish I could persuade Becky to come with me, but she insists on staying in Shropshire. Lord knows why. It's a mad, benighted county, always has been.'

John sipped his drink and frowned. 'I don't think I understand your relationship with Mistress Blanchard at all, not that it's any of my business. I got the impression that you'd left her for another.'

Blanchard smiled. 'I'm very fond of her, even though the true love of my life is my man. Notwithstanding that, I'd set up Becky nicely with her own home in London, as I have done at Hornspike. There's still love between us.'

John was left no wiser. 'I take it you've met Sir Moreton.'

'The first time I saw him was in the courtroom today.'

'Sir Moreton swore he'd not met you either, and yet, somehow, someone has managed to persuade him that Baccy isn't a witch.'

'I'm sure he still considers her a witch, but I left a message for him saying if he arrested, or in any way harried her again, I'd create a stink for him throughout this county. I'm wealthy and not without influence.'

John sighed. 'Spibey's a bully and won't stand against someone he thinks might best him. I don't suppose you'd make the same threat to him concerning Zipporah?'

'No, sorry. She may well be guilty for all I know.'

Johns stared hard at him. 'I take exception to that, Master Blanchard. You've seen Zipporah; you've met her. She's no witch. You'd have to be one of those whipped up fools from the mob to think she was.' John drained his tankard and slammed it down. 'Maybe you *are* just one of the idiots who's fallen for Spibey's baseless lies. So, if you won't help me, I'll have to think of some way to stop him myself.'

'You'll find it difficult. As far as I can see you've little wealth and no influence. As Spibey has made such a show of this trial, he'll want to see it through, even if you hang with her.'

'Well, you're a comfort to a man, Master Blanchard.'

'No point giving you false hope. Whatever his reasons, Spibey wants your wife dead. Find out why he's chosen her, and maybe you'll find how to stop him. I'd understand it all the better if it was the other way round. A man seeing the beauty and spirit of Mistress Carné might well want to be rid of her husband, to claim her for himself. Now, if *you* were on trial everything would make perfect sense.'

John buttoned his coat in preparation for the cold outside. 'I've stayed too long, I must visit my wife.'

Zipporah was gripping the bars of the door to her cell. 'I didn't think you'd come,' she said.

John motioned to the gaoler to let him inside, but the man remained at his station. 'Please, open the door,' said John.

The sergeant shook his head. 'No one's to go in or out, on the express order of Sir Moreton.'

'How much do you want?'

'I daren't disobey the magistrate. Not for all the gold in the world.'

John turned back to his wife. 'I'm trying to sort something out. I'll get you out of here.'

She shook her head. 'You won't.'

'Don't give up hope. You shouldn't have buried the children, though.'

'You shouldn't have told Baccy Blanchard you saw me kissing the devil's backside. Why did you say that?'

He rubbed his eyes, which were sore with the cold. 'I was angry, with Baccy and with you. I can't even remember exactly what I said. It was something such as, if you and Baccy didn't co-operate with me, I'd report you both to Spibey. It was a stupid remark, and I wish I hadn't said it. Now, would you care to explain why you put the dolls in Tom Perks's grave?'

She leaned against the bars and let out a long juddering sigh. 'I didn't want to destroy them. When they were real to me, they *were* real. I thought of my poor children cold and alone on the Moss and, yes, it was a silly thought, but it came to me that if I buried them properly it might make God look more favourably on my real babies. So I pushed them under the soft earth covering Perks's grave. I must have still been mad to do such a thing.'

'Hmm, I suppose I sort of understand.'

'How did your brother know about the dolls?'

John shrugged. 'I found him on the landing when he stayed on his way to Whitchurch. I didn't think anything of it at the time, now I can only presume he'd been in the nursery. As far as Dick's concerned, I held a viper to my bosom without knowing it.'

'I'm sorry. Yet my brother is no better. I'm only surprised he didn't testify against me himself.'

'We both have rotten siblings. What I need to do is persuade Sir Moreton that if he swims you tomorrow *he* could end up being guilty of murder.' He wiped his eyes again, which wouldn't stop watering. 'I cannot, I will not let this happen. I can't live without you, Zipporah.' He reached through the bars and ran his finger across her cheek.

She jerked away from him. 'Have you ever considered this is God's will?'

'No.' He scrubbed his hands across his eyes yet again. Salty tears were irritating the sore skin around them. 'I cannot— I refuse to think like that.' His scabbed knuckles were white as he clutched the bars. 'Gaoler,' he called over his shoulder, 'I plead with you, show some Christian charity, let me hold my wife.'

The sergeant looked away. 'I cannot, Sir Moreton has the keys.'

John reached through the bars. 'Come to me, Zipporah, my love.'

She shook her head. 'I'll keep my distance and not make things harder for you.'

'You're afraid, I can see it in your eyes. Let me hold you.'

'Go, John, you'll make me weep, and I want to be strong.'

'Why do you always have to be strong?'

'So I don't succumb to you, and drag you down to hell with me.'

'If anyone's going to hell it's Randall for poisoning your mind against yourself.' Then he stood in silence, memorising every detail of her face and body, unable to comprehend that soon she might be no more.

She looked up sharply. 'I've just thought of something.' She came close to the bars now, and though she resisted she couldn't stop him wrapping his arms around her neck.

'Be careful,' she whispered. 'Remember my suspicions. Molly Kade may have been strung up in our garden to implicate me, but she was killed for other reasons.'

'I don't care about the murders anymore, let me kiss you.'

'You should care about the murders. They're everything, I'm sure. Think, John, think. This is all about Margaret and her child. Perks must have known the child wasn't his; he's dead. Nanna knew the child wasn't Perks's; she's dead. Molly Kade would have realised the child she delivered was at least conceived before the marriage to Perks. Likewise, dead. Everything, *everything* is to ensure that Margaret maintains her reputation and the child is heir to Whixall. And who gains from that? Why, Margaret herself.'

John brightened slightly. 'Sam Blanchard said that if I could discover why Spibey wants you dead, then I might find a reason to make him stop this madness.'

She shook her head. 'I don't think Spibey particularly wants *me* dead. He wants a witch, to prove all his silly theories about devil worship and such like. Your brother gave him the evidence; my brother denounced me, and the dolls gave even more credence to their allegations.'

He rubbed his hand over his rough unshaven chin. 'Maybe. I'm going to see Spibey now. Keep hopeful.' And, as she was close and he was quick, he managed a clumsy kiss, though it fell on the end of her nose.

'But you take a care, John. I know you don't believe it, but Spibey may be the killer himself. Margaret is his daughter, and he'd want to protect her name and her inheritance. And you know my suspicions concerning Wellings.'

Crowther didn't know where to look. 'I'm so sorry, Master Carne. Sorry about everything. Sir Moreton says he'll not see you until tomorrow, after the swimming.'

'That's not good enough. Tell him if he won't speak to me now, I'll blacken his name throughout the county and beyond.'

Crowther nodded, turned and climbed the staircase, leaving John waiting in the doorway. When he returned he was unable to look John in the eye. 'Sir Moreton says he must pray. He says you can tell anyone anything you like, but as you know nothing, there's nothing to tell. And you are bewitched, so no one will believe you anyway.' He paused, wringing his hands in front of him, before, at last, looking at John. 'I am so sorry, so very sorry, Master Carne. How is your wife? Can I send anything to her, quietly, you know?'

'Keys would be good,' snapped John. 'I'm sorry, Crowther. This isn't your fault.'

'Sir Moreton has the keys to the gaol on his person at all times. If I could take them from him, I would.'

'Oh, you good fellow! I know you would,' John turned away, full of emotion. How was it that one sour bigoted man could hold the whole town in his thrall? Then he turned back, pushed past Crowther and hauled himself ungainly up the stairs.

The door to Spibey's private chamber was locked. He

hammered on it with his stick. 'Come out, Spibey, meet me man to man. I'll spend all night here and hack your door down bit by bit if you don't open it.'

'Go away, John.' He heard Randall's voice. 'You do no good.'

'*You* do no good, Randall. Send Spibey out now.'

He heard Spibey's muffled refusal.

'What do you say, Spibey, speak up!' he shouted.

'I'm not coming, John,' called Spibey. 'And it'll take you more than a night to hack through that oak. Pray, John, pray. Pray the Lord will make you see the light.'

'I'll pray all right, Spibey. I pray that you rot in hell. I pray that you never see light again, that demons rip your organs from you and constantly eat them before your eyes, and while you endure this torture you see in front of you the face of my Zipporah, the woman you're about to wrong and murder.'

'But see, Moreton,' he heard Randall say. 'Keep firm, he admits the witch is destined for hell.'

John continued to bash impotently against the door until his stick cracked. Then he stopped, fighting to control his breathing and emotions. Zipporah was alive; there was still hope.

'Promise me one thing, Spibey,' he called through the door. 'Make it a fair swimming. Don't use a rope so tight that Zipporah can only float. She must be allowed to sink, if that's God's will.'

He heard mumbling.

'John.' It was Spibey. 'Never accuse me of being unjust. I'll swim the witch fairly. Will you accept the result?'

'I believe you'll use no trickery in the swimming.'

'Master Carne, Master Carne!' It was Wellings, standing behind him.

John swivelled round.

Wellings spoke quietly. 'Master Carne, Margaret asks that you keep your voice down, you're disturbing little Thomas.'

'Ah, the indispensable Master Wellings.' John narrowed his eyes. 'You're everywhere these days, aren't you?'

Wellings indicated the stairs. 'Shall I see you out, sir?'

'You don't ask after Mistress Carne?'

Wellings expression was blank. 'I think we're all shocked by the revelations.'

'Oh, indeed we are. Shocked by the shameless way your beloved employer is destroying an honest woman, simply for his own gratification.'

'We know Sir Moreton is determined to vanquish evil wherever he finds it.'

'Then you'd best examine your own soul, Isaac, lest you're found wanting, too.' John stared hard at the man but his expression was bland.

'I demand you go now, sir. Margaret and the child need rest and quiet.'

John narrowed his eyes. This was a new side to Wellings. There was no pleasantness to him now.

'I'll see myself out. Remember what I said. Examine your own soul. If Zipporah dies it will be in every way a murder as foul as Perks's, Nanna's and Molly's. If you know more than you're saying about recent events, you should say so.'

Wellings remained impassive. John decided to press him. 'You may have been the last person to see Molly Kade alive.'

Wellings continued to stare straight ahead. 'You should go.'

'I can't really see the point of killing Molly. As long as you paid her a little more, that would have been enough. She'd have returned to Whitchurch happy and said no more.'

Did John detect a slight flash of anger, quickly controlled? 'I don't know what you insinuate, sir.' There was a great wail from the child. Wellings gripped John's arm. 'See, you've disturbed the baby. He's born before time and delicate.' He pushed John towards the stairs and once at the bottom opened the door. 'Sir Moreton has been lenient with you, Master Carne. That might not always be so. I see you have no walking stick, tread carefully, sir.'

Johns stepped out and the door was immediately slammed behind him.

The gaoler was even more reluctant to let John see Zipporah. He eventually relented, but said he would allow John only the shortest time.

'It's him. Wellings,' said John under his breath. 'I've just seen another side to him. It's all about the baby, I'm sure. We already know Perks had to be silenced because of what he knew, Nanna likewise. Molly Kade we suspect was taking money from Spibey to keep silence that the baby was full term. But why kill her?'

'In case she asked for more?'

John shook his head vehemently. 'I think Wellings didn't like what she said. It angered him. After all, if the child was conceived before Margaret arrived at Whixall, which we're sure it was, then the child is no more his than Perks's. He must maintain the myth that the child is early, even to himself.'

'So what are you going to do?'

'Spibey won't speak to me. And even if he did, and I told him who the murderer was, it won't help you.'

'We still don't know how involved Spibey is,' she said.

John reached through the bars. 'Come to me, my love.'

She did and allowed him to wrap his arms around her as much as he could. 'How can you be so calm?'

'I'm resigned. Nothing can save me.'

He stared at her beautiful, frightened face. 'I've not given up. I won't desert you.'

The gaoler slapped his hand on John's shoulder. 'Time to go.'

He didn't return immediately to The Dial. He trudged the streets for a while, thoughts and emotions tumbling around inside his head. He'd walked so mindlessly he found himself back in Noble Street, surprised he'd managed to go so far without his stick. He had to stop this aimless rambling and work out a way to rescue Zipporah. He went to the rear of Spibey's house and onto one of Laycock's fields. The flock of sheep wandered out of his way, except for a runty lamb who couldn't keep up. John caught it and slit its throat with his knife.

John had lost track of time, pacing up and down the room as he thought through the plan to save his wife. The door opened and Benbow came in on a blast of cold air. He went straight over to the fire and threw a log onto it. 'Mistress Carne hasn't been away a day yet and you're letting her fire die.'

John shrugged. 'I've more important things to concern me than the fire. Anyway, I thought you were out on a long patrol.'

'It was short in the end.' Benbow poured them both a mug of ale. 'I've spoken to Colonel Mytton by the way. He knows what's happening is wrong, but says he hasn't the jurisdiction to intervene.'

'That's true.'

'So, what's the plan then, Captain?'

John looked at him.

'Come on, Captain, I can't believe you haven't thought of a way to rescue Zipporah, Mistress Carne I mean.'

John sat at the table and rubbed his hands across his face. 'It's little more than an idea, and not a very good one. Spibey holds all the cards at the moment. What plan I have is quite mad.'

Benbow sat next to him. 'Good, we're dealing with lunatics, aren't we? Let's talk about it, shall we? I'm here to help in any way I can. Is that blood on your shirt?'

'Yes, I sacrificed a lamb.'

Benbow frowned. 'I see,' he said cautiously. 'Was this sacrifice to any god in particular?'

John smiled. 'No. I want to give Spibey something to think about. Now, while there's still some light, we must go to the river.'

It was just dawn. John saw a small crowd had gathered by the bridge across the river Roden, just before it spread out to form the mill pond. It was the only place where the water was deep enough to attempt any witch swimming. He saw the procession coming down Mill Street and gasped in revulsion. As a final act of humiliation Spibey must have ordered Zipporah to remove her dress, so she was left shivering in only her petticoat and corset. He was likewise chilled to the bone, since he wore neither hat nor cloak, both would be a hindrance to the execution of his plan.

She would think even he had deserted her. He looked on for as long as he dared. Then he turned away, not needing to see any more. He knew how it would end. He scuttled into the undergrowth.

He crawled away from the bridge and only when he knew he couldn't be seen let himself into the icy river and dipped under the surface, gritting his teeth as cold fingers of water crept inside his clothes. The ale-coloured liquid rendered everything about him into muzzy shapes, then a shadow above him told him he was under the bridge. Feeling along the bank his fingers clasped the rope he left there the day before and he pulled himself slowly up, using all his willpower not to gasp loudly as air flew into his chest. Not that anyone would have heard, such was the commotion from above. He pushed himself into the hollow between the side pillars of the bridge. From there he could just make out some people on the bank. The noise subsided. Zipporah must have arrived. Such was the bitterness of the day he knew she would be trembling uncontrollably from both cold and fear. He'd seen that her hands were tied behind her back and Spibey himself must have dragged her along the path to the bridge.

He heard Randall's voice, distorted by the echoes under the bridge. He was reading from Scripture. How John hated that man!

'If I die, you'll be a murderer,' Zipporah was shouting, presumably at Spibey. 'How will that sit on your godly conscience? And will you be quiet!' She must be screaming that at Randall.

John grinned bleakly. How she kept her spirit.

'See how the witch refuses the word of God,' he heard Randall say piously.

'I don't refuse the word of God. I refuse to hear it from you.'

Was it possible to love her more? She couldn't die. He wouldn't allow it.

She wasn't going to give up without a fight. 'Murder, Sir Moreton, premeditated murder, that's what you're committing. That's the sin you'll have to repent. But you won't need to repent if you stop it right now. Let me free. I'm going to hell if you kill me, and I'll be waiting for you there.'

'Murder is the killing of another human being. You may have the appearance of a woman, but you're all demon.' Was Spibey's voice trembling? Did John detect doubt? Was there a hope he might, at the last minute, change his mind?

'Then swim my brother, too, for we came from the same womb.'

If only we could just swim him, thought John.

'Shall I gag her, Moreton?' said Randall.

'Why, to stop me telling the truth?'

There was a short pause, what were they doing? His heart pounded and he felt sweat trickle down his back, despite the cold.

They hadn't gagged her for Zipporah spoke again. 'Why is it you want me dead, Sir Moreton? How, in any way, can I harm you? What threat do I pose? None. You know I'm no witch, yet you persist in this farce of so-called justice. To what end? Think of your own soul. Is killing an innocent woman marking you out as one of the elect, or one of the damned?'

John heard Spibey's voice but it was too muffled to catch the exact words.

'Self-righteous and self-deluded,' Zipporah spat.

How true, thought John. Once again he didn't hear Spibey's reply.

'What other crimes have you committed?' said Zipporah.

What had he said to her? Then he heard Spibey clearly. 'Gag her, gag her. Bind her feet, quickly, get this done.'

Lord, dear lord, help me, give me strength, prayed John as he slithered down the rope.

'Swim her, swim her. Swim the witch' was the last he heard before he put a thick reed between his lips and slipped under the water.

Chapter Twenty-Six

John tried to breathe through his reed, but could only manage shallow gasps. The noises above him were muffled now. He daren't move from under the bridge and risk being spotted.

Then there was a large splash, just a few feet away, as Zipporah plunged into the water. He had to move quickly. He'd gutted Laycock's lamb and tied stones to its feet, so it wouldn't float. He could make out the shape of his wife's body twisting frantically. She became even more agitated as he caught hold of her. Then she must have seen his face and allowed him to pull her under the bridge. He struggled with the gag. His hands were cold, sore from the cuts on his knuckles and swollen from immersion. He sucked in a long breath, took the reed from his mouth and tried to blow air into her nose. He had to get the sheep attached. It wouldn't be enough simply to free Zipporah from the end of the rope; he needed to frighten Spibey.

He returned the reed to his mouth and choked as he breathed again. The reed had been submerged and his mouth was now full of sour river water. He cut the rope from her and tied it to the lamb. Now he pulled Zipporah upstream and round the bend where the river split and ran along both sides of the mill. He blew more air into her, but she was frighteningly limp; there was no more struggle in her. Pulling against the flow, keeping close to the riverbed, he struggled on for what seemed an endless time, until at last he saw the marker he had left to show him he was out of sight from the bridge and it was safe to emerge from the water.

He tried not to grunt too loudly as he hauled her onto the bank. At last he could rip the gag from her colourless, motionless face.

'No,' he mouthed angrily. 'No, don't die, don't die.' He squeezed her tight in his arms. She was floppy as a rag doll, cold as ice and showed no signs of stirring or warming up. He rubbed her hands between his. 'Awake, awake,' he whispered urgently in her ear. Then he picked her up, held her shoulders and shook her, she twisted in his arms and a torrent of peaty water gushed from her mouth. A tremor convulsed through her, followed by a fearful gurgle, then she fell limp again. He shook her once more, another gout of water flowed, there was more choking, then a great shudder ran through her body, followed by a loud whistle as she sucked air into her lungs. He held her close as she coughed and gagged on his chest, but already her pale lips were becoming pinker and a slight blush was apparent on her cheeks. Eventually her eyes opened, she saw him and wrapped her arms around him.

'You are alive, my love,' he whispered.

She pushed her face close to his. 'I knew such peace, John, such warmth, such love. I dared to think I was in the arms of the Lord.' Her voice was hoarse.

'For a while you were, then I had the temerity to take over. Can you stand?'

She staggered upright, and began to shiver. He held her as tightly as he could. 'I didn't think Spibey so inhuman he'd strip you—' His mouth was on hers and for the first time they kissed as deeply as two lovers should.

John flinched as he felt a light tap on his shoulder.

'Captain, sweet as that must be, we should be away,' said Benbow softly.

Benbow was right and he reluctantly relinquished his wife, whom Benbow was already covering with a capacious lined woollen cloak.

'What's happened at the bridge, Jack?' said John.

'The lamb was an idea of genius. When it came out Spibey looked as if he was about to have a seizure. If your brother-in-law has a hair left on his head tomorrow I'll be surprised, such was his tugging of it. So, as we hoped, there is much confusion. We must go.'

Zipporah looked quizzically at both men.

'Jack will explain,' said John. 'He's taking you to Baccy's; you'll be safe there.'

'How can I be?'

'Mistress,' implored Benbow. 'We must get away and the captain must be back at The Dial, as that's the first place they'll look for you. Will you be all right behind me, on the horse?'

'Of course, I can ride astride as well as any man.'

'She's most precious to me, Jack, guard her well,' said John, holding the horse's bridle as Benbow mounted.

'You can take that for granted, Captain.'

With a hollow cough she allowed Benbow to pull her up behind him. She bent down to John. 'Our enemies are close to home,' she warned him. 'Before he pushed me, Spibey said what he'd done, he'd done for love. Is he the killer? Perhaps I was wrong about Wellings.'

'Spibey is the key, leave him to me. I'll come for you as soon as it's safe.'

'I'd rather be with you now, whatever the danger.'

John smacked the rump of Benbow's charger, and it cantered off. He plunged back into the river, easily swam across and returned to The Dial via the back alleys.

He waited longer than he thought he'd have to for the eventual noisy and unwelcome guests.

'Carne, John Carne,' bellowed Spibey.

John heard heavy boots on the stairs before the bedroom door was thrown open. John poked his head above the bedcovers. The time he'd spent in the freezing river meant he didn't have to try too hard to feign illness; his eyes were red rimmed and he had a sick grey pallor to his skin.

'What ails you?' boomed Spibey. Randall's hard-featured, wild-eyed face peered over the magistrate's shoulder.

'I'm ill. Is she drowned?' John sniffed loudly.

Randall dragged back the covers. John was in his nightshirt and he pulled the blankets back up. 'I'm freezing. What have you done with her? May I bury her properly?'

'She's gone,' said Randall.

John turned away from them.

'No, she's gone, Master Carne,' said Spibey. 'She was replaced by a lamb, by magic or design I've yet to discover. We must search this house and the outbuildings. Have you brought her here?'

'Look at me, I can do nothing. Leave me to my grief. Come back when you make more sense. Just let me know where her body is.'

Spibey gripped John's shoulder and turned him over to face them. 'Stop this charade. I know you, Master Carne, with your clever ways. You're sure to have tried something.'

'I did. I tried to reason with you and I failed. Leave me.'

'He may be speaking the truth. Perhaps the enchantment has left him,' said Randall.

'Enchantment?' said Spibey.

'Isn't that what we hoped?' said Randall. 'That he'd be freed from the witch's hold over him?'

'Oh, yes, *that* enchantment. Yes, of course, that might well be the case. I'll send Wellings over later to see how he is.' Suddenly Spibey's breath became ragged. He gripped the front of Randall's jacket. 'What if she wasn't a witch! You fool! What have you made me do? Has God deserted me?' He sped from the room, Randall clattering down the stairs after him.

John remained motionless as he listened to them leave. What happened? Had Spibey suddenly seen sense? That, he could hardly believe. Would Spibey still send Wellings to see him? Given Zipporah's suspicions over Wellings, he wasn't too happy at the thought of him being around. He got out of bed and put on clean clothes, retrieving his wet shirt and breeches from under the bed and hanging them in the nursery to dry. Downstairs the fire had all but died, though the log that Benbow had thrown on the night before still glowed, albeit dully. He added some kindling to it and some smaller woods, and began to coax it back to life. By now his wife should be safe with Baccy, as long as Mistress Blanchard accepted her. Benbow would see to it that she did.

Much as he wanted to go to Noble Street and beat the bone and guts out of Spibey, he knew he had to remain rational. He had to find out who was really responsible for the murders, prove it, and clear Zipporah's name.

He selected a pipe, and as he packed tobacco into the bowl, saw the papers Zipporah had used to try and solve the murders tucked underneath the rack. He pulled them out, lit his pipe and studied them. He thought about what Spibey had said to her, and her suspicion that he'd killed before. That was the hardest thing to believe. Much as he hated Spibey, he thought the magistrate acted as he did because he was an ill-informed bigot, happy to sacrifice an innocent person to further his career as a self-styled witchfinder. But Spibey had said he'd done what he'd done for love. What had he meant by that? He was speaking to someone he believed would soon be dead and would never repeat his words. Was that the chink in Spibey's armour that he had been seeking? Had he said something that would give him away?

He jumped as the door opened. Sam Blanchard sauntered in carrying a flagon of wine. 'Master Carne, I have to say I like your style,' he said, planting the vessel on the table and retrieving a couple of mugs from the sideboard.

John shook his head. 'It's nowhere near midday, far too early for me.'

Blanchard shrugged and filled his own mug to the brim. 'It had everything, suspense, drama, even a little comedy. And so perfectly tailored to befuddle the weak-minded, gullible Spibey and that proud pompous Randall Goodman.' He raised his mug. 'I salute you, Master Carne, a truly marvellous morning of entertainment.'

'I don't recall inviting you in,' said John. 'I'd be grateful if you left. My wife died today and all people will do is talk to me in riddles.'

'Oh, you're good,' said Blanchard. 'Have you ever appeared on the stage?' He leaned forward. 'Now *you* stop talking in riddles. If you're only half the man I think you are, you'll have sent the delicious Mistress Carne to the safest place I know: the home of my wife.'

'And why would that be safe? Now Sir Moreton's bagged himself one witch, who's to say he won't get a taste for it? He may have promised you he'll leave her alone but I wouldn't trust him.'

'How you keep your part, sir, but it's time to drop the act. While I'm around Becky is safe. Once I'm gone, well, she refuses my protection, but I still doubt he'll act against her, for I'd find out eventually and make good my threats. I could still ruin what he loves most.'

John stopped mid-draw on his pipe and coughed slightly as the smoke swirled around his mouth. 'What Sir Moreton loves most.'

Blanchard nodded.

'What does Spibey love most? God? He'd like us to think that. He loves himself and that's a fact.' John was thinking aloud more than talking to Blanchard. For some reason, his mind went back to the morning after the battle for the town, when Spibey was boasting of his new grandchild. The child that could not have been Perks's. 'Family's so important.' That's what he said. 'I'm so stupid,' said John. 'She's been there all the time, not the thing, but the person Spibey loves most. Not his soul, but his immortality.' He looked at Blanchard. 'I know London is a big place, but I believe you met Mistress Perks when she was there.'

Blanchard raised an eyebrow. 'London's large, as you say. And it's a godly town, but for those who enjoy the pleasures of the flesh, well, if you know the right places...'

'And though the love of your life is a man, you also take your pleasures elsewhere.'

'I prefer men – I prefer *my* man – but I can't help myself when I'm offered pleasure. My wife one night, those beautiful chubby whores at the Lion another, a lonely soldier, a magistrate's daughter... There's so little joy in the world these days, if two people make each other happy, if only briefly, how can that be bad?'

'And yet you consider yourself a godly man,' said John.

'So I am. If you accuse me of perversion or fornication, I'd have to confess, but Popery is the greater sin. The greatest sin. The bowing to idols, the belief in the magic of their cannibalistic Eucharist. That sticks in my gullet. Not to mention the thought of those ridiculous brocaded cardinals having some say in the running of this great country. The Old Queen would spin in her grave if she thought the Armada had been beaten for nothing—'

'Never mind that,' said John, testily. 'I'd hate to think we've been killing each other over a bit of brocade.' He sighed. 'Are you the father of Mistress Perks's child?'

'I doubt it.'

'But you could be?'

'I have known her certainly, or should I say carnally.' His mouth curled into a satisfied smile. 'I wasn't the first either, and there'll have been others after me, I've no doubt. When two experienced people come together it makes for a memorable coupling. Spibey needs to marry her off as quickly as he can. Now she's free of the child in her belly, it won't be long before she'll want to resume her adventures.'

John spread out Zipporah's pages. 'It still doesn't make sense. Spibey could have killed Perks, who, if he was impotent, would have known the child wasn't his. Nanna Grey somehow found out the mistress was with child before the marriage, so she had to be got rid of. Molly Kade would have immediately seen the child was full term, so she needed to be silenced.' He looked up at Blanchard. 'And you threatened to tell all and Spibey tried to kill you.'

Blanchard sat upright. 'I was set upon by brigands.'

John shook his head 'The surgeon found a thorn pressed into the flesh above your lip. You were thought to be dead, and your assailant was about to stitch your lips when he must have been disturbed by the soldiers.'

'You think that's Spibey's work? Damn the man, we had a gentlemen's agreement.'

John smiled. 'Both men need to be gentle for that to hold.'

Blanchard harrumphed.

John studied the papers again. 'But Spibey was definitely here at Wem when Nanna was killed. Are he and Wellings working together, and if so why?'

'I can't see why that lackey Wellings should be involved. Unless he's such a faithful servant he'll kill for his master.'

'We wondered if the child was his; you gave us that idea.'

Blanchard reached over and dragged the papers across the table and studied them for a moment. 'Means nothing to me, except for Becky and her sister.'

'Louisa. I did wonder if she was one of the bodies found in the Moss, but I reckon they were buried a lot longer than ten years ago.'

Blanchard laughed. 'It's more like twenty, and the rest, since Louisa ran off.'

'Then why would Baccy say ten?'

'Because she's vain, and she wants you to think she's younger than she is.' He frowned. 'Have you met Margaret Perks?'

'A few times. She doesn't look old enough to be "experienced", though her manner of talking can be blunt.' John thought for a while. 'She told me her father lets her do what she wants and she always gets her own way.'

Blanchard nodded knowingly at him. 'My theory could still be correct, you know, but the wrong way round.'

'What theory?'

'I told you. I could understand why someone would want to get rid of you to claim Zipporah for themselves. Perhaps Spibey wants to get rid of your wife so his daughter can have a handsome young husband. You're too close to have worked that out.'

John sighed and poured himself half a cup of wine. 'I suppose I must see Spibey, though I don't know what I can do. It'll be my word against his.'

'Why were the thorns used in all the murders, do you suppose?' said Blanchard.

'A warning to other people to be silent?'

Blanchard shook his head.

'No, you're right,' said John. 'That makes no sense. Also, I was with Spibey when we first saw Perks's body. He was shocked, truly shocked; there was no pretence. When I told him about Molly he was really shaken and crying "no, no, no"'

'The old man's lips were pierced, weren't they?' said Blanchard.

'Thorns, that's the theme, from the Moss bodies to Mistress Kade.'

They sat in silence for a while.

Eventually John spoke. 'You were attacked somewhere between Prees and Hornspike, weren't you?'

Blanchard nodded.

'Wellings was allegedly riding from Whixall to Wem, wasn't he?'

Blanchard shrugged. 'I've really no idea, being insensible at the time.'

John sketched a little plan. 'Theoretically, your paths could have crossed that night, and yet, I think it unlikely. I believe Zipporah's original idea is the right one. Wellings is our man. He was following you, tried to kill you, and when he was disturbed by the arrival of the troopers, made up some story about being on his way back to Wem.' John looked up at the ceiling. 'But that makes no sense, either. How would Wellings know you'd be out and about that night?'

Blanchard shrugged. 'Because I told him. The pretty factotum was there when I first called upon Sir Moreton. I said maybe the magistrate might out of courtesy call upon me, though I'd be busy in Prees all day on Monday.'

They both looked around as they heard a knock and the front door opened a little.

Crowther peered round. 'Master Carne, you live! You are recovering. Oh, what a day. Such dreadful—'

Blanchard was instantly on his feet and guided a staggering Crowther to the table.

'I don't know what's happening. Sir Moreton said you were looking sick enough to die. And then Mistress Carne. Oh, that it's come to this. Everything is so—'

John reached out and squeezed Crowther's hand. 'Mistress Carne is safe. I'll say no more, but you need have no worry for her.'

Crowther's eyes were moist. 'She lives! Oh, there is still some goodness in the world, praise the Lord for that. Sir Moreton returned from the swimming in a most deranged state. He said that God had spoken to him, that Mistress Carne was no witch and how evil resided at Noble Street ever since he'd brought those abominations from the Moss into his house. That last bit was the only sense he made.'

Blanchard pushed a mug of wine into Crowther's hand. 'Why does every lunatic in this country have to reside in Shropshire? Here, man, take a draught of that.'

Crowther nodded and took a deep gulp and looked at John. 'It only got worse, Master Carne. I'm at a loss to know what to do.'

'Go on,' said John, taking a sip of wine himself.

'Sir Moreton found Wellings in Mistress Perks chamber—'

Blanchard slapped the tabletop and hooted a laugh. 'I told you she'd soon be back to her tricks, but so soon after the baby—'

John held up his hand. 'Master Crowther, please continue.'

'Master Wellings had taken one too many liberties that time. There followed the most vile of arguments. Such shouting I've never heard the whole time I've worked for the magistrate. Sir Moreton calling Wellings every name under the sun. Wellings saying Sir Moreton should be grateful to him. Sir Moreton ordering him to leave. I couldn't hear half what they were saying, but Whixall was mentioned many times, as was Mistress Perks.' He sighed and took another drink of wine, his hand trembling.

John squeezed his shoulder. 'Take a breath, Master Crowther.'

The man nodded then resumed his story. 'By now your brother-in-law, Reverend Goodman had joined in – "If only Sir Moreton had kept faith in the Lord…" – well you can imagine the sort of things he was saying. Eventually he left saying he was going to the rectory. By now the baby was crying and Mistress Perks was in floods of tears, telling everyone to be quiet.'

Blanchard leaned back on his chair. 'My return to London cannot come soon enough. Madness, all madness.'

'So how did you leave things at Noble Street?' said John.

'Wellings said he was going. He told Sir Moreton that as usual he'd have to finish what Sir Moreton had started. He'd not take the blame, he said. The people of Wem wanted a witch and that was what he'd get them.'

John sat up. 'Where was Wellings going?'

Crowther shrugged. 'He mentioned Whixall enough times, I can only suppose he was going home.'

John stood. 'I'd better go and see Sir Moreton.'

Crowther looked up. 'He's gone, too. He went after Wellings.'

John frowned.

Blanchard leaned forward looking more interested that he had previously. 'Why?'

'I told you, sir, he's deranged. He kept saying God had spoken to him. Mistress Carne was no witch.'

John's mouth was dry. 'Did he say he knew where my wife was?'

Crowther shook his head. 'Wellings said something like one witch would likely be drawn to another.'

John gasped. 'He couldn't know Zipporah is at Hornspike, could he? I must go to her. Get your horse, Blanchard, your wife is at much at risk as mine.'

Blanchard leaned back in his chair, seemingly unconcerned. 'Spibey won't lay a finger on her.'

'*He* won't,' said John, reaching for his coat and hat. 'But Wellings will. Damn I need a horse. I'll have to take one from Spibey's stable.'

'Freddy's always available to you. Sir Moreton has not changed his instruction on that count.'

'I'd be faster walking,' said John, fastening his sword to his belt.

'There's Sir Moreton's hunting horse, but I've no permission to lend her to you.'

'Then look the other way, Crowther.' John picked up his pistol and put a handful of balls into his pocket.

'Her harness is hanging on a peg under the name Queenie. But I'll not look the other way – I'll help you.'

'I'll shake your hand now, then, sir,' said Blanchard to John. 'It's been a pleasure to make your acquaintance. I don't know how you can best a man like Sir Moreton, but I'll be interested to hear how it ends.'

'You're really not coming?'

Blanchard shrugged. John didn't press the point and rushed out of the door.

Chapter Twenty-Seven

John winced at the stabbing pain in his leg as with Crowther's help he hauled himself onto Queenie, a tall, dappled mare with a frisky manner. It was a long time since he'd ridden such a horse and he just about kept on the saddle as she lurched through the gate.

After about half an hour of hard riding, he pulled up, as much to take a breath as anything else. He listened, but heard nothing. Queenie could travel at a fair lick, but Spibey and Wellings must have been too far ahead to catch up. He spurred the mare on.

A few minutes later he reached Hornspike. Still no sign of Spibey. Was he too late? His heart thumped as he slithered shakily from the hunter, willing his leg to work. He pushed open the door to Baccy's house. The two women were sitting at the table, talking and laughing.

'Zipporah, thank God,' he cried, almost collapsing.

She rushed towards him and helped him to a chair at the table.

'Oh, you've not come to take her back already?' said Baccy. 'I was hoping to have her for a bit longer. She's such good company.'

John swallowed the ale Zipporah gave him and smiled at her,

relief flooding through him. 'How comely you look, wife.' She was wearing an ill fitted assortment of clothes, obviously borrowed from Baccy. The bodice was too wide and the skirt too short, but John was right, in a strange way they suited her. Despite their predicament, for a moment, all he felt was desire. 'How are you?'

'I feel rather better than you look! I've done little but sleep since I've been here.' She turned and grinned at Baccy. 'And drink some rather fine wine.' She stopped and coughed.

John looked concerned. 'Are you sure you're feeling all right? Your voice is hoarse.'

'I'm well, better than ever, in fact. This cough and hoarseness will pass soon enough.' Her smile was dreamy. 'Something happened when I nearly drowned. I tried to tell you but there wasn't time. I felt pulled towards a light full of nothing but love. I went willingly towards it. Then you were there, and all I wanted was for us to be together. I'm restored, John. I was never damned, a whore nor a witch.' She leaned towards him, her eyes sparkled and her lips grazed his cheek. 'Soon, soon, we'll be husband and wife as we always should have been.'

'Enough!' shouted Baccy. 'Now, Master Carne, tell us, what's happening?'

'I thought Wellings had deduced where Zipporah was hiding. I presumed he and Spibey were on their way here, but I didn't pass them on the road.'

'Well, if they do turn up, they won't be welcome,' said Baccy.

'Why would Wellings care where I was?' asked Zipporah.

'I think your suspicions about him are right. He and Spibey have had some dreadful falling out. Wellings said he was off to find a witch.' John blew out a long breath. 'But he's not here, that's the main thing.'

'You think he killed them all? Perks, Nanna, Molly?' said Zipporah.

John nodded tiredly and drained his mug. 'Crowther overheard the argument. Wellings had had enough of doing

Spibey's dirty work. Finishing off what Spibey started is how he put it. He wasn't going to take the blame, he said.'

Baccy looked puzzled. 'Why kill anyone?'

'It was all to protect Margaret Perks's reputation.'

Baccy blew out a plume of smoke. 'She's a reputation all right. Sam rated her highly in bedroom play.'

John and Zipporah exchanged glances.

'He told me that, too,' said John. 'Though he doubts the child is his.'

'So, Margaret has been free and easy with her favours. But neither can the child be Wellings's, unless he knew her before she married the squire,' said Zipporah.

'Whoever this Wellings may be, he may think the babe is his,' said Baccy. 'Men are stupid about that sort of thing.'

'I agree. I think he's desperate to believe the child is his.' John stood up and gripped his wife's shoulders. 'Blanchard thinks Spibey wanted you out of the way, so that Margaret can marry me, though I find that a fanciful idea. And according to Crowther, after your swimming, Spibey has seen the error of his ways. About you, anyway.'

'Is Sam still around?' asked Baccy. 'I thought he was already headed for London.'

'He'd like to be, though he waits to be escorted there by troops. You should go with him; I know he wants you to,' said John.

Baccy shook her head.

Zipporah was frowning. 'I think Master Blanchard's theory makes some sense. No matter the paternity of the child, Margaret Perks is now a respectable widow and mother of the heir to a profitable estate.'

'If she's got any sense she'll not remarry,' said Baccy, squinting as a plume of tobacco smoke drifted from her mouth into her eyes.

Zipporah continued. 'And if young Widow Perks takes a fancy to you, who better for Spibey to marry her to? His trusty assistant wed to his wayward daughter, perfect. You'd keep her on the straight and narrow.'

He rubbed his hands through his hair until it stood up in untidy spikes. 'Steady, steady, this is too much.'

'Have a smoke,' said Baccy. 'It'll clear your mind.'

'It'll take more than a smoke,' he said, lighting the pipe she gave him nevertheless.

'If only I had my charts, it would be easier to work out,' said Zipporah. 'But I think I see it now. Everything has been done to free Margaret from Perks and keep her reputation.'

'It's not about me, though,' said John. 'You were right all along, Zipporah. The person who has most to gain from all this is Wellings. He wants Margaret. I didn't realise that at first, but when I last saw him at Noble Street, it's obvious he's on close terms with her. And Spibey found him in her bedchamber, which caused their falling out. Spibey accusing you of the murders only helped him. No one would be looking anywhere else for the perpetrators, and Spibey, no matter what Blanchard thinks, can hardly let his daughter marry the husband of a witch. Even though he was so keen to tell everyone I wasn't to blame.' He leaned back in his chair and suddenly felt very tired. 'I've had enough. Why don't we escape this place, get a passage to the Americas?' He held her hand. 'When I thought there was no more hope for us staying together, I'd more or less decided to go there myself anyway.'

Now Baccy was frowning deeply. 'This Wellings you keep talking about, he's not the old steward at Whixall, is he? Don't tell me he's still alive.'

'I'm talking of Isaac Wellings, a young man, just in his twenties I suppose. He's the son of the person you're thinking of,' said John.

Baccy got up and started poking the fire. 'Wellings, New England,' she muttered to herself.

'Baccy, what do you know?' demanded Zipporah.

'No, it can't be.' She turned round and sat back at the table.

'Baccy,' said Zipporah, this time with an edge to her voice.

Baccy twisted uncomfortably. 'It's probably nothing. Years ago I had a letter from a man called Wellings from Whixall, saying that my sister had gone to New England with him and died there. I didn't believe a word of it, so I threw it on the fire.'

John leapt to his feet. 'Baccy, that's really important, why didn't you tell me before?'

'As if my sister would have run off with a humble servant, of course she wouldn't. She was taken by somebody, murdered I should say.'

'What do you mean?' said John. 'Last time we talked of it, you said Louisa could have run away with a gypsy.'

'I didn't mean it.'

Zipporah stood up and waved her hands excitedly. 'This could explain a lot. If Isaac is the son of Louisa, who may have been with child by Perks, could it be possible that he thinks he's the true heir to Whixall Grange?'

'Why not accept the obvious, that's he's the son of old man Wellings?' said John, reasonably. 'If he did kill anyone, it's been to protect Margaret, not get rid of her.' John rubbed his face again. 'The more I think about it, the more muddled I get. Come on, Zipporah, whatever happens, there's no life for us here anymore. Pack some food in a bag and borrow what warm clothes you can from Baccy. I've stolen Spibey's hunter and she's a good strong mare who can keep going all day, and all night if needs be. We'll easily make Chester before the morning.'

Zipporah opened her mouth but said nothing as a terrific bellow was heard outside.

Baccy went straight to the door and pulled it open.

'No!' shouted John, but it was too late.

Spibey staggered through the doorway, his face dripping with blood. 'I've been murdered!' he cried as he collapsed backwards onto the floor. He looked up. 'Mistress Carne,

Mistress Carne, you *are* alive, praise the Lord. Or do I meet you in Heaven?'

'Neither Heaven nor Hell, so I must be alive,' said Zipporah, peering over him. 'You've taken a bludgeoning.'

'I've been murdered,' Spibey cried again. 'I'm about to die.' He pulled himself onto his knees and shuffled over to her, grabbing the hem of her skirt, sinking his face into it. 'Mea culpa, mea culpa, mea maxima culpa—' He stopped short as Baccy kicked him sharply in the ribs.

'I'll have none of your blood and spit on my best dress.'

Spibey rolled around on the floor. 'Honourable Mistress Blanchard, good wife to my dear friend Sam, forgive me. Dear God, Lord Almighty, forgive me, take my soul.'

Zipporah reached down to him but started to tremble. She pulled herself upright jerkily and rushed to the edge of the room, staring out of the window, breathing raggedly and shaking visibly.

John hurried over to her. 'It's all right. He cannot harm you now,' he said softly, his arm wrapped comfortingly around her shoulder.

'It's not that. For one moment I pitied him. He tried to murder me and yet I felt sorry for him. I'm furious with myself.'

He kissed her forehead. 'You're so beautiful.'

'I've had enough, enough! Enough of you all!' screamed Baccy, stamping and slamming her fist down so hard on the table her pipe shattered. 'Now look what you've made me do. You can all go now.' She pointed at Spibey. 'I don't want you drooling over my newly waxed floor any longer. And as for you two –' she threw the remains of her pipe at John and Zipporah '– you'll not make love in the corner of my room, nor anywhere else in this house. Be gone all of you. Go and throw yourselves in the Moss for all I care. By God and all the saints if I had a pistol I'd shoot the lot of you.' She took a breath. 'Well, maybe not Zipporah.'

'Too late, I am dead already,' moaned Spibey.

'Not dead enough,' said Baccy, giving him another kick.

Zipporah walked to the fireplace and put the small cauldron on the trivet over the fire. 'Pull him up, John,' she said. 'I'll warm some water and clean his wounds, then we can see just how dead he is.'

John smiled and hauled the protesting magistrate into a chair. 'And while we're tending to your wounds, Spibey, you can tell us exactly what happened to you.'

Baccy snorted. 'Weak, weak, weak.' She lit another pipe and blew thick smoke into Spibey's face. 'Let's do the world a favour and finish him now.'

'Baccy, if you've some clean cloths, I'd be grateful,' said Zipporah

'I've some special linens which have been close to my arse; you can use them.'

'Baccy, get some clean cloth,' said John.

'Weak and mad, weak and mad,' she muttered under her breath, but she did bring some decent material, and soon Zipporah was gently bathing Spibey's face.

'Looks like our bludgeoner is losing his edge,' said John, peering at the gash on Spibey's temple. 'There's hardly a dint here. Master Blanchard's skull took a far heavier blow. So, you'll die all right, but not just yet. It's time to talk.'

'I'd suffer you for some wine, or ale. My tongue cleaves to my mouth,' Spibey croaked.

'I'll piss in a pot for you,' said Baccy.

'If that's all you have to offer, kind mistress, I'll have it,' he sobbed.

Zipporah filled a tankard with Baccy's best wine and thrust it towards Spibey. 'Slake your thirst, then talk.'

He took half the wine down in one gulp. 'Most assuredly, gentle Mistress Carne, you're the embodiment of Christian charity. How the devil has led me a merry dance about you.'

She reached up and pulled down a sharp long handled fork

341

that hung above the fireplace and jerked it towards him. 'Less of this flattery, you answer John's questions or you'll feel this pricking your flesh, if not your conscience. I shan't be gentle.'

'Now, that's more like it,' said Baccy.

'Steady, ladies,' said John. 'Right, Spibey, perhaps you'll tell us what happened between here and Wem. Who attacked you?'

'Why, that devil Wellings of course! To think I've nurtured Satan's spawn in my own bosom—'

'Or Perks's son,' said Zipporah.

Spibey's face clouded. 'How did you know that?'

'Never mind for now,' said John, motioning his wife to remain silent. 'Why did you leave Wem in such a hurry?'

'Because Wellings worked out where you were hiding Mistress Carne—'

Zipporah jabbed the fork into Spibey's sleeve.

He yelped.

'Why do you persist in lying?' she said. 'I don't believe you've ridden here to save me. Tell the truth or there'll be more of that.'

Baccy began to cackle.

'Zipporah, no more,' said John.

'It felt good,' she said, the fork still hovering over Spibey.

'Let me have a go,' said Baccy, sending another plume of smoke into the magistrate's face.

'Help me, John,' sobbed Spibey again. He hardly paused as Zipporah looked eager to jab him again. 'Wellings said he'd find the witch. But God has spoken, this lovely lady is not possessed.' He forced a sickly smile towards Zipporah, then looked at John. 'You know, don't you, the evil came into my soul from those monsters we brought back from the Moss.'

'Don't make excuses, Spibey,' said John.

'Prick him, Zipporah,' Baccy squealed in delight.

'Hold for the moment,' said John. 'So who really attacked you, and what's happened to Master Wellings? You left Wem before me, where've you been?'

'He's my murderer! I told you.'

John looked away. 'You're not telling the truth, not in any way, Spibey. I don't know what you think you'll gain by lying, but the time for dissembling has long passed. I need some fresh air. I'm sure these fine ladies will look after you while I'm outside.'

'No, no, for the love of God, please no,' said Spibey. 'Don't leave me, they'll finish what Wellings started.'

John shrugged and turned back to Spibey. 'Why should I protect you? If you'd had your way I'd be a widower by now. No, you've had your chance. I'll leave you to the women.'

Spibey dragged himself off the chair and dropped to his knees. 'I deserve everything they do to me, but spare me, John. I told you, the evil from the Moss bodies forced me to do what I did to lovely Mistress Carne. Your brother and Randall gave me more than enough evidence of her supposed witchcraft. How was I to know they were lying? But see, our wise and wonderous God has saved her.'

'My clever and brave husband saved me,' said Zipporah, the fork pointing at Spibey's head.

John stood by the doorway. 'I can never trust you, Spibey. There's no point. You're beyond help.'

Spibey clasped his hands in front of him. 'For the sake of my Margaret, spare me. Don't leave her a widow and fatherless, so that beast Wellings can claim her for himself.'

'And where is Wellings?'

'I don't know. I chased him, he led me a dance around the Moss. He knows his way around there, but I caught up with him. I challenged him, oh I did. You'll not touch a hair of Mistress Carne's head, I said. And for that he bludgeoned me.' He took a shaky breath. 'Let me return to Wem. I must protect my Margaret. He could be on his way back there. I must not let him have her.'

John walked back and crouched down in front of him. 'Now we're getting some sense out of you, at last. I know it's all about

Margaret. I know the child isn't her husband's and I guess she wants to marry Wellings.'

Spibey moaned.

John took his arm. 'Sit back at the table, take some more wine and tell us exactly what's been happening. Starting with when you found out your daughter was with child.'

The magistrate's head slumped towards his chest, but he complied, and with much grunting heaved himself back into the chair and choked a little as he drank more wine.

'You can hang up that fork now,' said John to Zipporah, and with a slight shrug she obeyed and took a seat opposite Spibey, her eyes never wavering from him.

'It was the day I first met you, Master Carne. I was congratulating myself on gaining the services of so able a man—' The expression on John's face was enough to make Spibey stop and collect himself. 'After you left, Master Carne, Tom burst into my room. He said my daughter was heavy with child, and as he'd never had the pleasure, he demanded to know whose it was, and what I was going to do about it.'

Zipporah's eyes narrowed. 'But surely you married her to Perks because you knew she wasn't pure.'

Spibey winced. 'I knew she wasn't a virgin. Perks seemed the obvious solution, and if everything said about him was true, he'd never discover her secret. He'd die soon and leave her a respectable widow. No one would dare to question her lack of purity, then. But I knew nothing of the child until Perks told me.

'Perks was demanding that I not only took her back and had the marriage annulled, but that I paid him compensation, as well. I knew he was in the right, but he was talking about my Margaret as if she was some defective farm animal I'd sold him. I tried to reason with him. "Look," I said, "Tom, old friend, you've everything you want. An heir by the name of Perks that no one can question. A child, at last, to leave your land to. Who cares how that child is got?" But he wouldn't listen to sense. He began to rant and rave. He threatened to throw Margaret out into the countryside in nothing but the clothes she'd arrived in. I grabbed hold of him, I was trying to shake some sense into the stupid man, but he pulled away from me and fell down, hitting his head on the side of the table.'

'Stone dead,' said Baccy, with a certain glee.

'No, not dead at all, but completely insensible. What could I do? I didn't want anyone to find him like that, so I locked him in one of the cellar rooms.'

'You could have called for an apothecary or doctor,' said Zipporah. 'As any normal person would.'

Spibey heaved another great sob. 'How could I? What if he spoke, and Margaret's secret became the talk of the town? No, I wouldn't let that happen. Tom regained little of his wits but simply lolled his head, dribbled and groaned. In the meantime I ordered Margaret's immediate return to Wem. When she arrived she was escorted by Wellings. I don't know how it happened, but immediately I trusted the man. I suppose that was the time the devil began to control events. I took Wellings into my confidence, telling him that Tom had taken a fall and had lost his mind, and was likely to make scurrilous accusations against my daughter. It was as if he instantly understood. He offered to take Tom back to Whixall. He assured me everything would be all right.'

'He knew about Margaret's condition before you did,' said Zipporah.

'He tells me he's the father,' said Spibey, draining his mug and holding it out for more.

'But you realised the child was conceived while she was in London, didn't you?' said John.

'When Margaret returned to Wem she confessed to me that she suspected her condition when she married Perks. She tried to rouse him, hoping to pass the child off as his, but to no avail.'

'My husband very much enjoyed poking your daughter,' chortled Baccy.

John held up his hand. 'Enough! Let's stick to the facts, shall we?'

'They are facts. He poked her and enjoyed it,' said Baccy, with a sulky shrug.

Spibey began to weep. It was a pitiful sight and Zipporah offered him a clean cloth so he could wipe his eyes and blow his nose.

'My Margaret had no mother to guide her. If she's wild, it's because I, her father, haven't given her the correct instruction.' He sniffed loudly. 'I took Wellings to the storeroom but Tom, poor old Tom was dead. Wellings said he'd take care of everything.'

'When he was discovered hanging at Hornspike, you were truly shocked, weren't you?' said John.

Spibey nodded. 'Wellings said he'd left him on the Moss. It would look like an accident. Which it was. I never meant to harm him, just to stop him saying those horrible things.' Spibey sobbed.

'So why string him up?' said Zipporah. 'It's perverse and makes no sense.'

'We need to know more,' said John.

Chapter Twenty-Eight

J ohn stared intently at Spibey. 'Perks was found hanging Tuesday morning. Though by the state of his clothes he *had* been in the Moss.'

'Wellings was pleased with himself. He said those evil bodies gave him the idea. It would point to witchcraft, and no one would ever suspect me, a professed witchfinder, of sorcery.'

'There's a logic to that,' said John. 'But it complicated everything. An old man has an accident and dies. Speaking brutally, I can see it was the best thing that could have happened to your beloved Margaret. She'd become what you wanted, a respectable widow, waiting to give birth to her dead husband's son.'

'I'm not so sure,' said Zipporah. 'What if Master Perks wasn't dead when the ever-helpful Master Wellings said he'd take care of him. Had the old man started to recover?'

Spibey's sobs deepened as if they echoed up from the depths of his soul. 'I was so frightened, for my dear Margaret, of course. Wellings said not to worry, that he'd never let anyone besmirch Margaret's name and the old man couldn't recover. I was so ·grateful, so happy to find someone who truly respected my daughter. I let the beast take him, and closed my eyes to what might happen. Of that I am guilty.'

Zipporah stood up and moved the cauldron away from the fire, as it had almost boiled dry. 'Where is he?' she said. 'Where is Wellings?' She turned back to Spibey. 'He knows you're alive I suppose? I mean, did he see you run away?'

'He struck me, and I spurred my horse on. As soon as I saw this house I knew I'd be safe,' sniffed Spibey.

Baccy snorted. 'I wouldn't be so sure. Master Carne and his wife may be full of forgiveness. I assure you I'm not.'

'Where *is* Wellings?' said Zipporah again. 'He has two options. Run away or kill us all, for he'll guess you've blurted the story out, Spibey.'

John pulled his pistol from his belt and felt in his pocket. 'I doubt he'll run away and lose everything he desires. Whixall, Margaret.' He felt in his pocket. 'I've ten balls and not much powder, and what little I have is probably damp.'

'We both have swords,' said Spibey.

'Is Wellings armed?' asked John.

'He has a sword and a pistol. No, he has two pistols for he took mine when he attacked me.'

'For the moment no one leaves this house,' said John.

Baccy was shaking her head. 'How many times must I say it? I've had enough of you all. I want you gone.'

Zipporah went over to her. 'Let's cook everybody something nice,' she said kindly. 'That might take your mind off things.'

'I've not much in the way of makings,' said Baccy. 'Anyway that silly girl from the village will be here shortly with my meal.'

'Hmm,' said John, twisting his lips. 'I don't think we should let her in.'

'I'm hungry,' said Baccy.

'But we only ate an hour ago,' said Zipporah. 'I was thinking of John; he must be starving.'

'I need my food, and besides, I've paid for it,' said Baccy. 'Send the idiot magistrate out when the girl comes. If he gets shot we'll know the murderer is out there. If he doesn't, you can all go.'

'We're not going anywhere. Keep Baccy calm,' said John to Zipporah, who shrugged back at him, but she did persuade Baccy to take her into the larder to see what they could find.

'Your wife's a wonderful woman,' said Spibey.

'Never mind that,' said John, nipping off a tag of lead from a ball with his teeth before loading it into his pistol. 'I quite like the idea of sending you out as a test, though.' He packed the ball down with the pistol's ramrod. 'I'd be able to pinpoint where Wellings is from the flash of his pistol and deal with him before he has time to reload.'

Spibey stood up and tried to pull his dishevelled clothes back into shape. 'You speak the truth, Master Carne. It's the least I can do, to sacrifice myself, so that you and your dear wife may have some chance of living. Just promise me one thing, if you do survive, will you protect my Margaret?'

'I didn't really mean—' John began, then he stopped, somewhat surprised at Spibey's out of character offer to lay down his life for another. 'I can't order you to go out, but yes, that way we would know for sure if Wellings is outside.'

'Where else would he be?' Spibey gulped some air into his lungs. 'I can do this, Master Carne.'

John went back to the window. 'No sign of our horses, someone's led them off. I think Wellings is out there all right.' He held up his hand. 'Hang on, there's a girl with a basket coming towards the gate.'

Spibey joined him. They saw her look over her shoulder. She screamed, dropped the basket and ran away.

'He's there,' said John, grimly.

'With our two swords and your pistol, we can go outside together. While we still have the light, we stand a chance against him,' said Spibey

Zipporah, now back in the room, pushed herself between

them. 'I've just found my husband. I'll not lose him on the day we're reunited.'

'Sir Moreton said he'll go first,' said John.

Zipporah jumped as they heard the unmistakable crack of a firearm being discharged and a glass pane shattering.

'Everyone all right?' called John, as they backed away from the window.

Baccy shrieked. 'Where are my babies, Master Pipkin, Colonel Jojo! Where are they? Look, my panelling has taken a cannon ball! Oh, mercy, mercy, where are my babes? And my window, have you any idea how much window glass costs?'

Zipporah ran to her and hugged her close. 'It's but a small shot, Baccy, it can be mended, and your cats are cats: they'll see to themselves. They'll be hiding and quite safe.'

'Everyone, keep away from the windows,' said John.

'He grows impatient,' said Spibey.

'That could be to our advantage,' said John, reaching sideways and gently prodding the window open. 'Wellings! Show yourself.'

'Is that you, Master Carne?' They heard a distant voice.

'It is. You know I'm here,' shouted John.

'Then help me, Master Carne, help me. Sir Moreton is possessed and hell bent on killing me.'

Spibey's trembling had almost become apoplectic, his face was a purplish red and his eyes bulged as big as plums. 'Don't you dare believe him over me,' he snarled. Then he shouted over John's shoulder. 'Come out and show yourself, you devil-worshipping, possessed idolater!'

'What, so you can get Master Carne to shoot me, for he'll have his pistol with him for sure,' Wellings shouted back.

'I'm not going to shoot anyone. Throw down your weapons, Wellings, and show yourself,' said John.

'No,' replied Wellings. 'My arm's already ripped by Spibey's ball. I'll not risk one to the head.'

John motioned Spibey away from the window. 'Did you shoot him?'

'I did,' said Spibey, under his breath, as if they could be overheard. 'He tried to knock my brains out. I managed to let off my pistol; it tore the flesh of his arm, certainly, but it's a wound of no consequence, though he fell from his horse. He was well enough to reach up and wrench my weapon from my hand, but it gave me a chance to gallop away. I'm telling the truth.'

John snorted dismissively. 'I'm surprised you even know how to pronounce the word, so distant is your acquaintance with its meaning.' He turned to Baccy. 'There must be another way out of this house?'

'Through the storerooms, yes,' she said. 'I'm not leaving my babies, though.'

'Your babies will be perfectly all right. You and Zipporah sneak out quietly that way and go to the Simmonds' house. Stay there till I come and collect you.'

'No, I'm not leaving you, John,' said Zipporah. 'You, go, Baccy, I'll look after your cats, I promise.'

'Go, both of you,' ordered John.

'I shall not,' said his wife. 'Wither thou goest, husband.'

'I'm not going anywhere,' said John.

'Wither thou stayest, then, husband.'

'I'm more than happy to go,' said Spibey. 'Dearest Mistress Blanchard, allow me to escort you to a place of safety.'

'You don't move from my sight,' said John.

Baccy stood close to Spibey and tapped his chest with the stem of her pipe. 'And if you're with me, then you are not in a place of safety. I'd happily see you die, happily kill you myself, if I could. You think nothing of imprisoning an innocent old woman, nothing of drowning a blameless young one. There's no good in you, Moreton, no good at all. Go outside, face Wellings and let the devil take you both.'

'Baccy, if you're going, just go, eh?' said John, but she made no move. He returned to his position at the side of the window and called out again. 'Wellings, what are you going to do? You can't stay there forever.' He peeped round the shutter. 'What's this?' he muttered, as the farmer, Simmonds appeared by the front gate. 'Have a care, Master Simmonds, there's an armed man abroad.'

'Who's that?' said the farmer. 'And what have you done with Mistress Blanchard?'

'It's John Carne from Wem, and Mistress Blanchard is here and in good health. Have a care, sir.'

Simmonds picked up the basket that his daughter had dropped, walked the few steps up to the front door and let himself in. His solid reliable presence in the room was somehow reassuring.

'What's going on?' he asked, looking from John, to Spibey, to Baccy and then frowning at Zipporah, presumably on account of her too-wide bodice and too-short skirt. Then he stared again at Spibey. 'You've a nasty wound, Sir Moreton. Do we have some royalist malignants left over from the battle?'

'This is my wife, Zipporah, by the way,' said John, as Simmonds' gaze returned to her again and again.

He nodded and put the basket on the table. 'I don't think your victuals are ruined, my lady,' he said to Baccy. 'Though my daughter's half out of her wits with fear. She said the devil whispered to her from a tree saying he was come for her soul to take her straight to hell. She's a silly girl, though.'

'It *is* the devil, the devil himself,' said Spibey, gripping Simmonds' shoulders. 'Disguised as Isaac Wellings.'

Simmonds burst into guffaws of laughter. 'Isaac Wellings the devil, the devil he is! You've had *your* wits well pummelled, Sir Moreton. That pretty boy isn't capable of a sour thought.'

'I believe he's murdered three people,' said John.

Simmonds looked surprised. 'Well, I trust you to have your wits about you, Master Carne, though with respect, I think you're mistaken.'

'Did you see anything on your way here?' asked John.

'Nothing at all, though I did wonder why the horses were tethered in that little copse, and not at the front of the house or put out in the paddock.'

'How many horses?' asked John.

'Three,' said the farmer.

'At least we still have mounts,' said John. 'Though Wellings must still be around.'

Simmonds frowned. 'We'd heard a rumour there was a witch to be swum at Wem this morning, what happened?'

'I sank,' said Zipporah.

Simmonds held up his hands and shook his head. 'I think it's best I get back to my farm. You're mistaken if you think Wellings is a wrong'un, you mark my words.' He went to the door.

'Simmonds, don't,' said John, but the burly man was already outside. He'd hardly taken a pace when they heard the echoing crack of the pistol.

'No!' cried John, leaping out of the house. Simmonds was on the ground, his face foaming red with blood. He was groaning.

'John, no,' screamed Zipporah, following him out.

'Back inside,' he ordered.

She called over her shoulder. 'Baccy, Spibey, make yourselves useful, the farmer still lives, help me pull him indoors!'

John headed towards the small copse to the side of Baccy's house. He could see the three horses tethered to trees at its edge. 'Wellings, show yourself,' he said, cursing that he hadn't brought his pistol with him. He heard a rustle and the jangle of harness, then saw a blur as a man leapt from the cover of the trees, and pulled himself onto one of the horses. John ran, as best he could towards them, but Wellings was already galloping down the track. John jumped as he felt hands squeezing hard on his shoulders. 'Spibey!'

'I'm leaving, get out of my way,' said the magistrate, pushing him aside and untidily clambering onto Queenie.

John lunged forward and managed to grab hold of the hunter's bridle, but Spibey jerked away and John tumbled to the ground. He rolled over and saw Spibey take off in the opposite direction to Wellings.

'You're headed for the Moss,' called John. 'Come back.'

John returned to the house. Simmonds was lying on the table. Bloodstained cloths surrounded his head.

The man groaned again.

'How is he?' John asked Zipporah.

'Baccy, have you warmed that spiced wine, and put plenty of brandy in it?' she said, before looking up at her husband. 'He may live, but his left eye is burst; he'll never see through it again.' She nodded to Baccy, lifted the man's head, and they gently poured the thick red liquid into his mouth.

'Sleep, Master Simmonds,' said Zipporah, stroking his forehead. She looked back to John. 'I'll try and staunch the bleeding. Spibey took your pistol, by the way.'

'Damn the man,' snarled John, under his breath. 'I'll go down to the farmhouse and let them know what happened.'

'Take care,' said Zipporah. 'Both Spibey and Wellings are out there and armed, and I don't know which of them I trust less.'

'At least they're running away from each other, and hopefully from here.'

Baccy shook her head. 'They'll meet. It doesn't matter which way you follow the track from here. One goes to Hornspike and then to Wem alongside the Moss. The other goes around the village and joins the other close to the Moss. If they haven't already killed each other, God willing they soon shall do.'

'Whatever,' said John, 'I owe it to Master Simmonds' family to let them know what's happened.'

'You do, John,' said Zipporah. Then she frowned as she saw him drag a chair to the doorway. 'What are you doing?'

'I need to get on the horse, come, Baccy, hold the beast while I climb on.'

'Baccy, do this; Baccy, do that,' she whinged, but followed him obediently enough.

John soon returned, Mistress Simmonds riding pillion behind him. It was instantly obvious she was a good and sensible woman, and she and Zipporah talked quietly together, often looking at the prone, but now mercifully unconscious farmer. The two women eventually embraced, just as a red-faced Jim, Simmonds' son, burst into the house.

'Pa! Pa!' he cried.

'Shh,' said his mother softly, rushing over to him before he could disturb the sleeping patient. 'Your father is strong, with love and prayer he'll live. Are your brothers bringing the cart?'

'They're on their way. Oh, my poor Pa! What happened?'

'He's been shot by Isaac Wellings.' said John. 'He got involved in an argument that wasn't his.'

They spoke no more as two of Jim's brothers arrived and, with much care, slid their father onto a hurdle, covered him with blankets and carried him to the cart.

It was quiet when the Simmonds left.

'I'd better tidy up,' said Zipporah.

Baccy shook her head. 'Leave that to me. I doubt there's two hours light left. Get yourselves back to Wem.'

John and his wife looked at each other with surprise. 'I know you keep telling us to go, but we really can't leave you like this,' said Zipporah.

'Of course you can,' said Baccy. 'I'm not as incapable as I make out. I can tidy everything.'

'I was thinking more that Wellings or Spibey might come back,' said Zipporah.

'I'll not let anyone in, I assure you. Once you're gone the door is barred. Go now. For once, will someone do what I ask?' Baccy crossed her arms and her lips tightened in an expression of utter stubbornness.

'I promised Mistress Simmonds I'd see justice done,' said John.

'And how will you achieve that? Not by tearing about on the Moss.' said Baccy. 'Go home, get some rest.'

'Baccy has a point,' said Zipporah. 'We've no idea where either Spibey or Wellings are, but one thing is for sure, if Spibey still lives he'll return to Wem as soon as he can, to protect his Margaret and I would be surprised if Wellings doesn't go back either, and for the same reason.'

'Very true,' said John. He wanted nothing more than to go back to The Dial, and clasp Zipporah close. And she was right, Spibey and Wellings, if they hadn't killed each other or got lost on the Moss, would return to Margaret. 'I don't want another innocent victim like Simmonds, though,' he said. 'And for that reason I'm not happy to leave you here alone, Baccy.'

Colonel Jojo and Master Pipkin chose that moment to saunter into the room and with loud meowing, claw at Baccy's skirt. 'Hungry babies,' she cooed. She looked up at John. 'My babies are here. Now I know I'm safe. Go, Master Carne, take Zipporah home.'

Chapter Twenty-Nine

J ohn and Zipporah headed out of Hornspike, riding Spibey's
cob, Zipporah behind her husband. They took their usual
path home, the one that led alongside the Moss. John hadn't
known that the two tracks outside Baccy's house converged until
she'd mentioned it earlier. He knew there was a danger they could
meet either of their enemies. He thought he'd prefer it to be
Spibey, but only just. More than once, he turned round, thinking
he could hear something, but saw nothing.

'Were Spibey and Wellings working together?' she said.

'I don't know. Spibey was truly shocked when he heard Perks
was hanging. He knew nothing about the old woman. He was
equally horrified when I told him about Molly. I don't know what
to think. I can't trust the man, and he tried to kill you, after all.'

'He swam a witch, the result was up to the Almighty. Would
he murder someone? I don't think so.' She was quiet for a while.

'Was Wellings working under Spibey's instruction or on his
own misplaced initiative?' pondered Zipporah.

'We'll be past the Moss soon,' said John, relief in his voice.

A pistol shot whistled by, inches above their heads. He spurred the cob on, but a second ball caught her neck, and she reared with a terrified neigh, tossing them both to the ground and bolting off

They untangled themselves, and pulled each other upright. All was quiet.

'They're reloading,' he said, under his breath.

'*They?*'

'Or one man with two pistols.'

'Wellings has two pistols,' she said.

They both jumped as the undergrowth rustled loudly, and two horses burst through. Then Spibey and Wellings were looking down at them, both pointing their pistols.

'The bastards were in it together all along,' John snarled. 'Stand behind me, wife.' He squared up to the men. Spibey dismounted first, keeping his pistol aimed at John. Wellings was soon by his side.

'So, what do you intend?' said John.

Wellings spoke. 'To end this. We've come across you with the escaped witch. I can see you're still in thrall to her. I have to destroy her, before she flees across the Moss to join her devilish master. To prevent more evil, she has to die.'

Spibey moaned. 'Do we have to?'

John spat onto the ground. 'What hold does this man have over you, Spibey? You've no stomach for this and you know it. Zipporah is no witch, God has told you that.'

'Too much killing,' said Spibey, his voice shaky.

'But Master Wellings needs us dead. He'll kill us all to protect himself, and win your daughter into the bargain.'

'Don't listen to him,' said Wellings. 'The witch has perverted him. We're working together, remember. For Margaret's sake.'

Spibey's jowls were shaking.

'You can't trust them,' said Wellings urgently. 'They'll tell everyone you were involved. It is I, not Master Carne and his wife, who's always been there for you. Done your bidding without question.'

John continued. 'I know you killed for Spibey, Isaac.' Zipporah prodded his back anxiously.

Spibey and Wellings exchanged glances.

John pressed on. 'You don't trust each other. Nor should you. I imagine Spibey has used you, Isaac, and you've deceived him. The child isn't yours, do you know that?'

'He is, Margaret told me. Through me he's the true heir to Whixall Grange,' said Wellings.

'How did he talk you round, Isaac?' said John. 'Earlier today you attempted to batter his brains out, now you work together.'

'We had a misunderstanding. Sir Moreton has now given his blessing to my marriage to Margaret.'

John laughed. 'And you trust a man to whom a lie comes more easily than the truth? Look where his pistol points, Isaac.'

Spibey's weapon was indeed now aimed at Wellings. 'You disgraced my daughter,' he said. 'Did you really think I'd let you have her? You, the son of a nobody? John, praise be that you're here to see how this man terrorises me.'

'What's going on?' Zipporah whispered in John's ear.

John said nothing. He was walking very slowly backwards, pushing Zipporah, hoping to enable her to make an escape into the trees that lined the path.

'You lied to me,' said Wellings to Spibey. 'You promised! I love Margaret and I'll have her. You'll die today, Spibey, as will John Carne and his wife. Then I'll wed Margaret and be squire of Whixall.'

'Never!' said Spibey, squeezing the trigger. The ball seemed to pass straight through Wellings's shoulder, who span around, involuntarily discharging his own pistol into the air.

John leapt towards Spibey, and Zipporah launched herself at Wellings, somehow gripping onto his back and pummelling his head with her fists. She even managed to pull the other pistol from his belt and throw it into the bushes. Strong as she was though, he was more powerful and managed to throw her off and flee onto the Moss.

'Stop him, stop him,' cried Spibey, as he broke free from John and ran off after Wellings.

'Shall we leave them to it and take their horses?' said Zipporah, breathing heavily.

'A very sensible idea.'

'But we're not going to be sensible, are we?'

John leaned forward and took a deep breath. 'I can't risk either of them escaping. I owe as much to Master Simmonds, not to mention you.'

She twisted her face and sighed. 'I suppose you're right, but I'm past caring what happens to either of them. The devil will claim his own, I'm sure. Though I'd have preferred Spibey to return to Wem and formally declare me no witch.'

'Quite so,' said John tiredly. 'And can we really stand by and do nothing? What if Wellings escapes? He should be brought to justice.'

Her shoulders sagged and she smiled resignedly 'You're right, of course, come on then.'

'No, you stay here with the horses.'

'I won't. Wither thou goest, husband, remember?'

Although they'd only just left the path, within a few paces they were in a different world. The Moss, a land with its own rules, its own nature. The already cold air became icier. Every noise they made, now magnified.

'Where are they?' asked Zipporah. 'Why can't I see them? This place is so large and flat and yet two men have disappeared without trace.'

'I know from my one visit to the Moss that it has hidden dips,' he said, jumping back almost immediately as a large dark waterfowl screeched and flew upwards. 'And that sort of thing happens, just to unnerve you further.'

'I'm not unnerved by a duck,' she whispered tersely.

'Head for that line of reeds,' said John, pointing ahead. 'Keep your head down, just because we can't see *them*, doesn't mean *we're* invisible.'

'Reeds, hmm, that means it's wet.'

'You're not afraid of a bit of water are you?'

'After this morning, who'd be surprised if I was? But no, it's not that. It's falling into a bog that sucks me down that bothers me.'

John could manage a sort of loping trot, and keeping their heads low, they crept until they suddenly halted as they saw Wellings some way in front of them. He was reloading his pistol.

'Two pistols against one sword,' said John, drawing his from the scabbard. 'God, what a mess.' He squinted as he heard the first loud blast of a pistol. 'Spibey,' he said softly, peering through the reeds. 'See him just over there, quick to load, terrible aim. Nowhere near Wellings.'

There was a dull hollow pop as Wellings's pistol misfired and he ran towards Spibey, holding his gun by the barrel. It must have jammed and was now being used as a club. Spibey took a hard thump to the side of his head, which sent him reeling.

Both men now unable to use their pistols, John walked towards them, despite Zipporah's vocal misgivings. 'Stop this now, both of you,' he shouted. 'It's over.'

'You have to die,' screamed Wellings, his voice hoarse, as he forced his ramrod down the muzzle of his weapon, trying to clear it.

'No, no' shouted John. 'Don't fire, you'll blow your face off.'

John noticed Spibey had pulled himself up and was reloading. He pushed him hard causing him to drop his weapon. Zipporah followed John and scooped up the gun, clasping it close to her bosom before taking a step back.

'You're going first,' Wellings shouted at her.

'What have I ever done to you?' she said, lunging towards Spibey again and pulling his powder pouch from his belt.

Spibey was rubbing blood from his forehead, where Wellings had struck him 'Stop this madness, Isaac,' he said eventually. 'Talk to me, I can sort something out for you.'

'Yes, my death,' said Wellings. 'And I didn't despoil your daughter; she'd been used, over and over again by the time I got to her. But I didn't care, because she's so beautiful, and when I told her I was the rightful heir to Whixall Grange she didn't laugh at me. She said one day it would be mine, doubly, through our marriage and through our child.' He continued to fumble with his weapon, tapping more powder into the pan.

Zipporah had reloaded Spibey's pistol.

'Down, Zipporah,' said John, and she dropped to the ground as Wellings took aim but apart from a click, nothing happened.

'It's jammed, Isaac,' said John. 'Sir Moreton is right, let's talk about this. Something can be done.'

'No! Nothing can be done. You have to die, all of you. Spibey's trying to persuade Margaret that she's in love with you, John Carne. She'll betray me. As my mother betrayed me by marrying a peasant bailiff instead of the squire. Everyone betrayed me.'

'John's right, let's talk. Things may not be as bad as they seem. Margaret will never marry John,' said Zipporah, pulling herself upright.

Wellings was shaking more powder into his pistol's pan, then he cocked the hammer.

John raised his hands to cover his face. 'Don't—'

There was a blinding flash followed by a splintering crack as the barrel of the pistol exploded, sending shards of shrapnel into the sky. Wellings was thrown backwards by the blast.

John looked to where Zipporah had stood. She was crouched down but mercifully unharmed. Spibey was likewise on his haunches though John suspected cowering rather than crouching. John heard a dull slurping sound as Wellings tried to stagger to his feet, but he made little progress as he was stuck fast in a bog. All three slowly made their way towards him, testing every footstep. Wellings was sinking quickly, his arms flailing.

John lay on the bank and reached out. 'Come this way,' he said, offering his hand.

With another foul-smelling slurp, Wellings sank further.

'Have you a rope on your horse?' John asked Spibey, who shook his head, his heavy jowls flapping loosely.

'I'll go and look,' said Zipporah. 'I'll bring the reins if there's nothing else.'

'Give me the pistol and take care,' called John, watching her as she skipped over the tussocks of reed and heather, occasionally stumbling but quickly pulling herself up.

'Help me!' cried Wellings.

'Keep still!' shouted John. 'Don't struggle, we've gone to find a rope. We'll pull you out.'

'No, let the Moss claim him,' said Spibey.

John looked up at the magistrate. 'There was a time when I almost respected you, Sir Moreton. No longer.'

'You wait until your wife has child after child and they all die. Margaret is flawed, I admit that, but I've not lost hope for her. She's all I have. Believe me, John, once you know a father's love then every other emotion pales in comparison. Everything I do is for her.'

John's face was limp with disbelief. 'No more excuses, Spibey.'

'Help me,' cried Wellings. Then he let out a sickening gag as his chin slipped beneath the mud and he tasted the bog. 'I'm descending into hell! Forgive me, Lord, forgive me! All I wanted was my rightful place in society. Help me, Master Carne, please.'

'Stop struggling, you'll sink faster,' said John, standing up and looking across the Moss.

Spibey was staggering all over the place. 'What to do? What to do?' he cried to no one in particular.

Zipporah appeared, panting hard.

'You've got a rope,' said John,

'No, no,' cried Spibey, trying to pull the rope from her. 'Let him drown!'

'Leave her,' said John, jumping to his feet, only for his leg to collapse under him and he fell onto Spibey with such force that Spibey tumbled backwards into the bog.

Wellings gave out a last agonised shriek before disappearing into the mire.

'Too late for him,' said Zipporah.

'We can save Spibey,' panted John, pulling himself upright, his leg held this time.

The side of her mouth curled. 'Should we?'

'Help me, help me,' called Spibey, his arms waving frantically in the air. 'I'll give you anything, anything!'

'Why do I feel pity for him?' she said. 'Considering what he's done to us and others, shouldn't we let him die?'

'Can you stand here and watch him drown?' said John.

She shook her head.

'Nor can I, though he must earn his rescue.' He raised his voice. 'When we return to Wem, Sir Moreton, you'll tell everyone that my wife is neither witch nor whore. Then you'll leave us to live our lives unmolested. If you keep your word, then I'll never tell anyone of Margaret's shame. Do you agree?'

'Yes, I'll agree to anything, throw me the rope, quickly.'

'One word out of place, Spibey, and the world will know that your daughter's a whore and you're a liar who got a man to kill for you, I promise.'

'Whatever you want. God damn it, man, throw me the rope.'

John turned away. 'That's not good enough,' he said.

'How can we trust you?' said Zipporah.

Tears etched rivulets through the mud on Spibey's face. 'I promise before God, I promise. I swear. May my daughter and grandson die an agonising death if I ever renege on my promise. This I swear before the Lord God Almighty and on the life of my daughter.'

'John?' said Zipporah.

'Now he means it,' he said, throwing out the rope. The magistrate grasped the end and between them they pulled him clear of the bog.

All that was left of Wellings was a hollow in the mud, that let off a plume of foul-smelling gas, before it rippled and then closed.

'I'm saved! I'm saved!' gasped Spibey. 'I didn't think you'd do it.'

'Well, I'm mad, that's my defence,' said Zipporah.

'You still have a family to look after,' said John. 'Do that, and do it well. You'll have to work out the rest of your guilt with the Lord.'

'You're merciful. You've forgiven me.'

'What makes you think that?' said Zipporah.

Chapter Thirty

Spibey, slumped on Queenie's saddle, sobbed all the way back to Wem.

They hadn't found Spibey's cob, but Wellings's horse was with Queenie and Zipporah rode behind John.

'I got it all wrong,' she said.

'I think you worked out most of it. Though Spibey's full involvement I don't think we'll ever know.'

'I did get it wrong, in that I thought there was some great plan. Some devious malefactor who planned everything. Now it just seems to be that one event lead to another. Margaret's silly selfishness, Wellings greed and envy, and Spibey's obsession with evil and overwhelming love for his daughter, all came together at the wrong time, with tragic consequences.'

'That's a way of putting it. What are we to do about Spibey?'

She pulled herself closer to him. Despite being cold and exhausted he felt desire. Her hands were round his waist and he transferred the reins in his left hand to his right, so he could give hers a reassuring squeeze. 'Would it have been better if he'd died in the Moss? I don't know, Zipporah, I just don't know. I doubt we can prove anything against him. And who would we report him to anyway? Another justice of the peace? Who'd believe us over him?'

'Whatever he has or hasn't done, I need him to publicly declare me no witch before we do anything. I don't want retribution, nothing like that. I simply want us to be able to live our lives without fear or suspicion.'

He clutched her hand even tighter. 'I'll make sure he does it, my love. You need have no doubt on that score.'

He felt her relax behind him. 'I love you, John Carne.'

At last they saw the shadow of the town in the moonlight. John had never been happier to see Wem and to pass through the makeshift defences.

'Anything I need to know, Captain?' asked the sentry anxiously.

'We got lost on the Moss, that's all.'

A sleepy Crowther, a blanket draped over his shoulders and a lantern in his hand, opened the door of the house in Noble Street.

'By all that's in heaven, what now?'

'Sir Moreton had a tumble in the Moss,' said John.

With a sigh Crowther helped his master down.

'Master Wellings was drowned on the Moss,' said John as he slipped from his horse, getting a balance on his legs and reaching up to help Zipporah down.

Crowther made no comment about that. 'You're soaked through, sir,' he said to Spibey.

'He'll need a warming pan or bottle in his bed,' said Zipporah.

'Of course, Mistress Carne. Please come in and warm yourselves.'

John said nothing. He was desperate to go home.

Crowther continued. 'Do you think we should tell Mistress Perks about Wellings, perhaps you could do that, kindly, Mistress Carne.'

'I think it's best her father tells her in the morning,' said John.

'Wellings was a beast, Crowther,' said Spibey. 'He killed them all. The Moss took him. Evil took its own.' He began sobbing again.

'Your master needs to rest,' said Zipporah to Crowther. 'It's been a difficult day.'

Crowther raised his eyebrows. 'For you most especially, my lady,' he said softly.

'We'll see you tomorrow,' said John. 'Zipporah and I need to be home.'

Spibey tore himself from Crowther and clumsily wrapped his arms around Zipporah. 'I killed no one. You believe me don't you. Forgive me. Have you forgiven me?'

She tried to push him away but he was heavy, already John and Crowther were pulling on his shoulders.

'It doesn't matter,' she said tiredly. 'It's over now.'

He let go of her and leant on Crowther again, though he still spoke to her. 'My Margaret knew nothing.'

Zipporah turned away.

'It's over, Sir Moreton, say no more,' said John. He guessed that Margaret had known a great deal, though whether she'd instigated anything he wasn't sure. Nothing would be achieved now by probing further. 'Home,' he said to Zipporah.

'Take the lantern,' said Crowther, bundling Spibey through the door. 'And have a care, it'll be slippery underfoot.'

John took a deep breath, though the sharpness of the cold air was painful. He looked back at the thick oak door as it closed behind them.

'I almost feel it's possible that house is cursed,' he whispered.

Zipporah gripped his hand. 'No you don't.'

The bright stars were now enveloped in cloud, and the light of the lantern shimmered in the mist. It was far too late for anyone else to be around and their footsteps echoed hollowly around the deserted street. They could have been the only two souls left in the world. John wrapped his arm around Zipporah, as much for support as love, for his leg pained him.

She broke the silence. 'When I had the dolls, though they weren't real, I loved them. I would have done anything to protect them and they were only bits of wood and rag. Spibey has many faults, but his feelings for his daughter are true. Isaac used Spibey's blind devotion for his own ends. All he wanted was to be squire.' She let out a long sigh. 'It was greed, pure and simple, that led to these crimes.' She kissed his cheek. 'And that's all I shall say on the matter. Now all I can think of is you. I want you, John. I want love. After all this, I *need* love. I need to lie in your arms. I need your kisses and your touch. I want us to be truly married. I want that more than anything.'

His heart beat fast, the promise on her lips and in her voice dispelled exhaustion and he no longer felt the ache of his leg as longing overwhelmed him. 'You're even more remarkable than I thought,' his said, his voice soft, for he could hardly speak.

Her cheek touched his. 'As are you to me.'

Although the fire had long since died there was warmth in The Dial.

'We're not moving away, are we?' said Zipporah. 'I love our little home.'

'No more talk,' he said, as he lifted the cloak from her shoulders and gently untied her scarf. His finger traced down from her mouth, along her slender neck and onto her breast.

She sighed and her lips sought his, their embrace becoming increasingly passionate.

'To bed,' he said breathlessly against her cheek.

John was vaguely aware of a tapping, far away in the distance. A woodpecker? No, it was nowhere near fast enough. Someone mending something? They were early; it was hardly light. He moved closer to his wife, the thrill of her soft naked flesh next to his was a wonderful reminder of the night before. He should have guessed that once she realised that a true expression of love was pleasure and not pain, she'd embrace him with passion. He relived every wonderful touch, every arousing movement and the deep fulfilment they both enjoyed. He sighed contentedly. He would be as enslaved to her in satisfaction as he had been in frustration, and he welcomed his servitude. The tapping continued.

She turned over, opened her eyes and smiled. 'Who knocks on our door?'

'Nobody,' he said sleepily, wrapping his arms around her.

'Master Carne, are you there?' A faint voice could be heard.

'It's our door, John.'

He shivered as he left the bed, and even more so as he opened the shutter to look out.

Crowther was below. 'Master Carne, are you still in bed?' he called up.

'I was,' said John, wryly. 'As should you be. Has something happened?'

'Sir Moreton is recovered and demands everyone's presence early at church. You and Mistress Carne most especially.'

'Very well,' said John resignedly.

Zipporah was sitting up, the covers pulled up to her neck, she was frowning. 'What does Spibey want now?'

'I don't know, we'd better be there, though.' He groaned. 'I had hoped not to think of him for a while longer.' His expression brightened. 'Never mind, at least I'll have the chance to let my fingers fumble lacing your best dress.'

'Your fingers never fumble, husband.'

He blushed to the roots of his hair.

The church was already full by the time they arrived. Spibey was standing at the front, looking in remarkably good spirits, with the rector and Randall a little away to the side. Spibey made a great show of beckoning them to join him.

'My dearest Mistress Carne,' he said solicitously, gripping both her hands. 'How do you fare?'

For once Zipporah was lost for words. They took their place next to Spibey.

'Thanks to you, I no longer feel comfortable staying with Moreton,' Randall hissed to John. 'He talks of Zipporah as if she were some saint, which clearly she's not, even if she might not be a witch, after all. I'm back to Nantwich as soon as I can travel with some troops. Even in church I feel that merely standing next to her my soul is in danger.'

'Any more talk of your damned soul and I'll dispatch you straight to the spirit world with my bare hands,' said John under his breath.

Randall made a choking sound and reached for the lectern, gripping it tightly.

Zipporah smiled angelically. 'Thanks be to God, I've been given a vision of Heaven, dear brother. And it's full of love and peace and happiness and not one godly person like you, with their mouths screwed as tight as a hen's arse.'

'We're in church, wife, mind your tongue,' said John.

'You're a fine one to talk after what you just said,' she whispered back. 'And you were more than happy with my tongue last night, I seem to remember.'

'Master Carne, do you have a fever, you look very red of face,' asked Spibey.

'I'm a little flustered,' he said. 'Wife,' he whispered in her ear, 'I need to talk to you when we get home.'

'You'll not talk when we get home.' She smiled triumphantly.

Spibey held his hands in the air. 'Good people of Wem, my friends,' he began. 'I come here to warn you against the works of the devil. I thought, as a godly person, I was immune from Satan's malign influence. I was wrong. The Reverend Randall Goodman was very wrong, too.' He shot a glance at Randall, who bowed and looked away. 'I was persuaded that this noble and blameless woman, Mistress Zipporah Carne, was both a whore and a witch. Let me here and now admit that I was mistaken, no, misled, totally and utterly and completely misguided by the dark forces that surround us. For as you can see, she is as good and decent a woman as any. True to her husband, true to God. And you, the good people of Wem, will treat her with the respect due to her.' He stopped to sniff loudly.

'Well said, for once,' called Farmer Laycock from the back of the church.

Spibey nodded graciously. John fought down bile. He had to do something about this sanctimonious hypocrite.

'Now,' continued Spibey, with another ostentatious sniff. 'I must inform you of truly dark matters. Master Isaac Wellings, from Whixall, was responsible for the terrible murders that have afflicted this county. I, we, that is Master Carne and myself, pursued him to the Moss where he was claimed by the devil that possessed him. He was sucked down into the bog and a great fart of sulphur was sent out as he returned to hell, to suckle on the sour-milked paps of his Satanic master.' He paused breathlessly, and looked around the church, his expression grave. 'For now the evil has gone. But be warned. We must *all* be on our guard.

'And now I have a personal announcement. I shall take my leave of you. My priority is my family. I shall be moving to Whixall at the earliest opportunity, to administer the estate there on behalf of my grandson.'

John and Zipporah exchanged astonished glances. John wondered if it was his way of admitting some responsibility for the crimes and removing himself from an office he was unworthy of. If so, Spibey might be a truly reformed man.

'You'll have no magistrate, for a while, and in these uncertain times, who knows when one will be appointed? Though my trusted assistant Master Carne will be here for you—'

'What!' John couldn't help exclaiming, but Spibey's hand landing hard on his shoulder not only silenced him but nearly knocked him over.

'Go to him as you would to me. Trust him as you trusted me. Now let us pray'

'Dear God,' whispered Zipporah, bowing her head. 'What are we to do?'

John squeezed Zipporah's hand. 'Whatever happens, we'll face it together and that's all that matters to me.'

Acknowledgments

I wrote my first novel when I was twelve. I'm in my late sixties now, so my path to publication has been long and not without obstacles. The number of people who helped me on this journey are countless. I haven't mentioned anyone by name, if I did the list would be never-ending and I'd be sure to inadvertently miss somebody out. So here, generally are my heartfelt thanks.

The team at One More Chapter have been unfailingly enthusiastic, helpful and patient with a rather low-tech person who's having to learn a lot of new skills.

The largest group to whom I owe gratitude are my friends. I include in this everyone – closest confidantes, former colleagues, even passing acquaintances who've done or said something to help and inspire me. You'll never know how much I appreciate you.

In the friends category I include tutors and fellow students in the Creative Writers course organised by the Take Part initiative at The Theatre Chipping Norton. Joining this group is one of the best things I've ever done. Being with other writers, sharing ideas, giving and receiving encouragement, is a complete joy.

It was one of my tutors who suggested I joined the New Writers Scheme of the Romantic Novelists Association. I attended their conference in 2023, where I met various industry professionals, which led to the offer of publication from One More Chapter. I'm proud to belong to such a supportive organisation.

My family mean everything to me. They've hugged me through rejection after rejection and urged me to carry on. How wonderful they can now pop champagne corks and celebrate. I love them.

Finally, special thanks to my long-suffering husband, who reads every word, offers criticism and encouragement and, most generously, never begrudges the hours I spend playing with my imaginary friends.

ONE MORE CHAPTER

The author and One More Chapter would like to thank everyone who contributed to the publication of this story...

Analytics
James Brackin
Abigail Fryer
Maria Osa

Audio
Fionnuala Barrett
Ciara Briggs

Contracts
Sasha Duszynska
Lewis

Design
Lucy Bennett
Fiona Greenway
Liane Payne
Dean Russell

Digital Sales
Lydia Grainge
Hannah Lismore
Emily Scorer

Editorial
Arsalan Isa
Charlotte Ledger
Federica Leonardis
Bonnie Macleod
Jennie Rothwell
Emily Thomas

Harper360
Emily Gerbner
Jean Marie Kelly
emma sullivan
Sophia Wilhelm

International Sales
Peter Borcsok
Bethan Moore

Marketing & Publicity
Chloe Cummings
Emma Petfield

Operations
Melissa Okusanya
Hannah Stamp

Production
Denis Manson
Simon Moore
Francesca Tuzzeo

Rights
Vasiliki Machaira
Rachel McCarron
Hany Sheikh
Mohamed
Zoe Shine

**The HarperCollins
Distribution Team**

**The HarperCollins
Finance & Royalties
Team**

**The HarperCollins
Legal Team**

**The HarperCollins
Technology Team**

Trade Marketing
Ben Hurd

UK Sales
Laura Carpenter
Isabel Coburn
Jay Cochrane
Sabina Lewis
Holly Martin
Erin White
Harriet Williams
Leah Woods

**And every other
essential link in the
chain from delivery
drivers to booksellers
to librarians and
beyond!**

ONE MORE CHAPTER

One More Chapter is an
award-winning global
division of HarperCollins.

Subscribe to our newsletter to get our
latest eBook deals and stay up to date
with all our new releases!

signup.harpercollins.co.uk/
join/signup-omc

Meet the team at
www.onemorechapter.com

Follow us!

@OneMoreChapter_
@OneMoreChapter
@onemorechapterhc

Do you write unputdownable fiction?
We love to hear from new voices.
Find out how to submit your novel at
www.onemorechapter.com/submissions